PROSECUTION
in the public interest

PROSECUTION
in the public interest

Susan R. Moody
and
Jacqueline Tombs

1982

SCOTTISH ACADEMIC PRESS
EDINBURGH

Published by
Scottish Academic Press Ltd,
33 Montgomery Street
Edinburgh EH7 5JX

SBN 7073 0321 4

© 1982 Scottish Academic Press Ltd

Printed in Great Britain by
Clark Constable (1982) Ltd, Edinburgh

CONTENTS

ILLUSTRATIONS

ACKNOWLEDGEMENTS

THIS BOOK would not have been possible without the full co-operation of members of the fiscal service, who freely and unreservedly gave of their time and experience to help us understand the practice of public prosecution in Scotland. In particular, the Crown Agent, Mr. W. G. Chalmers, has from the beginning given us his unfailing encouragement and assistance. We are also most grateful to those police officers, defence agents and social workers who provided us with valuable material for the study. Many colleagues both in government and the academic community, too numerous to be mentioned individually, have been helpful and supportive throughout.

Certain people, however, deserve special mention. To Theresa Stephenson who, as the research assistant involved in fieldwork, contributed so much to the study we owe a particular debt of gratitude. We are also indebted to Richard Scott, Sheriff Gerald Gordon and Chris Gane of Lancaster whose careful scrutiny of our drafts ensured that many inaccuracies and ambiguities were excised before publication. This book, then, while any remaining defects are solely our own, reflects the generosity of those who gave us the benefit of their knowledge and to all of them we express our thanks.

S.R.M.
J.T.

GLOSSARY

Advocates:	Scottish equivalents to the English barrister, members of the Faculty of Advocates who act as professional pleaders in all courts and prepare legal opinions for solicitors.
Advocates Depute:	Practising advocates nominated by the Lord Advocate to examine all cases reported to Crown Office with a view to solemn proceedings and other cases of doubt or difficulty and to prosecute cases in the high court; collectively known as crown counsel.
Complaint:	The statement of a lesser crime served on an accused person who is to be tried in a summary court and running in the name of the procurator fiscal.
Crown Agent:	The senior civil servant assisting the Lord Advocate in the prosecution of crime in Scotland.
Crown Office:	The Lord Advocate's permanent staff selected from members of the fiscal service and located in Edinburgh.
Crown Counsel:	See Advocates Depute.
Defence Agents:	Solicitors in private practice who give legal advice to accused persons and can represent them in Scottish criminal courts, except the high court.
Fiscals:	The generic term used to refer to procurators fiscal and their deputes.
Lord Advocate:	The principal Law Officer of the Crown in Scotland who is responsible for the prosecution of all criminal cases in Scotland and is the government's chief adviser on Scottish legal questions.
Marking:	The stage at which the fiscal decides whether or not to institute criminal proceedings against accused persons on the basis of reports concerning alleged offences usually compiled by the police.
No Pro:	The decision not to prosecute an accused person taken by the fiscal at the marking stage.
Petition:	The document containing the initial charges made against an accused person whose case in the fiscal's eyes merits trial on solemn procedure and who is served with the petition at his first court appearance, called the petition hearing.
Plea negotiation:	Agreement between prosecution and defence concerning the adjustment of charges whereby the accused pleads guilty and a trial is avoided.
Precognition, a:	A statement taken from a party or potential witness to discover the evidence which he is likely to give if a case goes to court.
Precognition, the:	The statements of witnesses and relevant background information forming the complete dossier of the prosecution case and submitted to crown counsel for their decision.
Procurators Fiscal:	Qualified solicitors employed as Crown servants who prosecute crime on behalf of the Crown in each sheriff court district.
Procurators Fiscal Depute:	Qualified solicitors employed as Crown servants who assist the procurator fiscal for each sheriff court district in the prosecution of crime.
Reporters:	Officials who receive reports on children in trouble and decide whether or not to refer such cases to a Children's Hearing.

Solemn Procedure: The trial of criminal cases with a jury either before a sheriff in the sheriff court or a Lord Commissioner of Justiciary in the high court.

Solicitor General: The junior Law Officer of the Crown in Scotland, depute to the Lord Advocate.

Summary Procedure: The trial of criminal cases without a jury before either the sheriff in the sheriff court or lay justices in the district court.

FOREWORD

THE CURRENT TREND is towards openness in government and although
the details of individual cases could not be disclosed publicly, it was nevertheless
considered to be most appropriate to allow Jacqueline Tombs and Sue Moody
to examine not only the procedures which operate within the Procurator Fiscal
Service but also the individuals who comprise the corps of full-time, public
prosecutors in Scotland.

From what I can gather, fiscals enjoyed being interviewed by the authors
and, indeed, judging by the statements recorded, the experience addled the
minds of some of them. From that the reader will gather that I do not accept
all the conclusions which the authors arrived at, particularly those relating to
the constraints on the use of discretion. Nevertheless they have done an excellent
job. They have stripped much of the mystery which has in the past surrounded
decision-making by fiscals and I sincerely hope that members of the public will
read this book and contemplate on the problems which beset fiscals in the
execution of their duties.

Certainly the findings will promote great discussion within the Procurator
Fiscal Service itself. I agree entirely with the authors' views that the Procurator
Fiscal Service as well as the whole criminal justice system in Scotland is now at a
crossroads. The old methods are simply not good enough for modern circumstances. The approach of fiscals to their work has changed, is changing and will
change even more.

With change in mind, it is essential to have a firm platform from which
to start and we in the Procurator Fiscal Service are therefore extremely fortunate
to have had the workings of our department examined in such detail and the
findings and conclusions so clearly spelt out by the authors. I trust that they
will come back again sometime. I can assure them that they will be most
welcome and also that they will see changes, hopefully for the better.

W. G. CHALMERS
Crown Agent
Edinburgh 1982

I

INTRODUCTION

THIS BOOK BEGAN AS A STUDY of the way in which Scottish public prosecutors, procurators fiscal,[1] make particular decisions in relation to the prosecution of criminal offences in Scotland.[2] The main thrust of our work centres on *marking*, the stage at which reports concerning alleged criminal incidents are considered and the fiscal decides whether or not to prosecute, on what charge or charges, by which form of procedure and in which criminal court. However, it became clear as the research progressed that the marking stage could not be isolated from the Scottish criminal justice process as a whole. On the one hand, decisions made at this point have a profound impact on all subsequent stages of criminal procedure. What the fiscal decides to do at the marking stage will, to a large extent, determine what happens to individuals reported by the police for alleged offences. On the other hand, the fiscal is himself dependent on other agencies for the information on which he bases his decisions. Above all, Scottish prosecutors operate within a particular ideological context which draws heavily on the rhetoric of the criminal law. Therefore, while the fiscal's task in marking remains the main focus of the analysis, other matters concerned with the nature of criminal justice generally are discussed: such issues as the role of the police as the servants of the fiscal, the legitimacy of pre-trial social work intervention and the place of trial-avoidance arrangements within an adversary system. This wider approach necessarily involves reference to the structure of criminal justice in Scotland and entails comparison with systems in other jurisdictions. In addition it attempts not only to provide descriptions of prosecutorial decision-making but also to offer explanations for the fiscal's actions.

THEORETICAL INTERPRETATIONS OF THE FISCAL'S ROLE

Little is known about the way in which Scottish prosecutors make those decisions which, to a large extent, determine how a case is dealt with by the

---

[1] *Procurator fiscal* is the term used for the chief prosecutor in each sheriff court district. He may be assisted by one or more *procurators fiscal depute*. The word *fiscal* is a generic term which may be used to describe a procurator fiscal or a procurator fiscal depute.

[2] The study did not include the prosecution of children.

criminal justice system in Scotland. The following remarks made by a former Solicitor General for Scotland, Lord McCluskey, underline this:

> although Scotland is an integral part of the United Kingdom it has a separate and distinct legal system from that which obtains elsewhere in the UK. And the feature of the criminal system which most distinguishes it from that of England is that, in Scotland . . . all prosecutions are undertaken by a public prosecutor, the Lord Advocate, acting personally or through his deputies (known collectively as Crown Counsel) or through local prosecutors called procurators fiscal . . . At the highest level, therefore, the decision to prosecute or not to prosecute is taken by lawyers wholly independent of the police. This system has been operating for centuries without serious adverse criticism despite the fact that Crown Counsel take their decisions in private and never give reasons for them. Thus it is difficult for the outside observer to discover the principles which Crown Counsel apply, or to detect if they vary from one period to another. What is certainly true, widely known and generally approved is that in deciding whether or not to institute a prosecution, Crown Counsel are not simply asking themselves the question "is there enough evidence to convict the suspect of a crime?" but are exercising a discretion. A public prosecutor in any legal system exercises some such discretion. If he decides to prosecute then, in a real sense, his decision is subject to a form of review; because the court will ultimately decide the issue of guilt or innocence. But if the prosecutor decides not to prosecute, his decision is not subject to review. Only a few countries allow the court to examine and reverse a decision not to prosecute; in most, as in Scotland, the prosecutor's decision is final. So that discretion and the manner of its exercise deserve examination. [McCluskey: 1979: 5]

The picture which emerges from textbooks on Scottish criminal procedure does little to increase our knowledge of prosecutorial decision-making in practice. Marking, for instance, in spite of its central importance in the processing of criminal cases, is only accorded a brief reference. It is striking to note the absence of legal rules in relation to decisions made by the fiscal before the accused's first court appearance. While the choice of charge and selection of procedure and court are to some extent limited by legislative provisions relating to the penalties for particular offences and the jurisdiction of the respective criminal courts, fiscals are under no obligation, either by statute or at Common Law, to prosecute nor are they bound in all cases to proceed against an accused person on the charge or charges selected at the marking stage. This latter freedom allows for considerable flexibility and facilitates negotiation between prosecution and defence often resulting in an arrangement to plead guilty thus avoiding the need for a trial. Yet the use of such broad discretionary powers is not generally subject to judicial review nor does the public have the right to be present when such decisions are made.

Scotland is not alone in its failure to examine the nature of prosecutorial discretion. It is only in the last ten years that the work of the public prosecutor and the key position which he occupies within the framework of criminal justice have become topics for research. Thus as recently as 1969 it was possible to say that 'of all the individuals and agencies exercising discretion in the criminal process, the prosecutor has received the least attention in the literature' and that 'the decision to issue a complaint, although the most important and least subject to continuing scrutiny, has been the area of least study'. [Southern California Law Review: 1969: 137] However since that time there have been a number of important studies examining different aspects of the prosecutor's work. While writers have generally concentrated on the office of district or federal attorney in the United States,[1] the prosecutor in Canada and in several Continental jurisdictions has also been studied.

Most commentators note the considerable differences between what the prosecutor does and what the legal literature and judicial decisions say he should do. According to one Canadian study:

> informal adjustments are continually made in order to cope
> with operational realities, while at the same time lip service
> is paid to officially stipulated means and required ends. It is
> not judicial theory which always determines the exercise of
> discretion by the prosecutor or the mode of his professional
> behaviour. Often it is the administrative demands made
> upon him and the informal social relationships which
> develop within his operational environment which control
> his decision-making processes. [Grosman: 1970: 500]

The same writer points out that this dichotomy between the ideals of the criminal justice system and the realities of pragmatic decision-making is not something of which the prosecutor himself may be aware since he is primarily concerned simply with getting on with the job. In the prosecutor's working environment, therefore, 'speculative qualities have little application to the critical contingencies of the here and now'. [Grosman: 1970: 500]

Decisions may be based on criteria other than those asserted by the formal requirements of the legal system but they do not, therefore, automatically become highly individualised and diverse. Research studies on the prosecutor do show that individual prosecutors vary in their assessment of particular cases, their willingness to negotiate with the defence, and their general attitude to the prosecutorial role, since:

> the law is written by legislators, interpreted occasionally by
> appellate courts, but applied by countless individuals, each

---

[1] For a useful bibliography see the *National Criminal Justice Reference Service: 1975*.

acting largely for himself and how it is applied outweighs
in importance its enactment or its interpretation.
[Baker: 1933: 770]

However, most writers maintain that there is a strong consensus among
prosecutors regarding the kinds of cases which merit prosecution. Such
consistency seems to be derived as much from the practical constraints which
dominate the criminal justice process and the strategies adopted by prosecutors
to deal with such pressures as from any legal requirements. Thus it appears
that prosecutors develop common perceptions of appropriate goals and methods
of achieving such goals, reflecting operational realities as well as the formal
requirements of the legal system.

The concept of a universe of shared meanings which is maintained by a
particular group in order to cope with social reality is now well established in
sociological theory. 'The range of human behaviour is so wide [that] social
groups maintain boundaries . . .; they try to limit the flow of behaviour within
a defined cultural territory.' [Erikson: 1964: 11] But it is clear both from
writings on prosecutors and general studies of decision-making in other areas
that it is generally not possible to isolate one coherent body of perceptions
which shapes all decisions made by a particular group. An examination of
prosecutorial decision-making is both more complex and more interesting
precisely because the prosecutor seldom operates with only one set of goals in
mind and with only one interpretation of the most appropriate way of achieving
such aims. Not only is he 'the pivotal figure in the justice process, he is also to
a considerable extent police, prosecutor, magistrate, jury and judge in one'.
[Moley: 1929] Thus, 'the multiple and often contradictory roles which the
[prosecutor] is expected to fill explain much of the power – as well as the
problems – of the office'. [Kress: 1976: 107] The procurator fiscal is, of course,
a qualified lawyer, but he is also a public servant and frequently exercises an
administrative function over junior fiscals and other staff. He is at one and the
same time a member of a profession which prides itself on its autonomy and
fosters the idea of equality among its constituents and part of a hierarchically
structured organisation which is accountable to the electorate through parliament. Thus different goals and interpretations can and do inform how a fiscal
makes choices.

The fiscal as lawyer

It is generally assumed that the label *lawyer* carries with it certain fundamental characteristics, regardless of the particular setting in which legal skills
are being utilized. This view persists in spite of the fact that lawyers function
in many widely differing occupational settings and may specialize in very
different aspects of the law. What supposedly unites them is a systematic body
of legal knowledge acquired through a common training both at university
and as apprentices and a code of ethical rules designed and policed by lawyers
themselves free from external interference. This almost myopic pre-occupation
with the technical minutiae of the law is designed to produce 'a disinterested

advocate concerned only with the legal process and not with the result of his or her interventions'. [Marks: 1972: 9–10] The possession of such esoteric expertise combined with his avowedly apolitical position ensures that the lawyer has traditionally enjoyed considerable prestige and public respect.

However, the image of the legal profession as the repository of unique specialist 'technical' skills essential to the operation of the law has been seriously questioned by several writers.[1] These studies suggest that, in fact, the lawyer's knowledge is not scientific but is concerned rather with the application of a body of social rules which reflects relative values and assumptions rather than absolute truth and seeks to ensure that the existing social order is maintained: 'the lawyer's role imposes on him a trusteeship for the integrity of those fundamental processes of government and self-government upon which the successful functioning of our society depends'. [American Bar Association: 1958: 1159] Furthermore, legal knowledge by itself will seldom be sufficient to ensure success:

> from the good lawyer we may therefore expect a generalised
> capacity for defining situations and a great variety of worldy
> knowledge . . . not based on systematic theory. Non-
> rationalised interpersonal skills . . . are of extreme
> importance in his relationship to the client, in litigation and
> negotiation. [Rueschemeyer: 1969: 271]

Research in Scotland suggests that Scottish solicitors use their technical knowledge of the law for something like one hour a week. 'The rest of their time involves little legal skills; either they use totally routinised legal knowledge or else move out of, or beyond specifically legal work.' [Campbell & Wilson: 1972: 209] While fiscals are not required to sustain relationships with clients, and are specialists in one particular branch of the law, they undergo the same education and training, use the same legal language and are members of the same professional association as the rest of the legal community. This community in Scotland has remained remarkably homogeneous since its inception in the sixteenth and seventeenth centuries. Students entering law faculties in Scottish universities are still predominantly middle-class, and very often will have family connections with members of the legal profession.

The fiscal as professional

However, lawyers, including fiscals, are not only a particular occupational category but also belong to one of the oldest and most respected of the professions. A great deal of sociological literature in recent years has been devoted to the notion of a profession and what effect, if any, the membership of a profession may have on working philosophies and practices. Writers stress 'the importance of professional associations in ensuring the adherence of members to a common set of values and behaviour patterns and socialisation into the service during a long period of professional training'. [Podmore:

[1] See A. S. Blumberg: *Criminal Justice*: Chicago: 1967 and J. R. Frank: *Courts on Trial*: Princeton: 1949.

1980: 1] There has been much discussion of the common attributes or traits that distinguish the professions as such from other occupations. These characteristics have been described as follows:

> members of professions receive systematic training,
> education, and socialisation; they possess special skills based
> on learning a body of knowledge. Their competence in
> these skills is tested and subject to review by the professional
> body whose control extends not only over specific technical
> activities but also the general conduct of the professional
> practice. Implicit in such codes of ethics is the notion of
> altruism, that members of professions supply a valuable or
> valued "service". Members of professions are not motivated
> by or concerned with simple monetary gain or making
> profits: their orientation is different and is reflected in the
> rules of obligation of each professional to other members of
> the same profession, to the profession itself, and to the
> community. [Campbell: 1976: 197]

The identification of a profession by particular traits, however, has become increasingly difficult, particularly since many professionals are now employed by large public or private bureaucracies and no longer operate independently. Arguably, a more realistic contemporary definition of what membership of a profession entails is provided by the notion of *occupational authority*. Where specific occupational groups have the power to control their work activities particularly in a practitioner/client relationship, they can obtain a monopoly and develop skills and an identity which tend to be jealously guarded. 'Professionalism arises where the tensions inherent in the producer-consumer relationship are controlled by means of an institutional framework based upon occupational authority.' [Johnson: 1972: 51]

Nevertheless the erosion of those characteristics commonly associated with the concept of a profession does not appear to have fundamentally affected the way in which professionals regard themselves and are regarded by others. There is in effect a time-lag between the present organisational settings in which many professionals work and the philosophy under which they operate.

> The persistence of 'profession' as a category of social
> practice suggests that the model constituted by the first
> movements of professionalisation has become an ideology –
> not only an image which consciously inspires collective or
> individual efforts, but a mystification which unconsciously
> obscures real social structures and relations. [Larson: 1977:
> xciii]

In the case of the legal profession this ideology is safeguarded by:

> differentiation and standardisation of professional services;
> formalisation of the conditions for entry; persuasion of the

public that they need services only professionals can provide;
and State protection of the professional market against
those who lack formal qualifications and against competing
occupations. [Abel: 1979: 84]

It appears that the pattern of responses for each individual member of a particular profession can therefore be seen as a relatively highly integrated and internally coherent belief system. As members of a well established professional group fiscals share in the prestige and the mystique which attach to such membership and which emphasise the importance of individual decision-making, specialist knowledge, loyalty to one's fellow professionals and service to the community.

The fiscal as bureaucrat

The procurator fiscal in a large office is also required to play the roles of administrator, organiser and supervisor of both professional and non-professional staff. As such, he is located within an organisation which is increasingly hierarchical in nature and which exhibits many of the attributes of a modern bureaucracy. Much has been written about the way in which particular organisational structures may shape the way in which decisions are made. Several major sociological studies have discussed in detail the nature of bureaucracies which are so characteristic of state and private organisations in the twentieth century.

Precision, speed, consistency, availability of records,
continuity, possibility of secrecy, unity, rigorous
co-ordination, and minimisation of friction and of expense
for materials and personnel are achieved in a strictly
bureaucratised administration conducted by trained
officials. [Weber: 1954: 669]

Of particular importance in a study of decision-making such as this is the impact which bureaucratic organisations may have on individual autonomy. Bureaucracies are hierarchically structured and great stress is generally placed on what Weber has called the 'calculability of rules' and the importance of 'the routine element in decision-making . . . the various routine practices of the decision-makers and the context of their occurrence'. [Bloor: 1978: 41] This is certainly at odds with the professional orientation which has already been described where members are not restricted by the orders of a superior or by formal regulations.

Bureaucracies within the criminal justice system have particular problems requiring solutions which may conflict with those espoused by the lawyer/professional. Both American and British studies have documented the need to maintain a continual flow of cases through the system, to meet the expectancies of agencies other than one's own, and to categorise cases. 'Organisational goals and discipline impose a set of demands and conditions on the respective professions in the criminal court, to which they respond by abandoning ideological and professional commitments.' [Blumberg: 1967: 16] A recent analysis of criminal justice in England and Wales demonstrates that:

> the concepts of truth and justice far from providing any
> absolute standards for the conduct of the actors are often
> used in a rhetorical manner to legitimate the pursuit of
> institutional and social objectives [and that] encouragement
> and rewards are given to procedures, strategies and
> decisions which save time and expedite the processing of
> cases, devices which reduce conflicts to the minimum and
> ways of stifling any threats to smoothness of the
> proceedings. [King: 1981: 1–2]

This recourse to supposedly rational and value-free ways of working helps to mask the highly political nature of the criminal justice process: 'crime is itself a socio-political concept which is the product of the structure of social values and attitudes in a society . . . all decisions in the penal process reflect a variety of social and political values'. [Bottomley: 1973: xvii] Thus fiscals in their capacity as administrators may make decisions in particular ways to satisfy the bureaucratic requirements of the criminal justice system.

Members of the professions and, similarly, people employed by bureaucracies make a strong claim to be regarded as apolitical in their working life. While we have already discussed the notion that, in fact, professionals, including lawyers, may 'closely reflect the interests and needs of established groups in society' [Tomasic and Bullard: 1979: 419], the professional's or administrator's own view would generally be that he eschews politics in making decisions. However, the fiscal is in the peculiar position of being enjoined to take considerations of public interest into account in his work. 'The procurator-fiscal is entitled to have regard to the public interest . . . consideration of the public interest may outweigh the desirability of strict enforcement of the law.' [McCluskey: 1979: 7] While the fiscal is not regarded as a party political figure, it is important to remember that the Chief Law Officer for Scotland, the Lord Advocate, is almost invariably a member of the ruling party, is a Minister of the Crown and is answerable for all procurators fiscal in parliament. Since 1975 every prosecutor in Scotland is accountable for the conduct of prosecutions to Crown Office,[1] the Lord Advocate, and through him the general public. Thus a chain of supervision and control now exists through which Crown Office endeavours to ensure that there is some consistency and similarity in prosecution policy.

Thus the fiscal operates within a number of different and potentially conflicting ideological frameworks and in making decisions in relation to prosecution is subject to the constraints imposed upon lawyers, professionals and bureaucrats. A valid interpretation of prosecutorial decision-making therefore demands a methodological approach which can do justice to the complex structure within which the fiscal works.

---

[1] *Crown Office* comprises the Lord Advocate's permanent staff who are civil servants appointed from the fiscal service headed by the *Crown Agent* and located in Edinburgh.

METHODOLOGICAL APPROACH

An approach which would permit fiscals themselves to present their interpretations of prosecutorial decision-making was explicitly adopted in this study from the outset. While the focus of the research was therefore on qualitative and impressionistic material, there was also a need for some preliminary work which would provide a systematic national picture of the kinds of decisions which the fiscal has to make in relation to prosecution. A statistical exercise[1] was mounted to collect information from all fiscal offices on the following:

i. a breakdown of reports received, giving details of the number and type of charges, the number and sex of accused persons, their status as cited or custody cases[2] and the reporting agency involved;

ii. a description of what happens to a report and why, whether proceedings are instituted, by what procedure and in which court, whether the charges originally specified on the report when first received are amended and in what manner;

iii. an analysis of how fiscals make such decisions, sketching patterns of consultation and contact with colleagues, seniors and relevant outside agencies;

iv. a brief biography of all fiscals who mark reports, providing information on both legal and other job experience outwith the fiscal service and on their careers as fiscals.

The rather one-dimensional picture generated by our Census was offset by the wide variety of other sources which were tapped at the exploratory stage of the study. We exploited the generous access accorded to us by Crown Office and the sympathetic co-operation of the fiscal service to the full. We observed fiscals at work in fiscal offices and courtrooms throughout Scotland, attended training sessions for junior fiscals and seminars for their seniors, studied reports and records relevant to every aspect of the prosecutorial function and held informal discussions with many Scottish prosecutors.

Finally, on the basis of this wealth of information a group of offices was selected for more detailed study. These offices differed considerably in geographical location, caseload size, numbers of staff and links with Crown Office. Interviews with fiscals in these offices form the central core of the research.[3] Although structured questionnaires were not used, all the fiscal interviews explored the same themes – the particular prosecutor's legal background and experience; attitudes towards marking in general; organisation of marking within the office; approach to particular marking decisions; relations with

[1] See Appendix *Decision-making by Fiscals: a Census of Prosecution Decisions.*

[2] A cited case is one where the accused is at liberty and will, if prosecuted, be served with a citation to appear in court on a particular day; a custody case involves an accused who is in custody and therefore must appear in court on the next lawful day or be released.

[3] Unless otherwise stated, all quotations in this book are taken directly from these interviews with fiscals.

Crown Office; relations with the police, defence agents and social workers; plea negotiation. Thus fiscals were given ample opportunity to present their own interpretations of the prosecutor's job. At the same time, interviews were also conducted with others in the locality, police officers, defence agents and social workers, whose work brings them into contact with the prosecutor and who therefore are able to provide alternative understandings of the prosecutor's role.

THE STRUCTURE OF THE BOOK

The analysis of prosecutorial decision-making presented in this book aims to articulate the way in which certain decisions of central importance in the processing of criminal cases are made. Chapter 2 begins by outlining the general features of different prosecution systems and then considers the historical development of the Scottish prosecution system and the nature of the fiscal service today. The substance of our research is contained in Chapters 3–6 which discuss the way in which fiscals make particular decisions. Much of the material presented in these chapters consists of direct quotes from our interviews with fiscals, defence agents, police officers and social workers. Chapter 3 explores the structure within which decisions are made at the marking stage, describing general patterns, local variations and the limitations which are placed on the fiscal's freedom of action by a variety of factors. Chapter 4 focuses on the decision whether or not to prosecute, exploring possible explanations for the overwhelming presumption in favour of prosecution which seems to underpin the Scottish criminal justice process and examining those rare instances where a prosecution is not instituted. In addition, this chapter discusses alternatives to prosecution and how acceptable the introduction of diversionary schemes would be to fiscals. Chapter 5 is concerned with the Scottish prosecutor's selection of the appropriate form of procedure and court in the trial of certain criminal cases where a choice of court or procedure exists. In particular, fiscals' assessments of the district courts, where lay people administer justice, are considered. Chapter 6 centres round the negotiation of guilty pleas, a practice by which the accused is encouraged to plead guilty and thus obviate the need for a trial in return for certain concessions. The first section presents a comparative review of trial-avoidance arrangements in different jurisdictions and subsequent sections detail the forms of plea negotiation practised in Scotland, ways of negotiating and the perceived benefits of such arrangements for prosecution, defence and accused persons. Finally Chapter 7 considers the main conclusions to be drawn from the research and relates these findings to wider questions about the changing face of Scottish criminal justice.

2

SETTING THE SCENE

THIS CHAPTER SETS THE RESEARCH on decision-making by procurators fiscal in context by providing background information on the nature of public and private prosecution in general and the particular system which operates in Scotland. The first section describes the models of prosecution adopted by different jurisdictions, the next considers the historical development of the office of procurator fiscal, the public prosecutor in Scotland, and the last section examines that office in its present form.

PUBLIC AND PRIVATE PROSECUTION

Criminal justice systems have traditionally been classified as adopting either an inquisitorial or an adversarial approach to the processing of criminal cases by writers concerned with comparing and contrasting different systems. The term inquisitorial is generally used:

> to describe a system in which the state, rather than the
> parties, has the overriding responsibility for eliciting the
> facts of the crime [and in which] the judge is expected to
> carry the factfinding initiative at [the] trial, using the file
> prepared by an examining magistrate or public prosecutor.
> [Goldstein and Marcus: 1977: 242]

Adversarial systems, on the other hand, have been characterised as being concerned 'not with an inquiry into all the facts and circumstances of a case, but with a contest between the prosecution and the defence to prove to the satisfaction of the jury on the evidence before it that the accused person committed the crime of which he has been accused'. [Justice: 1978: 1] The adversary approach is essentially a product of English Common Law.

One of the principal factors which would appear to distinguish an inquisitorial from an adversarial approach to criminal justice is the existence of a public official with responsibility for initiating and conducting criminal prosecutions. However, several legal systems which are adversarial in relation to trial procedure and have developed a criminal justice system reflecting many Common Law characteristics nevertheless retain public prosecutors. Thus in Scotland, Canada and the United States of America a system of public prosecution operates within an adversarial framework. American legal historians record that public prosecution is a relatively long established institution in that country. As early as 1704 the first public prosecution statute was enacted and by the end of the nineteenth century official prosecutions in the majority of the independent United States were conducted by public prosecutors. One writer suggests that this was:

> partly a product of a permanent hostility towards all things
> English and a certain enthusiastic interest in French
> institutions since the American prosecutor, both federal and
> state, was patterned after both the English Attorney General
> and the French Avocat General and Procureur du Roi.[1]
> [Grosman: 1969: 13]

Public prosecutors may therefore be a feature of what appear to be radically different criminal justice systems. But there are certain common factors that underpin the office of public prosecutor in different jurisdictions. Thus public prosecutors are invariably state servants attached to particular districts as in Denmark and Sweden or to particular courts as in Scotland, the Netherlands and France. They are always qualified lawyers and enjoy considerable status. The French prosecutor, the *procureur de la république*, for example, is regarded as a member of the magistracy and remunerated accordingly. In the Netherlands prosecutors must undergo the same specialised legal training as a judge and prosecution services are organised along hierarchical lines often under the control of a minister for justice or some other political appointee. In addition there are regular meetings between that ministry and the prosecution service to determine policy guidelines.

There may be several layers of prosecutors, as in the United States where the Department of Justice under the supervision of the Attorney General of the United States deals with federal prosecutions. United States attorneys appointed by the president with Senate approval are chief federal law enforcement officers in each of the ninety four federal judicial districts. Their duties include providing assistance to other law enforcement agencies such as the Federal Bureau of Investigation, developing cases presented to them by such agencies and representing the United States in criminal proceedings. Local prosecutors, district attorneys, act in their own counties within each state of the Union independently of federal control and are elected by the local citizenry.

In contrast, where a state monopoly on prosecution does not operate the machinery for initiation and conduct of prosecutions is more piecemeal and even somewhat confusing. For example, in England and Wales:

> the right to begin criminal proceedings belongs to everyone,
> whether as an individual or acting in groups, and whether
> in a private or public capacity. As a consequence there is not,

---

[1] However it is worth noting that prosecutors in the United States and in Scotland have no responsibility for civil matters unlike the French procureur. A useful comparative study of the Scottish and French prosecution systems is provided in A. V. Sheehan: *Criminal Procedure in Scotland and France*: HMSO: 1975.

as in most other countries, one or a very limited number of prosecutors acting in the public interest, but a great variety of them. Even the private citizen can prosecute in the public interest. Apart from the role of the Director of Public Prosecutions (which is comparatively limited in the number of cases that come his way though they are usually significant in substance), arrangements for police prosecutions are, by and large, at the discretion of and under the control of the local chief constable and the police authority for each of the 43 separate police force areas. It is not a system in the sense of being uniformly organised and administered in each of these areas and it does not rest on a single legislative foundation. The majority of forces have prosecuting solicitors' departments, that is solicitors in the local authority service who act on behalf of the police in advising on prosecution decisions and presenting cases in court on which the police have decided to proceed. But a significant minority do not, and instead use local firms of private solicitors to advise and act for them. Even among the majority there is little pattern in the structure, administration and function of the prosecuting solicitors' departments. Only one feature is common. The relationship between the chief constable and his prosecuting solicitor is one of client and solicitor. The solicitor acts upon the instructions of the police; the solicitor may advise, but the chief constable is not bound by that advice. So, the arrangements are characterised by their variety, their haphazardness, their local nature and, at least so far as the police are concerned, by the unitary nature of the investigative and prosecutorial functions, with primacy of responsibility for the decisions on prosecution being vested in the police and not in the legal profession. The present arrangements have grown gradually and piecemeal, adapting themselves to changing conditions, over the 150 years since an organised modern police service was first created. [Royal Commission on Criminal Procedure: 1981: 126–7]

The police carry responsibility for both the investigation and prosecution of crime, excluding a small number of cases.[1] 'The DPP plays only a very small part, numerically, in the prosecution of crime . . . in 1978 8% of indictable prosecutions passed through his office. His fundamental role is to undertake prosecutions of importance and difficulty and to advise the police.'

[1] These cases include complaints against the police which must be referred to the Director of Public Prosecutions (known as the DPP) unless a chief police officer is positively satisfied that no offence has been committed.

[Hetherington: 1980: 8] The Attorney General is answerable in parliament for the Director of Public Prosecutions.

While the police frequently employ prosecuting solicitors or use the services of a private solicitor for courtwork, it is the senior police officer in charge of the case who decides whether a prosecution should be brought and there is no obligation on the police to consult their solicitors or having consulted them to follow the advice tendered. This concentration of power in the hands of the police has been the subject of some criticism and the Royal Commission on Criminal Procedure in England and Wales, which included an examination of the prosecution system within its terms of reference, received many submissions supporting change. In its final report the Commission recommended that:

> there should be no further delay in establishing a prosecuting
> solicitor service to cover every police force. This should be
> structured in such a way as both to recognise the importance
> of independent legal expertise in the decision to prosecute
> and to make the conduct of prosecution the responsibility of
> someone who is both legally qualified and is not identified
> with the investigative process; to rationalise the present
> variety of organisational and administrative arrangements;
> to achieve better accountability locally for the prosecution
> service while making it subject to certain national controls;
> and to secure change with the minimum of upheaval and
> at the lowest cost possible. [Royal Commission on Criminal
> Procedure: 1981: 144-5]

While the powers of the police vary considerably in different public prosecution systems, the prosecutor or the examining magistrate is generally regarded as exercising control over the police. In some jurisdictions the prosecutor is very closely involved at the investigating stage but generally the police prepare a case up to the moment when key decisions regarding the institution of proceedings have to be taken. In France a specially constituted police force with legal qualifications, the police judiciaire, is charged with determining whether or not a criminal offence has been committed. Prosecutors in the Netherlands exercise day-to-day supervision over police work by means of logbooks documenting police activity.

The latitude enjoyed by the police in reporting or not reporting alleged offences and the degree to which the police themselves can determine a case vary in different jurisdictions reflecting different attitudes about the validity of out-of-court settlements and the degree to which extra-legal factors, such as police manpower levels, are regarded as legitimate criteria in deciding whether or not to pursue a case. In the Netherlands, for example, the police have considerable powers not to report certain offences, such as petty theft, minor domestic disputes and public nudity, though discussions must take place with the prosecutor before such policies can be established. Where minor offences are concerned police in Denmark have a number of different options open to

them in dealing with alleged offenders, such as fining on-the-spot or issuing a
warning. Similarly in Sweden cases designated 'summary' may be dealt with
by the police who impose a set fine. Police officers may indeed actually present
the prosecution case in criminal proceedings themselves, as in Denmark when
minor offences only are in issue, and in Germany under a special criminal code.
The point is frequently made in writings on these procedures (for instance
Hermann's study of the scope of prosecutorial discretion in Germany) that
they involve minor offences only but it is often difficult to give a precise
definition of this category. [Hermann: 1974]

   One of the central issues in any discussion of criminal prosecution is the
degree of autonomy enjoyed by decision-makers in the system. In many
jurisdictions the prosecutor's scope for discretion is, in theory at least, severely
curtailed by the operation of the *legality principle*. One commentator explained
the principle as follows:

> the key to most systems of continental criminal procedure is
> to be found in several connected principles. The Penal Code
> is the foundation of legal authority: judges and prosecutors
> have no "inherent" power to take positions that modify or
> nullify the Code's requirements. The primacy of the Code is
> said to be enforced in Germany and Italy by the "principle
> of legality", which makes prosecution compulsory and
> discretion in charging impermissible unless specifically
> authorised by statute. Even where some prosecutorial
> discretion is accepted, as in France, it is construed narrowly.
> [Goldstein and Marcus: 1977: 246–7]

   According to Article 152(ii) of the German Code of Criminal Procedure
the German prosecutor 'is obligated, unless otherwise provided by law, to take
action against any activities which may be prosecuted and which are punishable
in a court of law, to the extent that sufficient factual particulars may be obtained'.
The advantage of compulsory prosecution[1] is that it acts as a counterweight
to the considerable powers which reside with the prosecutor. One writer
describing the German system of criminal justice states that 'the rule of compulsory prosecution appeared both to rid the prosecutor's monopoly over the
formal criminal process of its dangers for the citizen and to protect the prosecutor
from political intervention'. [Langbein: 1974: 450] While the principle of
legality does not require that every offence be prosecuted, it may discourage

---

[1] It should be noted, however, that the rule of compulsory prosecution has been
considerably eroded in recent years particularly in Germany by the introduction of
alternative procedures such as a tariff system of fines and the use of warnings in cases
involving *Ordnungswidrigkeiten* (petty infractions). Such procedures are administered by the
police or other enforcement agencies and cases only come to the attention of the prosecutor
if the accused refuses to comply. In addition under article 153a the prosecutor himself may
decide not to prosecute in certain incidents of petty criminality, such as shoplifting. See
Sessar: Prosecutorial Discretion in Germany: In *The Prosecutor*: McDonald (ed): Sage:
1979.

consideration of the accused and his circumstances as valid criteria in deciding the appropriate course of action. Thus prosecution and punishment come to be regarded as essential ingredients of the criminal justice process.

In other jurisdictions, including Scotland, the principle of compulsory prosecution does not operate. The latitude in decision-making afforded to prosecutors where there is no legality principle may be considerable. The prosecutor's right to waive prosecution is arguably the key variable which distinguishes such systems. For example, according to Article 723, Paragraph 2 of the Danish Code of Criminal Procedure prosecution may be waived where special mitigating circumstances exist and waiver would not be against the public interest. A sample of Danish cases where prosecution was waived[1] suggests that the major criterion is the mental state of the accused and that usually committal to a mental hospital will be preferred to prosecution. The power may also be used in cases where a serious traffic offence has resulted in grave bodily harm or manslaughter of a next-of-kin of the accused person. It also appears to have been invoked in several cases involving sexual intercourse with a child under the age of fifteen where it was clear that the victim had consented. It appears that both the police and the prosecutor are sympathetic to those accused persons who appear to be mentally disturbed even if only slightly and even if such mental disturbance could not be regarded strictly as the cause of the offending. This may be contrasted with the approach towards mentally abnormal offenders who commit offences in France where the legality principle operates.

It has been argued that the emphasis in the Netherlands, where the prosecutor exercises considerable discretion, is on the question 'why prosecute?' rather than 'why not prosecute?' Even in serious cases the prosecutor may be entitled not to proceed. Recent research by the Netherlands' Ministry of Justice has demonstrated that in cases involving maltreatment of children, family assaults, theft and criminal damage, over a quarter of all reported offences were not proceeded with. It appears that the important variables are the value of the property stolen or damaged, the relationship between the victim and the suspect and the social class of the accused person. In such systems the prosecutor may regard himself as a quasi-social worker, not as an authority figure with an absolute duty to uphold the law.

However, a certain amount of concern has been expressed by writers and practitioners alike over the apparently unfettered use of discretion by prosecutors, particularly in the United States. Like his Scottish counterpart, the United States prosecutor has complete discretion in deciding whether or not to prosecute and may enjoy considerable freedom in the choice of charges, procedure and court and in the negotiation of pleas. In addition, the United States prosecutor has the responsibility of recommending sentence. In spite of attempts to bring the prosecutor's decision under judicial review, it appears that the United States Constitution based on the notion of the separation of

---

[1] From *The Management of the Prosecution Process in Denmark, Sweden and the Netherlands*: L. H. Leigh and J. E. Hall-Williams: James Hall: 1981.

powers precludes any such review. Nevertheless the US prosecutor has been enjoined to consider whether:

> a prosecution will promote the ends of justice, instill a
> respect for the law and advance the cause of ordered justice
> having regard to the degree of criminality, the weight of
> the evidence, the credibility of witnesses, policy, the
> climate of public opinion, timing and the relative gravity
> of the offence. [Pugach *v.* Klein 193 F Supp 630 (SDNY) 1961]

The American Bar Association has issued guidelines to assist prosecutors in deciding whether or not to prosecute and it has been suggested that reasons should be recorded and made available to the public where a decision not to prosecute is taken. When considering these suggestions it should be remembered, however, that the American system must be distinguished from other jurisdictions in certain important respects. For example, there are numerous obsolete unworkable and antiquated laws still extant on the statute book in the United States, prosecutors could not possibly handle all cases referred to them by the police and the district attorney is not answerable to any central authority and must be aware of the demands of his electorate.

Even where there is no corps of public prosecutors, as in England and Wales, similar tensions may arise. The problems of accountability and the justice or otherwise of responsiveness to local conditions and consideration of humanity in individual cases were also raised by the Royal Commission on Criminal Procedure. Caselaw has certainly indicated the right of the police in England not to prosecute: 'in carrying out their duty of enforcing the law, the police have a discretion with which the courts will not interfere' [Denning MR in R *v.* Metropolitan Police Commissioner *ex parte* Blackburn [1968] 2 QB 118][1] and text books have outlined valid reasons for not prosecuting, for example, where the accused has already suffered enough or where the evidence has been obtained by unfair means.[2]

The private/public distinction is therefore not always clearcut. In a public prosecution system it would seen axiomatic that only the prosecutor can prosecute alleged offences and that the wishes of the victim should not be considered. Quite apart, however, from the powers available to the police to handle cases themselves and the right to waive prosecution enjoyed by prosecutors in some jurisdictions, both the complainer/victim and the accused have the opportunity in some Continental systems to appeal against a prosecutor's decision. For example, in Denmark a victim must be informed if a prosecution

---

[1] Though Lord Denning went on to say that in this area there were 'some policy decisions with which the courts [could], if necessary, interfere'. For example, were a Chief Constable to direct that the theft of goods valued at less than £100 should not be prosecuted this would constitute a breach of the police officer's primary duty to enforce the law. There have been no recent Scottish decisions on police discretion in the reporting of offences.

[2] For a more detailed examination see A. M. Wilcox: *The Decision to Prosecute*: Butterworth: 1972.

C

is abandoned and may complain to a superior prosecutor; in France, a private person with a substantial interest may prosecute as a *partie civile*[1] and in certain cases a prosecution in Germany can only be instituted if the victim agrees. On the other hand, in Sweden an accused person can appeal against a decision to institute proceedings. Similarly, the power which the prosecutor is presumed to hold over the police may be more apparent than real. Assumptions are made that the existence of a public prosecutor, as an office separate from the police, ensures that police involvement in prosecution must be very limited but this, as has already been pointed out, is not necessarily the case.

The office of procurator fiscal in Scotland has features in common with public prosecutors in other jurisdictions. However, both in origin and development, it can be clearly distinguished from other systems, whether inquisitorial or adversarial, as a brief review of the historical development of the office and the powers and duties of Scottish public prosecutors today demonstrates.

HISTORICAL DEVELOPMENT OF THE OFFICE OF PROCURATOR FISCAL

The origin of the office and even the derivation of the expression 'procurator fiscal' are, according to legal historians, rather obscure. The first documented reference appears in the Records of the Scottish Parliament for 22 August 1584 naming several procurators fiscal in Edinburgh. One reliable source states that 'the fiscal was originally the servant of the inferior judge (the sheriff) and his appointment was a matter for the latter's discretion'. [Irvine Smith: 1936: 436]

His responsibilities appear to have included the collection of fines and, by extension, providing assistance to the sheriff in criminal proceedings. While the procurator fiscal was not in principle involved with the preliminaries to prosecution, such as receipt and handling of criminal complaints and the examination of witnesses, until the Sheriff Courts (Scotland) Act 1876 (since prior to that statute the sheriff was regarded as responsible in law for the prosecution and trial of all crimes falling within his jurisdiction), as early as 1701 the fiscal is described in legislation as the 'pursuer for criminal cases' in the sheriff court. [Journal of Jurisprudence: 1877: 25] In practice, by the early nineteenth century, the sheriff had delegated these functions to the fiscal: 'the procurator fiscal is the public prosecutor appointed by the sheriff. Criminal prosecution must be at his instance, or with his concourse.' [Barclay: 1853: 43] There remained a limited right for injured parties to bring a private prosecution[2] but the vast

---

[1] The partie civile, any person who has sustained damage or loss as the result of a criminal offence, may enter an appearance in the relevant criminal action (which will settle the civil issues) or institute criminal proceedings against the accused in addition to his right to raise a civil action.

[2] This right still exists but is rarely invoked. Proceedings can only be brought with the consent of the Lord Advocate or the high court by a person directly aggrieved who must present an application for leave to bring a private prosecution, called a *Bill for Criminal Letters*. In 1982 this procedure was successfully invoked for the first time in over seventy years by the complainer in a rape case.

majority of all prosecutions were in the hands of the fiscal with the exception of cases dealt with in the lowest courts where, until the District Courts (Scotland) Act 1975, local magistrates appointed their own prosecutors.

Until the end of the nineteenth century, the fiscal continued to be appointed by the sheriff, with the consent of one of Her Majesty's Principal Secretaries of State, and held office in the same manner as a judge *ad vitam aut culpam* (for life during good behaviour). This gave and continues to give the procurator fiscal a great degree of security in the holding of his office since 'no procurator fiscal shall be removed from office except by one of Her Majesty's Principal Secretaries of State for inability or misbehaviour, upon a report by the Lord President of the Court of Session and the Lord Justice Clerk of the time being'.[1] In 1907 the right of appointment of procurator fiscal to the sheriff courts was finally vested in the Lord Advocate under the Sheriff Courts (Scotland) Act.[2]

The development of the office of the procurator fiscal was matched throughout this period by the expansion in the office and authority of the Lord Advocate in Scotland. The holder of this office, 'the absolute monarch of the Great Department of Criminal Justice', [Ritchie: 1824: 363] is a member of the Faculty of Advocates, the Chief Law Officer of the government in Scotland, a political appointee and usually a member of the ruling political party. From its earliest days[3] this office has always been concerned with the prosecution of serious crime. Indeed 'every offence prosecuted in the High Court of Justiciary [the highest criminal court in Scotland] is charged in the name and conducted by the directions of the Lord Advocate'. [Ritchie: 1824: 365]

By the nineteenth century it was necessary for the Lord Advocate not only to appoint practising advocates, called advocates depute, to assist him in conducting such cases but also to establish an office in Edinburgh to provide support facilities both for himself and his advocates depute. This office, called Crown Office, also became the link between the Lord Advocate and the procurators fiscal, who had come under his immediate control and could be appointed and removed by him. Hume states that 'should the instructions of the Lord Advocate be neglected [by a procurator fiscal] a complaint will be presented to the court of Justiciary'. [Hume: 1797: 90] A rather piecemeal pattern of command and control over the prosecution of crime in Scotland was therefore gradually replaced by a more unified structure under the Lord Advocate. The advocates depute, known collectively as crown counsel, were authorised to issue recommendations to the procurator fiscal with regard to all cases of serious crime meriting trial by jury.

The administrative side of Crown Office was already firmly established by the end of the nineteenth century. Requirements that statistical returns be made by fiscals to Crown Office and the issuing of circulars, 'suggestions for the

---

[1] See Section 5 Sheriff Courts (Scotland) Act 1876.

[2] The relevant statute is now the Sheriff Courts and Legal Officers (Scotland) Act 1927.

[3] References to the King's Advocate are to be found as early as the fifteenth century and an Act of 1587 expressly conferred power on the Lord Advocate to pursue *all* criminal prosecutions independent of the wishes of the injured party.

assistance and guidance of procurators fiscal', were already common practice by the 1860s. Crown Office also issued to fiscal offices directions from the Lord Advocate such as the following sent out in 1868:

> where the procurator fiscal is credibly informed of the
> commission of any crime falling under his cognisance, he
> ought to take prompt and immediate steps for approaching
> the party accused. In doubtful cases, or where any unusual
> difficulty occurs, he should take the advice of Crown
> Counsel. [Journal of Jurisprudence: 1877: 27]

Such directions and circulars became embodied in what has been termed *the fiscal's bible*, the Book of Regulations. By the beginning of this century the office of Crown Agent, who is, in effect, the head of the fiscal service and in charge of administrative matters at Crown Office, had become an accepted feature of the administration of justice in Scotland.[1]

Some disquiet was expressed in legal and political circles during the late nineteenth century about the extension of government control over criminal prosecution. The Faculty of Advocates, for example, feared that the development of a unified prosecution service would 'enable Government to interfere with the administration of justice and the conduct of prosecutions in a manner unconstitutional'.[2] Those who favoured private prosecutors pointed to the dangers inherent in the appointment of a Lord Advocate who was also a government minister within the ruling party.

However, it was argued that the politically accountable nature of the office actually operated as a check on corrupt practices. Lord Normand, himself a former Lord Advocate, stressed that:

> the conduct of so important an official as the public
> prosecutor is subject to the criticism of Parliament and it is
> manifestly advantageous that the public prosecutor [the
> Lord Advocate] should himself be in Parliament and able to
> answer in person any attack made upon him there.
> [Normand: 1938: 354]

Nevertheless the same Lord Advocate emphasised that 'if the administration of justice is not to be corrupted by political and party considerations the public prosecutor should exercise his powers judicially and he should not be interfered with in his duties by the executive Government for political reasons'. [Normand: 1938: 354] There had been several instances where it appeared that the Lord Advocate had acted unjustly and in a partisan manner, for example in 1802 it was alleged that he refused to prosecute when several people were shot by the military. However, it was generally admitted even at that time that 'the

---

[1] It is thought that the expression *Crown Agent* may derive from the fact that in law the Crown Agent is the solicitor who briefs the Lord Advocate and is therefore the Crown's law agent.

[2] See *Notes on Bill to amend the law in relation to the appointment of sheriffs substitute and procurators fiscal* 1877: evidence submitted by Faculty of Advocates.

practice of the office has, in ordinary cases, been judicious, moderate and impartial'. [Ritchie: 1824: 370] In support of his contention that the office of public prosecutor, both at local level in the form of the procurator fiscal, and centrally in the office of Lord Advocate, had contributed much to the fair administration of justice in Scotland, Lord Normand cites Baron Hume:

> on the one hand, the inhabitants of Scotland have nothing
> to fear and in truth have never suffered (since the revolution
> at least) from the privileges of this office; on the other hand
> it is impossible to deny the high and expensive benefits
> which attend it, in maintaining the police of the country
> and securing the prosecution of every criminal whose case
> requires it, without any trouble or expense to the party
> injured. [Hume: 1797: 67]

In any case such criticism did not prevent further developments in the growth of the Scottish public prosecution service. In 1927 the final step was taken in the establishment of a corps of public officials, designated procurators fiscal, when the Sheriff Court and Legal Officers (Scotland) Act established that all fiscals appointed on a full-time basis 'shall be deemed to be employed in the civil service of the state'. They were to be paid out of central government funds allocated by parliament and the Act consolidated the position regarding the Lord Advocate's right of appointment and removal of procurators fiscal and their deputes. The majority of fiscals, then, were henceforth barred from holding any other office or doing any other legal work. It is interesting to note, however, that the post of Crown Agent remained a part-time one held by a political appointee until 1945.

The debates in the House of Commons on the 1927 Act do certainly suggest that its innovations were not universally welcomed. It was considered by some that the duties of the public prosecutor and those of a mere servant of the administration were incompatible. It was suggested that fiscals should be independent solicitors entitled to undertake other legal work and remunerated by fee rather than salaried government officials occupied full-time with prosecution work. One member of parliament expressed his misgivings thus:

> if you have a man who performs the duties of that office
> [the office of procurator fiscal] alone he lacks elasticity, or
> the generosity of mind which comes from private practice
> which brings a man into contact with all classes. Part-time
> appointments are desirable in the interest of the accused
> person. [Mr. Kidd: 1927: Hansard 23:3]

The majority of members, nevertheless, could see the advantages in having a public prosecutor. It was argued that:

> the procurator fiscal is, in his own district, just as important
> in the administration of justice as the Lord Advocate is in
> Scotland generally. There is no person who holds the lives

and characters of his fellow citizens more in the hollow of
his hands. He is in a sense a quasi-judicial person, therefore
it is with him that complaints and information are lodged,
and he has it in his power to make or mar the reputation of
every citizen in his locality. It is quite right that the
appointment should be in the Lord Advocate's hands and
that he should continue to have the protection which he has
at present. [Mr. Macquisten: 1927: Hansard 23:3]

Following the passing of the Act virtually all those who had held positions
as procurators fiscal or deputes prior to 1927 accepted their new role as Crown
servants, two-thirds being appointed full-time and the remainder being per-
mitted to operate a private practice also.

THE OFFICE OF PROCURATOR FISCAL TODAY

There are forty-eight district fiscal offices throughout Scotland situated in
a variety of settings ranging from the largest office in Glasgow City with a
professional staff of over fifty to the smallest on the Isle of Skye with a single
procurator fiscal. Since the reforms of 1927 there have been several factors which
have contributed to the significant increase in the number of fiscals within the
service. A rise in the level of reported crime,[1] the creation by parliament of
numerous new statutory offences and the assumption by the fiscal of responsibility for the prosecution of offences formerly prosecuted by government
departments (for example, offences under the Factories Acts, abuses of Social
Security legislation and breaches of Agricultural Regulations) have all added
considerably to the fiscal's workload. The number of fiscals has increased quite
dramatically since the prosecution of cases in the district courts became the
responsibility of the Lord Advocate. In 1975 the fiscal service had a professional
complement of 130; by 1982 it had risen to over 200.

Recruitment is generally from among graduates of Scottish universities
who have qualified as solicitors in Scotland, though advocates are also eligible
and occasionally appointments are made of people who have legal qualifications
from another jurisdiction. Selection is made by a Civil Service Board, though
the Lord Advocate exercises formal control over the procedure. Until 1971
there was an age bar which prevented people under twenty-six from entering
the service but now successful applicants may be in their early twenties and
are not required to have any professional experience before entry other than
an apprenticeship, which may have involved little or no criminal work.[2] The
Royal Commission on Legal Services in Scotland was:

concerned to discover just how inexperienced are most of
the recruits to the service. In the three years 1977–79
[Crown Office] recruited 67 new fiscals . . . two-thirds

[1] See Diagram 1 *Trends in Crime, Scotland 1970–80* p. 23.
[2] See Appendix *Biographies of Marking Fiscals* p. 143.

Diagram 1 Trends in Crime Scotland 1970–80

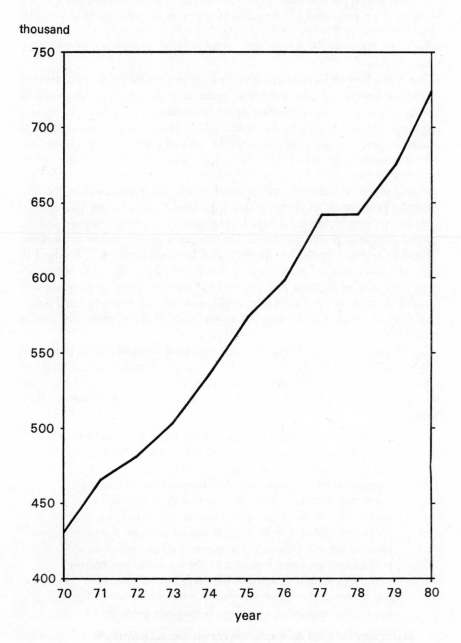

(adapted from Criminal Statistics 1979 Cmnd. 8215:11)

were newly-qualified solicitors; only 6% had more than
five years experience. [RCLSS: 1980: 281]

Successful applicants usually enter the service as legal assistants and after six
years may be promoted to the rank of senior legal assistant. It is possible,
however, for a legal assistant who is judged of exceptional ability by a specially
constituted Treasury Board to achieve accelerated promotion within three
years of entry.

A Civil Service Department investigation in 1977 led to the restructuring
of the fiscal service. Each fiscal office, apart from the offices in Glasgow and
Edinburgh, is now graded as either upper or lower and the procurator fiscal is
remunerated accordingly. In the smaller offices there is a procurator fiscal in
complete charge of the office, who has the rank of a senior legal assistant, and
one or more deputes, who are usually legal assistants.[1] In the larger offices
experienced fiscals may be designated *assistant procurators fiscal* or *senior deputes*
and will supervise different areas of work. Each procurator fiscal has control
over the prosecution of crime within a particular sheriff court area and, in
addition, six procurators fiscal have been assigned to particular regions and are
known as regional procurators fiscal. The office of regional procurator fiscal was
created in response to the reorganisation of local government in Scotland in
1973, and was envisaged as an advisory one. According to the Book of Regulations the duties of regional procurators fiscal include 'acting in a consultative
capacity throughout the Sheriffdom, deployment of staff, issuing general policy
guidelines, attendance at meetings in Crown Office to discuss policy and similar
meetings of all district procurators fiscal'.

The role of Crown Office has also expanded considerably over the last
fifty years. The volume and diversity of work require that the modern fiscal and
his staff be kept constantly informed of any new developments in the law and
in some areas must co-ordinate their activities in line with Crown Office
requirements:

> regulations are issued by Crown Office to procurators fiscal
> giving them specific instructions in relation to some matters
> and general guidelines in relation to others. Thus, for
> example, they are given clear orders as to how to deal with
> claims for diplomatic immunity so that there may be no
> uncertainty. When some special feature comes to light,
> procurators fiscal may be asked to report all cases of certain
> kinds to Crown Office. At the moment all cases of obscene
> publications are being reported to Crown Office not because
> we enjoy examining indecent literature but because there
> was a known divergence of opinion among procurators fiscal
> as to what constituted obscenity. [Chalmers: 1978: 7]

In this way the Lord Advocate and crown counsel may in effect shape what
constitutes the criminal law in Scotland without recourse to parliament or the

[1] See Diagram 2 *Structure of the Fiscal Service* p. 25.

Diagram 2 Structure of the Fiscal Service

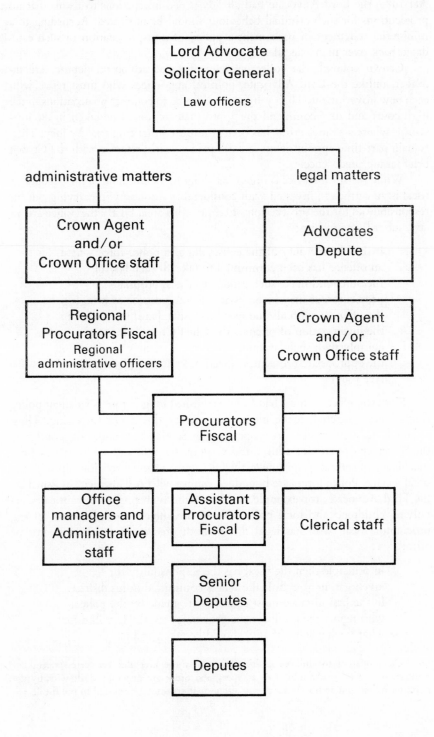

judiciary. For example, although homosexuality between consenting adults in private remained an offence in Scotland until the Criminal Justice (Scotland) Act 1980, the Lord Advocate had already issued instructions to fiscals that no prosecutions for such criminal behaviour should be instituted. According to a ministerial statement in parliament a policy of non-prosecution in such cases dated back over many decades.

Crown counsel, the collective name for the advocates depute, are no longer, unlike the Lord Advocate, political appointees who must retire with each new government. Their job continues to be to conduct prosecutions in the high court and to recommend the appropriate action to be taken in circumstances where a serious crime has been committed meriting trial by jury. They remain part-time appointments and are paid a yearly retainer with the Crown brief taking precedence.

While the fiscal service is organised along hierarchical lines, the procurator fiscal is, nevertheless, invested with considerable autonomy in carrying out his responsibilities for the prosecution of crime in his area. Firstly the police are, in law, subordinate to him:

> It shall be the duty of the constables of a police force where
> an offence has been committed to take all such lawful
> measures and make such reports to the appropriate
> prosecutor, as may be necessary for the purpose of bringing
> the offender with all due speed to justice [and] in relation to
> the investigation of offences the Chief Constable should
> comply with such lawful instructions as he may receive from
> the appropriate prosecutor. (Section 17 Police (Scotland)
> Act 1967)

Since the office of fiscal had been established long before permanent police forces were instituted in the nineteenth century this is not surprising. Thus, although the eight police forces operating in Scotland are under the control of the Secretary of State for administrative purposes only and are not part of the machinery of central government, they do enjoy a special relationship with the fiscal service. Police forces are bound to comply with any instructions issued by the Lord Advocate, for example, regarding the reporting of certain cases involving children,[1] and local police officers are subject to the control of the procurator fiscal, who has legal title as both prosecutor and investigator of crime.

> In principle then the fiscal has the responsibility for
> investigating all criminal offences committed in his district.
> In the first instance most enquiries are made by the police,
> who report the results to the procurator fiscal. He will direct
> what further steps (if any) should be taken and has the

[1] Cases relating to children under sixteen or those juveniles between sixteen and eighteen who are already subject to a supervision order are generally dealt with by the Reporter to the Children's Hearings but certain matters must be referred to the fiscal.

power to issue instructions to the police. In certain instances
he may also take charge of the inquiry from the moment
when the offence was discovered. He may also examine any
witnesses and must do so in all cases to be tried on
indictment (i.e. before a judge and jury). [Sheehan: 1975:
112–3]

In practice, the police bear the major burden in collecting and sifting
evidence. They have developed specialisms in such diverse fields as possession of
drugs and fraudulent dealings and the CID officers who carry out criminal
investigations operate independently from the fiscal except in very serious
matters such as rape or murder. Their expertise and first-hand knowledge of the
circumstances of a particular case will carry considerable weight in the prosecutor's eyes. In carrying out their duties the police have powers to arrest and
charge suspected persons. They do not, however, hold any brief in relation to
the actual decision whether to prosecute or not, unlike their colleagues in
England and Wales. They may and usually do charge a person whom they
suspect of having committed an offence but the charges may be dropped,
modified or changed by the procurator fiscal. There are also groups other than
the police who report certain types of offences directly to the procurator
fiscal, such as the Health and Safety at Work Executive and the Television
Licence Records Office.

Procurators fiscal and their deputes are responsible for the prosecution of
all offences committed within their district. The fiscal makes the initial decision
whether or not to prosecute.[1] If he decides that there is *prima facie* evidence of
the accused's guilt he must then determine the appropriate forum for trial
subject to certain statutory restrictions,[2] and to review by crown counsel in
certain cases. The accused has no right to choose the court of trial. The vast
majority of criminal matters are tried in courts of summary jurisdiction after the
accused has been served with a summary complaint running in the name of the
procurator fiscal. The fiscal himself conducts the prosecution case either before
lay justices or stipendiary magistrates in the district court or legally qualified
sheriffs in the sheriff court. Summary procedure is relatively straightforward
and is aimed at encouraging the speedy processing of cases. The prosecutor in
Scotland may appeal from an acquittal in summary cases only.

Solemn procedure, trial by jury in the high court or the sheriff court, is
reserved for more serious cases. When the fiscal decides that a case warrants
trial by jury he prepares a preliminary indictment, called a petition, and lodges
it with the sheriff at a petition hearing. Once the accused has been committed

---

[1] Except in those instances where a fixed penalty system operates under which alleged
offenders are offered the opportunity of the discharge of any liability to conviction by
payment of a fixed penalty.

[2] Exclusive jurisdiction has been granted to the high court in cases of murder, treason,
rape, incest, deforcement of messengers, breach of duty by magistrates and in certain
statutory offences, for example under the Official Secrets Acts 1911–39. Conversely, some
statutory offences can only be tried summarily, for instance careless driving under Section
3 Road Traffic Act 1972.

for trial the fiscal investigates the case fully, interviews witnesses and obtains statements from them, called precognitions. He then presents the complete file, called 'the precognition', to crown counsel for their decision. If they decide that the accused should be tried in the high court the indictment is prepared and the prosecution case conducted by an advocate depute. Where the case is to be heard before a sheriff and jury the precognition is returned to the fiscal who deals with it thereafter in court.

If the procurator fiscal decides not to prosecute he may refer the matter to the police and request them to administer a warning, he may send a warning letter to the accused or warn him personally. The warning is a slightly am-biguous device since the accused may not have admitted his guilt and so the presumption of innocence still applies. Crown Office circulars state that 'a warning should not be administered unless the Procurator Fiscal has sufficient evidence to justify taking proceedings' but 'a warning may be administered whether or not the accused is alleged to have admitted or denied the offence'. However, if a person is charged with an offence but is warned as an alternative to prosecution Crown Office recommends that the procurator fiscal should advise the accused that proceedings may be taken in court should a similar report be submitted in future.

In carrying out those duties which relate directly to the prosecution of crime the procurator fiscal is answerable to no-one but his own superiors and the public is not entitled to know the reasons for his decisions. An apparent abuse of his discretion will be investigated by Crown Office but it is the Lord Advocate in parliament who carries responsibility for any malpractices. There-fore, while criminal trials in Scotland are heard in public, the important decisions which precede any such hearing (the decision whether or not to prosecute, the choice of charge, the choice of court and the choice of procedure) will be made in private. It is striking that in only one case this century has the conduct of a procurator fiscal been the subject of public criticism.[1]

The other duties which the procurator fiscal has include responsibility for investigating all sudden, unexpected or suspicious deaths; presenting evidence at all fatal accident inquiries; investigating all fires and explosions where there is substantial damage or suspicious circumstances and investigating all other unusual or suspicious occurrences; investigating *ultimus haeres estates* where a person dies intestate leaving no known heirs and the estate is due to fall to the Crown; dealing with articles of treasure trove; at a local level giving legal advice concerning criminal matters to the police, the Customs and Excise, the Post Office, government departments and officials and investigating complaints against the police, especially if there is a suggestion that a police officer has been guilty of a criminal offence.

In relation to all his duties it has been stressed that the procurator fiscal must adopt an impartial role. Lord McCluskey, a former Solicitor General for Scotland, stressed the importance of impartiality in the following terms: 'the tradition is that the prosecutor in Scotland must regard himself as exercising the

---

[1] See W. Park: *The Truth about Oscar Slater*: Psychic Press: n.d.

role of the 'Minister of Justice' rather than as a lawyer acting for a client'. [McCluskey: 1977: 45] Thus the fiscal has an obligation to lay before the court both during the trial and after conviction any facts known to him but not to the defence which are favourable to the accused. Indeed, the quasi-judicial approach which the procurator fiscal should adopt is regarded as the justification for the comparative freedom which he has in decision-making. In McBain v. Crichton, for example, the Lord Justice General expressed this view as follows:

> the basic principle of our system of criminal administration in Scotland is to submit the question of whether there is to be a public prosecution to the impartial and skilled investigation of the Lord Advocate and his Department, and the decision whether or not to prosecute is exclusively within his discretion. This system has operated in Scotland for centuries, and the results have completely proved the justice of these principles for such has become the public confidence in a decision of the Lord Advocate and his deputes on the grounds of prosecution that private prosecutions have almost gone into disuse. It is entirely inconsistent with such a system that the court should examine, as it was suggested it would be proper or competent for us to do, the reasons which affected the Lord Advocate in deciding how to exercise his discretion, and it would be still more absurd for this court to proceed to review their soundness.[1] [McBain v. Crichton 1961 JC 25, L J-G Clyde at page 28]

Unlike his counterparts in certain Continental jurisdictions, the fiscal is not bound by the principle of legality which demands that the prosecutor must pursue a charge to the highest that the evidence will support so that it is perfectly within his competence either not to institute proceedings at all, to abandon proceedings before the trial or to amend the charge or charges. Although Scottish criminal procedure is adversarial in principle, the vast majority of accused persons plead guilty (nearly 60 per cent of persons tried in solemn courts and over 80 per cent tried in summary courts in 1978)[2] and few cases actually go to trial. Accused persons may simply decide to plead guilty but a substantial number of trials appear to be avoided as the result of plea negotiation, arrangements between prosecution and defence that the accused will offer a plea of guilty to an amended complaint or petition.

Discussions between fiscal and defence agent will generally revolve around the nature of the charge or charges. The defence will usually seek to have

---

[1] This case is not entirely supported by more recent pronouncements which suggest that the Scottish prosecutor's decisions may be open to questions in the courts. See Meehan v. Inglis and Ors 1974 SLT (Notes) 61, H.M. Adv. v. Stuurman and Ors 1980 SLT 182. In addition the *Glasgow Rape Case* in 1982 reversed crown counsels' decision not to proceed and, for the first time since 1909 the Scottish prosecutor's exercise of the discretion not to prosecute became a matter for judicial scrutiny.

[2] See *Criminal Statistics Scotland 1978*: Cmnd. 7676: HMSO: 1979.

the number of charges cut down or a serious charge such as assault to the danger of life reduced to something less, for example, assault. The fiscal, on the other hand, seeks to ensure that those charges should stand which can be substantiated evidentially so that the accused will be convicted for the offence or offences which best reflect the circumstances of the criminal incident. The prosecution is under no legal obligation to accept a plea of guilty in return for amendment to the charges as libelled, though pressure on court time makes it essential that large numbers of people should decide not to go to trial.

CONCLUSION

> The most striking feature of Scottish legal development is that Scotland has its own legal system, its own system of courts, its own system for the administration of criminal justice, its own system of law in spite of the fact that the Kingdoms of England and Scotland were united over 270 years ago. [Hunter: 1978: 5]

Public prosecution in Scotland, then, is grounded in an adversarial philosophy of criminal justice and yet bears comparison with the inquisitorial systems of Continental Europe. The procurator fiscal would appear to be in the unique position of enjoying a wide measure of autonomy in making decisions regarding prosecution without the restrictions imposed by a criminal code, as in Germany, or the need to satisfy an electorate, as in the United States. There is, according to the textbooks, no principle of legality which demands prosecution nor pressure from the police or other reporting agencies to institute proceedings. Prosecutorial decisions at the pre-trial stage are not subject to judicial review, are determined in private and may be scrutinised only by the Lord Advocate. Parliament alone can question the legitimacy of such decisions and indeed has confirmed the independence of the procurator fiscal in statute. The nature of the discretion vested in the Scottish public prosecutor and how it is structured in practice form the central theme of this book.

3

MARKING IN CONTEXT

THIS CHAPTER DESCRIBES the manner in which decisions made by fiscals concerning prosecution are shaped. It looks first of all at factors which are common to all fiscal offices and then discusses the variety of environments and organisational settings within which public prosecutors in Scotland work. Finally it discusses the way in which parameters are placed on decision-making by criminal law and criminal procedure, the criminal justice process, the fiscal service and fiscals' perceptions of the prosecution task.

INTRODUCTION

The focus of this chapter is on the particular task of marking, which is a crucial part of the fiscal's job as prosecutor and also a vital link in the processing of cases through the criminal justice system since the fiscal's decisions at the marking stage help to determine the direction which a case will take thereafter. When a fiscal scrutinises reports concerning alleged offences and decides whether an accused person will be prosecuted, on what charges, and in which court, he is, in fiscal terminology, marking. The origin of the expression probably lies in the fiscal's practice of underlining the important words or phrases in the report which will be regarded as crucial in presenting and establishing the prosecution case in court. Marking may also refer to the notes made on the minute sheet (attached to the back of the report) which record, in a kind of fiscal shorthand, the processing of the case. For example, the note *Sh Smy Cite*[1] is both a record of the fiscal's decision to prosecute an accused in the sheriff court by means of a summary complaint and an instruction to fiscal support staff to arrange for the issuing of such a complaint. The decision which the fiscal makes when marking a report will largely determine how a case is processed: 'marking is the start of anything which the fiscal does'; 'it's the initial stage, it starts off a case or doesn't start it off and that is a vital decision that you're making'.[2] Any mistakes in marking may materially affect the successful prosecution of a case: 'if you put in the wrong charge or draft it badly, you usually suffer at the end of the day for it'; 'it's the substance of our court

---

[1] Sheriff Summary Cite.
[2] Material in quotes is drawn from interviews with fiscal staff. See also pp. 9–10.

work and if it isn't given the consideration it should be you are undermining your own responsibility'.

Marking is something which takes place in private and is solely the prerogative of the prosecution service. However, it is important to remember that in marking the fiscal is largely dependent on the reporting agency for the information upon which he rests his decision. He is also keenly aware that in deciding which specific charge or court is appropriate in a particular case he is limiting the sentencing options open to the court in dealing with that case subsequently. In marking he is, therefore, standing as a bridge between the police as investigators on the one hand and the court as adjudicator on the other. But he may himself be required to act as both investigator and judge in making those decisions which are relevant to marking. Thus he must weigh up the evidential value of the information presented to him and decide if there is a *prima facie* case. In addition, if he considers it necessary and feasible he may direct the police as to the nature of any further information required. Marking is a task in which all fiscals at one time or another must be involved and it is one which is central to the consideration of the different philosophies which fiscals bring to bear on their work.

THE GENERAL STRUCTURE OF MARKING[1]

Bundles of reports are received by fiscal offices daily (or several times a day in the larger offices) and are generally given a unique number by the office staff who then pass them through to the fiscals for marking. Custody cases, where the accused is in the custody of the police, take priority and are marked first, usually by the fiscal who will be appearing in the custody court that day, though arrangements do vary from office to office. In cited cases, where the accused is at liberty, there is not the same pressure on the fiscal to make a decision. However, where there has been some delay on the part of the reporting agency between charging a person with an offence and reporting the matter to the fiscal, the marking of cited cases may also require to be done speedily since most statutory offences have to be prosecuted within a stated time period, usually six months from the date of the alleged criminal incident.

In our Census[2] 63 per cent of all cases were marked on the day of receipt and only 5 per cent took longer than eight working days: 'reports are generally marked within a day or two of coming in unless there's something particularly complicated'; 'marking is a "today" thing, stuff that comes in today is marked today'; 'marking is done daily so that there is never any backlog of work – a case is marked as soon as it's reported to the fiscal and a decision is made . . . sometimes it gets spilled over till the following day if we are short – somebody is ill – but it's done really very rapidly'.

The focus of virtually all fiscals' working day is on the court and marking generally has to be fitted in between court sittings and the preparation of cases.

---

[1] See Diagram 3 p. 33.
[2] See Appendix *Decision-Making by Fiscals: a Census of Prosecution Decisions.*

Diagram 3 The Prosecution Process in Scotland

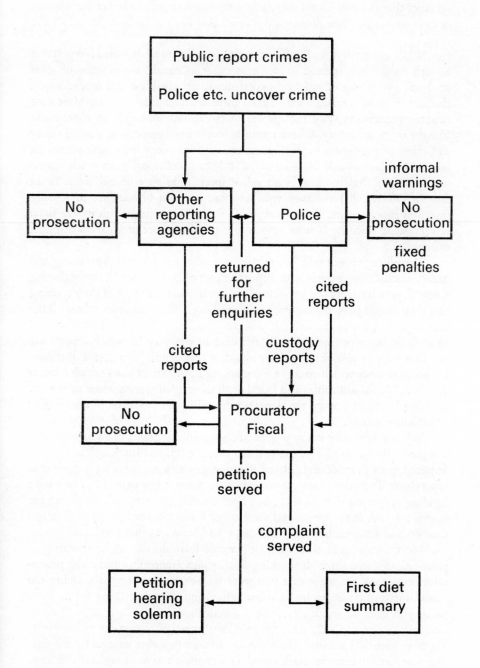

D

While marking is a sedentary activity, then, this does not mean that reports are left unmarked for long. There is an everpresent impetus to keep the flow of cases moving which reflects the nature of the criminal justice process as a whole: 'you get a report from the police and you just look at it and decide whether there's a case and if there's a case you go ahead'; 'a broad mainstream of cases are simple, straightforward matters that have to be brought before the court'.

While the professional staff in the fiscal service are all qualified lawyers and as such might be expected to work together as equals, the absence of solid academic grounding or practical experience in criminal law and procedure on the part of most entrants encourages a more hierarchical structure. Most new deputes, particularly since the age bar of twenty-six was lifted in 1971, come straight from university, where criminal law is only one course among many and criminal procedure hardly figures at all. While they must have served an apprenticeship, this may have involved little or no criminal court work (unless the apprentice has worked in an office specialising in criminal work or in Crown Office itself) and they will have had no right of audience to actually present a case in court. Yet the range of criminal cases dealt with by the fiscal is very wide since he is now responsible for the prosecution of *all* criminal offences.

Therefore, it is not surprising that procurators fiscal regard the training and supervision of new deputes as an important part of their work: 'at the beginning a new depute is supervised very closely . . . it is essentially part of their training that they should have the experience of marking'; 'this is an office where all the deputes have been young and fairly inexperienced and therefore I have wanted to exercise strict control'. This is reflected in the way in which reports are distributed by procurators fiscal for marking between the deputes: 'I distribute to them the cases which come in for marking . . . I extract cases which I know will have special difficulties and I deal with them'; 'all reports come to me . . . marking is undertaken by the deputes who will refer any cases of complexity or difficulty to me'.

While offices vary in the degree of responsibility granted to a new depute, it is generally accepted by these entrants that the skills of marking can only be acquired with practice and, in the initial stages at least, with an experienced supervisor: 'I've been sharing a room with a more senior depute . . . he's been handing me over a few cases . . . he's been checking it with me and giving me advice'; 'I look at the report and then realise I don't know how to draft it and then go and ask somebody else to draft it and learn . . . that way'.

Most fiscals agree that the best way of learning the art of marking is, paradoxically, not through marking but by appearances in court: 'the procurator fiscal took the view that you were far better off doing trials, seeing the complaints and trying to prove them before you started marking them. Then when you came to mark them you'd a better idea of just how to draft them because you knew exactly what the problems were and to that extent it more or less came naturally because you'd become so used to seeing charges by the time that you actually came to mark cases.' This approach to marking underlines the ongoing nature of the exercise which is essentially geared towards the *prosecution* of crime rather than the use of alternative measures.[1]

The marking process is completed by returning reports to office support staff, who then follow the regular procedures for the issuing of a complaint or petition against an accused person unless the case is dropped or further information is required. It is clear from observation and discussion with the staff, however, that their system also is orientated towards the prosecution of cases in the courts rather than any other means of disposal.

VARIATIONS

While this general outline of the organisation of marking holds true for all fiscal offices, there are interesting variations between offices in the detailed implementation of the general model. Variations in the organisation of marking appear to be related to several factors, both quantitative – the number of reports received by each office, the size of the professional staff complement deemed sufficient to deal with the caseload – and qualitative – the approach adopted by procurators fiscal, the experience and attitudes of deputes and the local environment. Organisational differences, then, are affected both by external concerns over which fiscals would appear to have little control and internal matters which the procurator fiscal and his staff may directly determine. A typology of five different organisational styles is used to explore these variations more fully and is shown in Diagram 4 on page 36.

Single fiscal offices

The traditional notion of the organisation of Scottish public prosecution was perhaps best reflected in the television series *Sutherland's Law* in which the fictional procurator fiscal worked in a rural community and handled all cases himself. In twenty-one offices this pattern still persists: 'the reports come in here, they are given a serial number, they arrive on my desk . . . there is no one else to involve'; 'I have full responsibility for running the actual mechanics of the office'. From annual returns made to Crown Office it appears that these single fiscal offices handle under 2,000 cases per annum, the average weekly caseload being about thirty reports, which can generally be accommodated by the criminal courts in two or three court days per week. There is little doubt that because of the small number of reports received by these offices and the nature of such reports marking is usually not carried out under pressure. In those offices which contributed more than fifty cases to our Census, 28 per cent of their reports were custody cases which required to be dealt with speedily whereas in offices of caseloads with less than fifty the percentage of custody reports was 11 per cent. Furthermore, the low volume of reports and the fact that one person controls their processing means that it is not essential to streamline the handling of cases. Fiscals in these offices talk informally about mulling over cases: 'you occasionally have naughty ones which you tend to leave lying on your desk for a while or take them to bed with you'.

---

[1] This point is expanded further in Chapter 4.

Diagram 4 Typology of Organizational Styles in Marking

Type	Organization	Fiscal Staff	Annual Caseload	Location
Single Fiscal	All cases marked and prosecuted by PF	PF only	<2000	Rural community
Pupil-Teacher	Cases marked by depute supervised by PF	PF LA	<4000	Small town
Senior-Junior	Cases allocated by PF between more experienced and new deputes according to degree of difficulty	PF SLA LA	<6000	Medium sized town
Marking Deputes	All cases marked by deputes allocated to marking for specific period	PF SLAs APF LAs	<20000	Large town
Marking Team	All cases marked under SD's supervision by summary team of 4-5 deputes with team leader teams rotate SD remains	PF APFs SDs Team leaders Team members	>20000	City

PF Procurator fiscal   APF Assistant procurator fiscal   SD Senior depute   SLA Senior legal assistant   LA Legal assistant

The same person is responsible for a report from initial receipt to eventual disposal, which ensures a certain continuity in approach sometimes lacking in a larger office. The single fiscal also has to develop an understanding of administrative matters, which is not so essential for the deputes in a larger office. A fiscal who had moved from a post as depute in a large office to procurator fiscal in a small office described it thus: 'when I came here I became more involved with administration, the actual mechanics of running an office which are largely unknown to the deputes running the court side of things in a large office . . . my predecessor had come from a large office and he didn't know much about running an office . . . in X papers arrived, you dealt with them, papers departed and that was it'.

Not surprisingly the lone fiscal is likely to have more knowledge of and greater involvement in the local community than his urban counterparts: 'it's rather like a large village here . . . a large proportion of the population are in some way related . . . I may well know the accused . . . in fact half of the regulars speak to me in the street'; 'I tend to get very much involved in cases which appear to me to be patently petty but to the person who makes the complaint it seems the antithesis of that'. While fiscals traditionally have been expected to remain somewhat aloof from local matters, they are aware of local feeling about particular cases and this awareness may be heightened in a small closely-knit community: 'at the moment I have a serious and particularly awkward road traffic death . . . a very popular local was knocked down by a stranger . . . the locals are desperate that the case should be heard before a jury'.

In marking, then, the single fiscal will have both sufficient time to weigh up the merits of individual cases and enough knowledge of the parties involved and the background to the offence to make an informed decision. For example after a minor offence of obstructing the highway was reported to a fiscal operating in a one-man office he considered it necessary to drive the fifty miles to the scene of the accident to inspect the locus. This zealous attention to detail was prompted by the background to the incident involving a feud between rival cafe owners in a tourist resort which was causing bad feeling and needed to be resolved, but not necessarily by a prosecution. Thus such fiscals may place more emphasis on keeping the peace within a community than in enforcing the strict letter of the law.

However, it is sometimes difficult for the fiscal to be seen as impartial and his decisions occasionally become the subject of considerable criticism. One lone fiscal explained his position thus: 'if one, for example, takes the city situation, one has the hope of complete anonymity. The opposite applies here. One has to be seen as Caesar's wife, above suspicion, not as the local persecutor but just simply as the prosecutor and be seen to be fair on all hands.' There is also a greater possibility that the fiscal in a small office will have to prosecute someone with whom he is personally acquainted. In an attempt to ensure impartiality fiscals may consciously omit to look at the name of the accused until they have reached a decision: 'about the last thing I look at is the name on the complaint, it's a sort of instinctive reaction'.

The impact of the local setting on these small offices contrasts with a sense of remoteness from Crown Office, the organisation at the centre of the fiscal service. There is also a feeling that close-knit communities effectively police themselves: 'there isn't a great deal of actual crime here – being islanders they've got to live together . . . people tend to sort things out for themselves. They only call on the police because they cannot.' Therefore while fiscals might consult Crown Office about a case with ramifications outside the local community, for example, 'a case involving an environmentalist group with the ear of the press', generally they do not need to seek outside assistance.

Pupil/Teacher offices

While the one-man office still represents the organisation of public pros-ecution in many areas of Scotland, it is apparent from the growth of the fiscal service in the last ten years that this picture is changing. The increase in crimes made known to the police and the expansion of the fiscal's prosecution responsi-bilities has resulted in a doubling of the numbers of professional staff since 1970. For example, one of the smaller offices we visited had trebled its annual return in the ten years between 1968 and 1978 for reports of alleged offences. Many single fiscal offices can no longer cope alone so deputes have to be allocated to such offices. Here is the experience of one depute recently recruited to the service who was assigned to what had been a one-man office: 'this office is a good office to learn in because there is only one fiscal and one depute so any training that the fiscal is going to do I benefit from. The fiscal is very keen on training, letting you do the job and making sure you're fit to do the job.' The procurator fiscal in this office described the pupil/teacher relationship thus: 'I will give the depute the reports which come up daily to mark and he will pass them through to me and then he will come in and I will go over each report with him to point out any matters which have to be corrected or changed'.

The definition of the new depute's status as that of a pupil ensures that the procurator fiscal remains in command and the relatively low volume of reports received (under 4,000 a year, about seventy a week) makes it possible for him to supervise all cases: 'I see everything that goes through this office because of its size. I can control things and the same applies to all offices smaller than this but when you get into the larger offices there must be more than one person marking the reports.' Since new deputes appear to assimilate fairly quickly the habits and attitudes of their superiors, differences of professional opinion are rare, according to one depute: 'he's taught me all I know and I operate his system, using his ideas'.

While such close supervision may be necessary and acceptable where deputes are new and inexperienced, it is probably important that the procurator fiscal devolve responsibility for marking and other duties as his depute gains expertise. One procurator fiscal explained his attitude thus: 'as time progresses the depute becomes a little more experienced and I pass more on to him but even after two years here I still checked everything that came up so that when he marked the reports initially he passed them through to me and I would initial them just to see that he was not missing something'.

As with the single fiscal office, the procurator fiscal emphasises his authoritative position: 'here the big advantage is that I am in charge of my own office . . . it's big enough to provide quite a variety of work and yet, at the same time, it is small enough to be able to control everything personally'.

Senior/Junior offices

A further group of offices stands midway between the small offices located in relatively homogeneous rural communities and the large offices which serve the urban centres of population in Scotland. The organisation of marking in these offices has features in common with the two models already described. Marking is generally delegated by the procurator fiscal to the two or three deputes working under him. But the procurators fiscal we talked to considered it an important part of their job to oversee the process both before the deputes actually receive the reports and after the essential decisions have been made. The procurator fiscal himself may allocate the reports when they come in or will occasionally do even the routine marking. Such day-to-day supervision is possible because caseloads generally do not exceed one hundred per week: 'normally it's the deputes who do the marking but I do all the signing so that at least my eye goes over the results and I can pick up mistakes'.

One procurator fiscal introduced a system of organisational notes: 'so the deputes are not in any doubt as to what they must do in this office: this one is allocation of office duties . . . it says "marking is to be undertaken by the two deputes who will refer any cases of complexity or difficulty to the PF" and they are told that if in any doubt at all refer it'. The deputes working in his office were able to state very clearly what this meant in practice: 'anything we consider no proceedings, anything that we think needs a warrant, anything on solemn procedure'. The more junior depute had some additional cases which she personally referred to the procurator fiscal: 'any case involving the police, any case involving children or indecency'.

In another office, there appeared to be an implicit understanding of the kinds of cases the procurator fiscal should see: 'he keeps an "interested" tab on the stuff which either he knows is coming on or which I draw to his attention . . . anything that I think is of substantial interest or importance I would ask him if he wanted to see it'.

Since it is generally the pattern to allocate to these offices one fairly junior and one more experienced depute, there may also be a second supervisory level interposed between procurator fiscal and depute, with the new depute being trained by both the experienced depute and the procurator fiscal. However, there is still a very clearly defined chain of command which vests the final decision in the procurator fiscal and this is either made explicit by the procurator fiscal: 'the depute might have one idea of what should be done and I might agree or take an entirely different view . . . if it came to the crunch it would be my decision that would be implemented' or assumed: 'the deputes know basically what my feelings are about cases . . . they are told what my policies are . . . they can put these into effect in particular cases'.

Both procurator fiscal and deputes can see the logic behind such controls.

As one procurator fiscal said: 'the rationale behind this is consistency . . . this is an office where, until very recently, all the deputes have been young and fairly inexperienced and therefore I have wanted to exercise a fairly strict control'. His deputes agreed: 'I take the view that the procurator fiscal, who carries the can, can say "this is the way I want a case marked"'; 'uniformity is crucial. I think it is disgraceful that one man will be prosecuted for an offence because the procurator fiscal marks the report and another will not be prosecuted because I mark it . . . it has to be standard if justice is going to be fair and be seen to be fair.'

However, such restrictions on the deputes' freedom to make decisions is regarded as irksome by a few deputes since what consultation with the procurator fiscal actually entails is acceptance of his decisons. For an experienced depute in particular this may rankle: 'my great grouse is that the procurator fiscal draws into himself the interesting and important stuff . . . that is a bit of a bind to a senior depute and you really want to do the stuff with a bit of a bite – I disagree on odd things and I am conscious that when I mark these particular things I mark them on what we talk about as office policy'.

Nevertheless, it is important to remember that in senior/junior offices with moderate caseloads, marking is only one aspect of the fiscal's work, which can be very varied: 'here you have to be a Jack-of-all-trades by doing marking and being in court every day. In a smaller office such as this one you're getting to grips with the practical difficulties which usually never come to a depute in a larger office'; 'you see the whole process not just a little bit of it . . . you start things off which you see right through to the end and that encourages responsibility . . . it has its own in-built sanction – you are the one who has to stand up in public.'

Marking depute offices

The effects of expansion in the fiscal service are most noticeable in the large urban offices and, consequently, there have been important changes in the organisation of marking in these offices. It is clear from an examination of figures for reports received by all offices over the last ten years that the increase has been particularly marked in the ten offices with the biggest caseloads. Fiscals who have been in the service for some time are keenly aware of this. One procurator fiscal made some interesting comparisons: 'things have changed very rapidly since the time I was at X in early 1970. It was then a very small office processing just over 5,000 cases. There was only myself and a depute and I was very involved in court work.' Now the office he described has a professional staff of one procurator fiscal and four deputes who handle almost 9,000 cases annually. Inevitably, these larger offices have developed systems of dealing with reports which are in contrast to the organisation of marking in the offices already described. Firstly, the procurator fiscal is less likely to be closely involved with the daily routine of marking and court work and becomes more of an administrator: 'I still mark a few just to keep my hand in but I'm much more involved in administration – it's almost a different way of life entirely'. Keeping track of reports as they come in and are processed becomes a more pressing problem necessitating the employment of more clerical and administrative staff who report directly to an office manager.

The procurator fiscal must ensure that the work gets done: 'that's the essential side of the administrative side . . . getting the work through'. He may delegate to one of his fiscal staff not only the day-to-day responsibility for marking but also the supervision of deputes and may confine himself to administrative duties: 'I used to have time for discussing cases with deputes and training deputes by taking them into court with me but my days of sitting in with them are over'. Deputes may be encouraged to consult another depute or assistant procurator fiscal rather than the procurator fiscal and such responsibilities may even be split between two experienced deputes, one person dealing with solemn cases: 'in relation to my actual job I supervise the serious stuff . . . deputes bring me cases they consider to be difficult' and another with summary cases: 'I am responsible for all the summary work. I am available for consultation.'

It appears that most large offices regard the traditional practice of allocating individual cases to deputes from initial reporting to final disposal as unworkable. Division of labour is deemed essential though it is also regarded as important to provide a variety of experience, especially to new deputes: 'there's always something different to do . . . you are either in the office, in the sheriff court or at a district court . . . the more experience you have the more responsibilities you have'. Therefore deputes are frequently allocated in rotation to undertake particular duties such as marking. Allocation of work in this way does mean that cases are rarely followed through by the same depute: 'you come to cases very cold here, in a smaller office you can keep track of things much better'; 'in a great big office very often you are just doing one bit of a case and not seeing it again'.

Some offices have introduced the concept of a summary team, consisting of two or more deputes: 'the cases reported by the police and other agencies each day are collected by the office staff and brought to the summary team'. Ideally this team should include one senior and one relatively inexperienced depute so another tier is added to the hierarchy: 'within our office I am fourth from the top of the tree . . . being in charge of the summary team presents scope for developing responsibilities. As the senior person I endeavour to oversee the marking.'

The learning process for new deputes in these offices is still an informal one, however: 'at the time I joined I was in a room with two other deputes . . . in effect we operated a summary team . . . it was just simply a question of asking and getting answers to your questions'; 'this is the first week I've had of constantly marking charges – I've been sharing a room with a more senior depute and it's been a case of handing me over a few cases and saying "you mark it" and then checking it and giving me his advice'.

Marking team offices

There are two fiscal offices in Scotland where the organisation of work and the structure of marking does not conform to any of the four models already described. The volume of reports and the number of professional staff needed to cope with the workload in these offices has led to the introduction of teams of about four to six deputes headed by an experienced fiscal called the team leader. These teams are allocated to, for example, marking, sheriff and jury trials, summary trials and district court work on a rota basis. Since each of these areas of work has a specialist senior depute or assistant procurator fiscal permanently assigned to it some continuity can be maintained as teams move on to their next assignment. One such specialism is marking and court work following prosecution. While involved in this area of work the team is designated the summary team and is allocated to the summary room.

The senior depute in charge of marking in one office explained his position thus: 'when I came here the senior deputes were given particular areas of responsibility . . . I am responsible for all the work of the summary team . . . if a disaster occurs, I carry the can'. While members of the team divide their time between courtwork and marking, the senior depute generally remains in the office. This is regarded as a necessity: 'now I can't be doing court duties and be responsible for what is happening here . . . it's not the ideal solution, but it is probably the best solution here'. In this way he can acquire considerable expertise across a wide range of cases from largescale frauds to breaches of health and safety at work regulations and will have the time to read up relevant statutes and case law. In addition he can develop useful links with the different reporting agencies and they in turn know whom they can consult.

Responsibility for the work is shared with the team leader: 'whilst I am in charge of the summary team the team leader leads the team . . . the normal chain of command is team to the team leader to me and I don't interfere with how he organises the team during the four weeks they are in the summary room. He splits up the duties in different ways.' However, the way in which supervision is divided between senior depute and team leader is not rigidly defined, as the senior depute explained: 'there's seven teams . . . the experience of the team leaders varies . . . team leader X for example . . . I would never have questioned his decisions . . . he'd know as much as I did. Others I keep a closer eye on because they are less experienced.'

The physical lay-out of the summary room reflects the way in which marking is organised. The four or five members of the team, the team leader and the senior depute all share one room. The senior depute explained: 'I have a room of my own across the corridor . . . I don't like that . . . I try to be here because I can hear things being said. I can sit in if I think a wrong decision is being taken . . . I am here all the time.' The availability of the senior depute is important for deputes who may not be very experienced and will certainly need time to adjust to the summary room: 'coming here was traumatic . . . the place is just different from any other place I have ever been'; 'it was a very big change . . . when I first arrived I felt very lost . . . coming from where there was five of us . . . you were able to keep track of things much better. It is so different here from the other places . . . it's got to be seen as having its own special problems.' The senior depute himself was very aware of the difficulties which a new depute assigned to the summary room might face and might even lay down specific guidelines in such instances: 'there was a fellow who was a month in the fiscal service . . . he was appointed to the summary team. I said to him "if there are any cases which you mark no proceedings I will see them all".'

Generally, however, consultation is a more informal matter: 'you consult in the summary team situation because you are all sitting there and you just pick something up and shout it out to somebody'. Fiscals assigned to marking regard this as valuable: 'it tempers the use of your discretion and I think it can only be a good thing'.

The working atmosphere in the summary room contrasts markedly with the slow pace in a single fiscal office. There may be a hundred custody cases received at nine o'clock in the morning to be marked and prepared before two o'clock the same day and three times that number of cited cases: 'it fluctuates, one can't say one is under pressure every day and every hour but there can be intensive spurts of pressure . . . one can possibly get eight murders in a month'.

Thus it is clear that the organisation of marking within fiscal offices varies considerably. However our research shows that, despite this variation in approach, all fiscal offices operate within certain general parameters which ensure that decisions made by fiscals are remarkably consonant across the whole country.

SETTING PARAMETERS TO THE MARKING TASK

Criminal law and procedure

The fiscal operates within the framework provided by the criminal law and must follow the rules of criminal procedure. However, this is not as confining as might at first appear. Criminal law in Scotland is concerned with offences at Common Law, which, as the legal texts on criminal law admit, are often difficult to define: 'it would be a mistake to imagine that the criminal Common Law of Scotland countenances any precise and exact categorisation of the forms of conduct which amount to crime'. [McLaughlan *v.* Boyd 1934 JC 19, L J-G Clyde at pp 22-3] There is even a latent power residing with the court to create new criminal offences. This residual power has rarely been exercised in the twentieth century[1] but it provides an indication of the flexibility inherent in this branch of the law. In Common Law offences the fiscal is free to frame charges as he wishes. An offence such as breach of the peace can be used to cover a wide variety of different situations which are regarded by the police and subsequently by the fiscal as matters requiring criminal sanction: 'the crime of breach of the peace covers a very wide range of conduct varying from drunken behaviour to offences of an indecent nature'. [Sheehan: 1975: 100] Statutory offences are usually more narrowly defined but even here there may be room for manoeuvre.

Similarly, the restrictions which the rules of criminal procedure place upon decision-making by fiscals may be more apparent than real. Certainly there are

[1] But see the offence of taking a motor car without the owner's consent first recognised as a criminal offence in Strathern *v.* Seaforth 1926 JC 100.

procedural requirements governing the framing of a summary complaint or petition and the jurisdiction of the different courts is limited by statute.[1] But the fiscal is under no legal obligation to prosecute and is not required to give reasons for his decisions in any instance. In general therefore the fiscal is not bound by any overt restrictions stemming from criminal law or procedure in the most vital decision which he as to make – whether or not to prosecute.

There is little doubt, however, that there are strong pressures upon the fiscal to make decisions in certain ways and these are derived from the logic of the law itself. Criteria of relevance, for example, are largely determined according to traditional ideas of legal logic. For instance, the emphasis on the criminal incident itself rather than the circumstances surrounding it or the characteristics of the parties involved and the inclusion of a wide variety of different fact situations under the one offence heading is a reflection of the lawyer's need to simplify and categorise complex events.

Again a rise in the number of statutory offences where a standard form of charge, called a style, is often included in the schedules to the Act has had an impact on the breadth of prosecutorial decision-making. When the police define an incident as coming within the ambit of a specific statutory offence there is less latitude for variation in charging and the scope for description of events is limited. Increasingly statutory offences are being substituted for Common Law crimes, for example, the Common Law crime of fraud which can cover a multitude of situations is very rarely invoked nowadays, since the most common types of fraud, malpractices in financial dealings, are specifically covered by statute.[2] The proportion of charges in our Census relating to statutory rather than Common Law offences was over 60 per cent.

The criminal justice process

While the powers of the fiscal appear to be very extensive and he is in theory given wide autonomy to make decisions independently, it is most important that he should not be regarded in isolation from the criminal justice process as a whole, since this exerts considerable pressure upon him to perform his work in particular ways and to strive for particular goals. For example, the fiscal does not himself collect the information upon which he relies in making marking decisions. This is in practice the prerogative of the police, even though the fiscal in theory is entitled to intervene and direct their investigations. There are other agencies which report directly to the fiscal but the vast majority of reports received for marking are submitted by the police. During the week of our Census 92 per cent of all reports received by fiscal offices were submitted by the police, 3 per cent from the Television Licence Records Office, 3 per cent from the Traffic Commissioners and 1 per cent from the Department of Health and Social Security. The remaining 1 per cent came from a wide variety of different agencies, including the Health and Safety at Work Executive and Local Environmental Health Offices.

[1] See Chapter 5.
[2] See for example Supplementary Benefits Act 1976.

Bundles of police reports, called police informations, are received by fiscal offices daily or more often in a larger office. This is generally the first intimation the fiscal will have of the alleged criminal incident unless the reporting police officer wishes to discuss the case with him before making a formal report. For example, in a complicated fraud case the CID officer involved in the investigation came to discuss with the fiscal the kind of information which would be needed to sustain a conviction. Again, a police officer sought a fiscal's advice regarding an allegation of rape where medical evidence was ambiguous. In that case, no report was submitted since the fiscal recommended that there was insufficient corroboration to support a prosecution. In a few offices there is a great deal of contact with the police before reports are actually submitted: 'where there is something specific which a reporting officer wishes to discuss with the fiscal, he will bring the report in himself . . . if it is something fairly serious he will want to speak to me about it'.

For the most part, however, fiscals do not speak to the reporting officer before marking a case and they rely on the police report solely in making decisions concerned with prosecution. If one accepts the premise that 'the quality of decision-making in most social contexts is directly related to the amount of relevant information available to decision-makers' [Bottomley: 1973: 98], it follows that the role of the police as reporters is a crucial one. Research on the creation of written records has shown that in encapsulating an actual event on paper ambiguities and inconsistencies are usually lost particularly where the writer is attempting to contain his description within a standard format and to suggest one course of action rather than another:

> in everyday life precise delineations are not made: vague
> stereotypes seem to be used. Control agencies in our society,
> however, in defining and classifying become responsible for
> drawing clearer lines than in fact exist in everyday life.
> [Freidson: 1973: 125]

In the case of police reports, for example, most police forces present what they judge to be relevant information in a similar way. Cited cases, reports concerning an accused person who is not in custody, state the accused's name, sex, age and address, the charge or charges which the police deem appropriate and a summary of the alleged criminal incident. Use is sometimes made of a section headed *Comments* where the police may include some further observations about the accused or his family. Generally, however, the report focuses on the offence itself and the ingredients deemed necessary for proving the offence. The language is stereotyped and the thrust of the presentation is towards minimising uncertainty and maximising the strength of the case for the prosecution: 'reports are stereotyped. In fact you will find out only that the accused is aged such and such, employed as so and so, has so many children.' Fiscals remark that only occasionally do the police express any doubts: 'two boys charged with assaulting X and X charged with assaulting one of these boys . . . the police clearly can't make up their own mind, that's why they have split this into two counterclaims'; 'occasionally we have cases where there is a charge and countercharge, the victim in one being the accused in the other, . . . we have a discussion with the police as to credibility, as to whom we should proceed against'.

Police officers may occasionally consider that it is in their own interests to inform the fiscal of police links with particular accused persons: 'where the accused in one case has, for reasons best known to himself, perhaps to ingratiate himself with the police, given them information as a result of which other accused persons have been reported, the police have quite properly submitted both informations together. I have a word with them about . . . whether they were expecting me to do any particular favour in relation to the accused or whether there was any particular order in which the cases should be taken so as not to prejudice a potential witness.'

Reports where an accused is in custody tend to be, if anything, briefer since the reporting officer may have apprehended the accused only hours before the fiscal receives his report: 'so many are drawn up – 20, 30, 40 reports a night that obviously they must become stereotyped'. Under Scottish law the accused who has been arrested and held in custody by the police must be brought before a court on the next lawful day (excluding weekends and public holidays) or be released by the fiscal. The custody report contains the same information as in a cited case, though the police may also include *full statements*, verbatim accounts obtained from witnesses to the incident.

Statutory offences are more amenable to standardisation than Common Law crimes and this is reflected in the use of pro formas by the police in reporting such offences. For example, in a speeding case the reporting officer uses a standard form to report the offence. The form gives a statutory definition of the charge and the officer merely fills in the blanks left for name, age and address of the accused, the number of his car, the locus where he was stopped, the time of day when the incident took place and the speed at which the accused was alleged to be driving. The same is true for an increasing number of statutory offences under road traffic legislation, the Vehicle Excise Acts and the Wireless Telegraphy Acts. Such forms are intended to reduce police time spent preparing reports and to ensure that there is uniformity both among individual police officers and between different police forces in Scotland.

In our Census 13 per cent of all reports received by the fiscal related solely to speeding and parking offences which makes a sizeable proportion of his marking caseload appear very routine: 'many of the cases are run-of-the-mill, like speeding and drunk and incapable offences and don't require much skill at all in marking'; 'marking is actually necessarily largely routine because a lot of the cases are straightforward – there is not a great deal you can think about with the statutory ones'. This mundane aspect of the work is often accentuated by the fact that cases concerned with one type of statutory offence are generally reported en bloc: 'it depends on the type of case and the volume one has of a particular type of case. I mean, you can't get terribly excited about careless driving when it comes in in piles of fifty'; 'you mark a lot of cases which really just take a second or two to look at . . . people think we decide individually on every case but the evidence is there on most of the statutory things'. Fiscals disagree on the general legitimacy of using pro formas, but it is clear that some regard such devices as appropriate in certain statutory offences. This is particularly evident in relation to cases which they define as equivalent to petty misdemeanours where no moral blame can be imputed to the accused: 'statutory ones do not involve much moral blame'; 'a lot of the road traffic stuff, it's called criminal. I just don't think it is criminal, speeding . . . you do it, I do it . . .'; 'it's the kind of thing that you or I could do or someone who is otherwise a respectable citizen.' They are prepared to accept a standard, brief presentation of the facts from the police in such cases since a conviction for such *minor* infringements of the law does not carry with it the same public condemnation as *serious* crime.

They are less happy about the use of the pro forma in Common Law offences and perceive a tendency on the part of the police to present the minimum amount of information when writing reports generally. Theoretically, the fiscal can ask the police to investigate the case further or obtain full statements from witnesses before he decides to prosecute. If there is some glaring evidential flaw or very obvious mistake in police procedure the fiscal will look behind the report and request further information. In our Census this occurred in 6 per cent of all reports and not surprisingly these were generally cited cases which were not reported on pro formas. Fiscals admit that informed decision-making may be hampered where the report is very brief: 'it's very dangerous . . . take, for example, a shoplifting reported on a pro forma. None of the real details are explained to me. A policeman can produce to me on a pro forma something that looks so simple and straightforward – straightforward shoplifting – and it may turn out to be nothing like that'; 'my problem is not having sufficient knowledge of the facts. You can say that the fiscal's discretion is often, maybe too often, exercised in an ill-informed way through no fault of his own. A Reporter to the Children's Hearings gets a social background report before he decides whether to proceed or not.[1] Why shouldn't I? Because if I have the full information, with my experience and my general views on the preservation of life and property, I really feel that I am hardly likely to make the wrong decision.'

The submission of a report by the police inevitably involves a strong presumption in favour of prosecution since fiscals regard it as unlikely that the matter would otherwise be reported to them. Scottish prosecutors generally hold the police in high regard: 'I have always been pro police. They have got a damned difficult job to do and while I don't think it's desirable for the fiscal to regard himself as a jumped up policeman, I think it's bad to consider oneself as so neutral that one is always against the police.' Nevertheless fiscals note that the reporting officer may screen out information which a prosecutor might consider important: 'the police can withhold information . . . they don't usually do it deliberately, but they can do it because they think the fiscal doesn't want to

---

[1] The Reporter to the Children's Hearings in Scotland receives information from the police, social workers and others about children in difficulty. In each case, he must decide whether to take no action, to involve the social work department or to refer the child to a Children's Hearing – see *Children's Hearings* Scottish Information Office Factsheet.

know that or doesn't need to know that'. In this way the police may, albeit inadvertently, undermine the fiscal's position as independent prosecutor: 'we have to rely on the police doing more and more . . . we're giving up our true constitutional function of investigating crime and are almost acting as a rubber stamp for police officers'.

Reporting agencies differ in the way in which they present information to the fiscal. The TV Licence Records Office and the Traffic Commissioners, for instance, generally use pro formas and do not submit reports personally to the fiscal. However, other recently established agencies where there is new legislation to be applied, for example, the Health and Safety at Work Executive and Consumer Protection Departments, would appear to involve the fiscal from the early stages of an investigation and to look to him for guidance thus giving the fiscal considerable control over the way in which such offences are reported: 'we have been trying to introduce a process of education to do with the local authority agencies, environmental health and so on. In particular, we have been trying to educate them into reporting the cases in a form which we find convenient. We will ask for statements from witnesses, a draft charge and any comments which they may have. It's really a question of getting them to structure their thoughts on the matter, it's also easier for us to deal with.' Presentation of reports, then, is a key factor in shaping fiscals' decision-making.

There are other aspects of the criminal justice process which tend to shape and possibly limit the fiscal's discretion in marking such as the volume of work with which some offices must cope. In the ten years between 1970 and 1980 the number of reports received by fiscal offices almost doubled.[1] In the same period the number of professional staff attached to the fiscal service had increased by more than 100 per cent. Some fiscal offices such as Glasgow and other large urban centres now handle over 1,000 reports per week.

The kind of pressure which this exerts on prosecutors has been well described in sociological literature which suggests that there is a tendency for the process itself to take over encouraging a constant flow of cases and leading ultimately to a conveyor-belt system of justice. [Blumberg: 1967] The inevitable pressure towards uniformity and streamlining which such large numbers create is reinforced by the nature of modern bureaucratic organisations preoccupied with the saving of time and expense and the encouragement of order, uniformity and predictability within the system. [King: 1981: 104] Individual exercise of discretion is regarded as both politically dangerous and an inefficient way of spreading resources and therefore something which should be kept under control. Members of organisations must be able to account for their actions within a particular bureaucratic framework and those explanations must square with the requirements of efficient processing. Even the smallest fiscal office has felt the impact of such bureaucratisation in the form of particular returns which have to be made and forms which are required to be completed for each case. One fiscal reckoned that when the fiscal office serves a complaint on an accused person that office may be required to provide the person with ten

[1] See Diagram 5 p. 49.

Diagram 5 Reports received by Scottish Prosecutors 1970–80

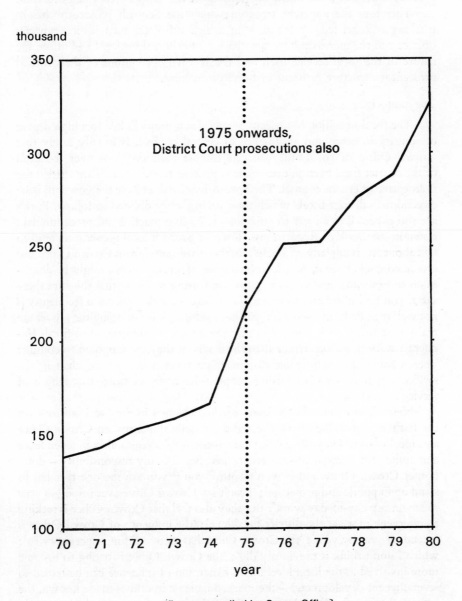

thousand

1975 onwards,
District Court prosecutions also

year

(figures supplied by Crown Office)

E

different completed forms. New legislation in the field of criminal justice, for example under the Bail (Scotland) Act 1980 and the Criminal Justice (Scotland) Act 1980, requiring forms to be completed at particular stages in the criminal process, underlines this tendency towards more formality in recording decisions.

Therefore the apparent freedom which the Scottish prosecutor has in marking is restricted by the way in which other criminal justice agencies operate and the increased bureaucratisation of criminal justice. In addition, the nature of the fiscal service itself and fiscals' own perceptions of their role as prosecutors structure prosecutorial decison-making.

The fiscal service

The fiscal's position historically is one of autonomy linked to a high degree of security in office and an absence of central control. It is only rarely that Crown Office or the Lord Advocate impose their decisions over the head of the district fiscal even in cases such as petition matters which are strictly the prerogative of crown counsel. The Lord Advocate does have the power to issue directions to district fiscals which they are in theory obliged to follow. Fiscals are also expected to adhere to guidelines regarding practice and procedure laid down in the Book of Regulations. However Scottish local prosecutors tend to talk about receiving 'advice', 'help', 'back-up assistance' from Crown Office and crown counsel rather than orders: 'in a spate of unusual cases I might be doubt-ful as to procedure and consult'; 'it is comforting to know that they are there when you find it difficult to make a decision'. To seek advice too frequently is not well regarded: 'in a sense it is passing the buck, it is not doing the job *we* are really here to do'. It is pointed out by some that, in any case, local fiscals fre-quently have more experience than those whom they are supposed to consult: 'there's something a little bit inappropriate when some young chap in the service a year or two is advising people who have six times that length of service'.

Nevertheless some fiscals detect marked changes in the fiscal service over the last ten years which have affected the relationship between Crown Office and local offices. They are quick to stress the fiscal's continuing independence and authority: 'there is no-one else to involve, it is my responsibility – don't bother Crown Office and it won't bother you'; 'you are the one that has to stand up in public and prosecute'; 'I can't say Crown Office ever impinges very much on my day-to-day work'. But they also feel that Crown Office is seeking to intervene more at the district fiscal level: 'the influence of Crown Office is extending year by year'; 'the Crown Office has an overriding supervisory role which I don't think it previously did'; 'the Crown Office is trying to become more involved at the local level'. This expansion of influence can be traced to several recent developments – the marked increase in crimes made known, the extension of the fiscal's jurisdiction to include the district courts, the increase in the number of statutory offences, and a greater awareness on the part of the public of their rights with regard to the law. Thus fiscals report cases to Crown Office which may be of particular public concern or be the subject of contro-versy at a national level: 'I report cases with very strong political overtones, something which goes beyond local interest, cases that will cause trouble'; 'a delicate, difficult or sensitive case – Crown Office acts as a filter so that it is unlikely that a seriously mistaken course of action will be decided upon'. This seems to have encouraged more formalised channels of communication between Crown Office and local offices and 'a tendency to try to get standard practice in certain types of cases'. Whereas formerly there seem to have been unofficial mechanisms for obtaining advice outwith the office, 'there was a system we used to work in the old days . . . X was the kind of person many people would have phoned up and said, "look I have got a problem, what's the answer?" ', nowadays fiscals perceive a need in some cases to obtain Crown Office approval for a particular course of action possibly as the result of public pressure to 'justify what you have done because of repercussions from one side or another that produce publicity'.

The role of the regional fiscal may also have important repercussions in relation to implementing national prosecution policies: 'the old concept of the fiscal being a separate entity with his own deputes and no one can intervene except at Crown Office level is gone'. This office is described as a purely administrative one, dealing with the allocation of staff and other supposedly non-contentious matters, but it is likely that regional procurators fiscal in future will be required to adopt a more assertive role in disseminating Crown Office policy. While we came across few cases where district fiscals felt that either the regional procurators fiscal or Crown Office were trying to impose their own decisions upon district offices, it is possible to discern a certain trend towards encouraging district fiscals to be aware of the potential political ramifications of their decisions and to balance this against the importance of individual discretion: 'policy matters come into it . . . would it be policy to take this case . . . difficulties in local relationships'.

Fiscals' perceptions of marking

Fiscals themselves have complex and often contradictory notions of their task in marking, reflecting both the ideal-typical notions of a prosecutor skilled in law and expected to exercise his judgment in the public interest and also practical matters concerned with getting the work done quickly and efficiently. These conflicting perceptions inevitably shape both the form and content of decision-making.

Fiscals are unanimous in their assertion that marking is a most important part of their work and one which requires the specialist skills of a lawyer: 'it demands the skill of reading fairly quickly and assimilating the information and deciding on the salient points – whether an offence has been committed in law – if there is sufficient evidence in law to prove it – the police do a good job but they are not lawyers – *you* have got to know the legal requirements'; 'the ability to see the matter very clearly, to get into it right away, to understand what you are dealing with, knowledge of the whole subject, knowledge of case law, of practice within the courts . . . a vast number of factors'.

The drafting of charges is regarded as one aspect of this expertise: 'one of the arts of a solicitor is craftsmanship – if you get an intriguing charge to frame in marking, it is a good exercise'. This is particularly so with Common Law offences: 'it's a drafting challenge . . . in the same way as a conveyancing solicitor would enjoy conveyancing simply because of the ability to exercise his style so it is in drafting'. The fiscal also draws on his legal skills in establishing if there is sufficient evidence to prove the case: 'our main angle is evidence – I think the police sometimes forget that we've got to prove it'. Supposedly straightforward legal concepts, such as sufficiency of evidence or standard of proof, are not always easy to define in practice: 'when you're considering whether you can prove it . . . one person might say "it's impossible to prove that" and somebody else might say "I know it can be proved"'.

It is generally accepted that there is also another facet of the marking task which does not relate to purely legal criteria but involves consideration of an individual's circumstances and motivation for committing a crime: 'you need a good knowledge of human nature . . . you have got to consider the circumstances in depth'; 'you have got to have some understanding of human relations'. This extra-legal dimension is regarded as particularly relevant in certain types of cases such as domestic violence. It permits the fiscal to exercise not only legal but also moral judgment: 'I don't take the letter of the law as the law . . . part of my job is making value judgments day in and day out'.

Marking is essentially a low-visibility activity and fiscals' decisions can only become the subject of public scrutiny when questions are asked in parliament. Emphasis is therefore placed on the individual fiscals' judgments rather than on the imposition of strict guidelines and in fact there are few formal rules governing decision-making at the marking stage: 'you just can't lay down a hard and fast rule, ten to one the next case that comes along will be on the wrong side of the line'. The freedom to make decisions is regarded as one of the positive features of the job: 'you do have a great deal of responsibility. You have a great deal of decision-making to do at various times or in various matters . . . it's demanding but extremely satisfying because your decisions are helping to shape the judicial process.' Most fiscals are totally opposed to the idea of restricting this freedom by the introduction of standard instructions: 'standardisation is a dangerous thing . . . it takes away from the fiscal his independence and individual discretion'.

Fiscal offices are located in very different parts of Scotland, ranging from remote island communities to large cities. It has been established that such variation affects the organisation of marking within offices but it may further be suggested that the particular locale influences the nature of decision-making. Certainly in the one-man offices the procurator fiscal is very aware of the need to consider the local context, as here where a procurator fiscal is marking: 'the next one is a drunk and incapable case occurring at X. When I get cases from X, I have to bear in mind the transport problems. I always say to myself "I wonder where the accused would prefer to go – the court in Y or Z?".'

Variation is accepted as inevitable: 'if you start to look for uniformity you tread on dangerous ground . . . you have got to take account of the variability of fiscals and the varying geographical differences and mores of the area'. There are differences between offices: 'there are bound to be regional variations –

in the Western Isles context behaviour A is really serious, behaviour B is not serious. In Edinburgh, it is the other way round' and between fiscals: 'the criteria in each district must vary according to the attitudes of the fiscal'; 'all fiscals are individuals, they all have their particular idiosyncrasies'. For example, a fiscal may have his own way of classifying assaults: 'there are some assaults that I feel are so distasteful – assaults on women, girls and children – they must go to the sheriff court'.

The value placed on individualized decision-making may be traced back to the fiscal's membership of the legal profession. Among professional groups of whatever kind there is usually a preference for what has been described in the literature on professions as *horizontal* rather than *vertical* interaction:

> under professionalism, a continuous and terminal status is
> shared by all members. Equal status and the continuous
> occupational career are important mechanisms for
> maintaining a sense of identity, colleague-loyalty and shared
> values. [Johnson: 1972: 55]

Emphasis is placed on the peer group rather than on a hierarchical structure so that decisions are made by individual members often in consultation with others but without pressure to accede to a fellow professional's assessment of the situation. Fiscals, even relatively new recruits, are very aware of this: 'I personally will go ahead and make my own decision no matter what anybody else says . . . there is no way that I would be pushed into doing something which I just didn't believe was right'; 'you tend to consult with people, if I had an awkward Social Security case I would discuss it with people'; 'it appears to be an independent but consultative system here. If I am in some doubt, I consult but it's my decision at the end of the day.'

This emphasis on individual decision-making and professional competence contrasts sharply both with our observation of the actual marking process itself and remarks made by fiscals themselves about the practicalities of the task. Thus: 'each case that comes in should be looked at closely and sympathetically so that decisions can properly be made. Now of course that's the ideal world'; 'it can be very routine when you're faced with a pile of fifty speeding cases to mark . . . that is something which a clerical officer can do'. Legal expertise in drafting and sufficiency of evidence lose some of their importance when it is remembered that charges may be drafted in a standard way commonly referred to by fiscals as a *style*: 'for a lot of statutory stuff there are styles and I have a large book of styles'. Similarly proving a case is often straightforward: 'most of the cases are probably fairly clearcut . . . a crime has been committed, there's evidence against the person that appears to have committed it . . . it's usually on that sort of basis that I personally operate'.

The primary skills which must be learned to do the job are not necessarily those which fiscals themselves emphasise in describing the ideal approach to marking. It is here that the routine nature of the task becomes important. The presumption in favour of prosecution and the tendency to elide ambiguity are themselves knowledge which has to be learned and applied and the most effective way of achieving that is generally by simplifying and categorising cases. It is true that fiscals claim to be alert for certain cues which will make them think twice before simply processing cases in the normal way, for example, a technical hitch in procedure or lack of evidence. But these cases are not the norm: 'we are always looking for funny ones but I think it's proper to say that the funny ones are very much at the edge of a very, very broad mainstream of cases that are simple straightforward matters that have to be brought before the court'.

This process of assimilating prosecutorial norms and rendering the unfamiliar familiar is reflected in fiscals' comments about the importance of experience: 'there is a skill in marking which is acquired through length of service'; 'some deputes are relatively wet behind the ears . . . they have not got the experience or the confidence that a more senior fiscal has in marking reports'. A very experienced fiscal remarked: 'having a new depute means that I am constantly looking at routine marking with a new depute's eye . . . you forget that things have not always been seen by you as routine'. There is no doubt that both the assimilation of particular work routines and the acquisition of certain skills are essential to marking, enabling the fiscal to make those decisions seen as appropriate for the processing of criminal cases. Fiscals note the problems for new deputes which unfamiliarity may bring. As one recent recruit said: 'I think most of the decisions are difficult for me at the moment. I know I spend far more time looking at them than the others do mainly because they know exactly what to do with them as soon as they see them.'

Most fiscals consider that there is a large measure of cohesion among Scottish prosecutors with regard to the *correct* decision: 'it's usually a fairly unanimous decision . . . we have fairly uniform views'. A number of reasons are put forward for this. For example, some fiscals regard the law as an objective fact and see little opportunity for deviation: 'there might be variations in the phraseology of marking but the end product of the charge is static throughout the service – there are only so many Common Law offences and so many statutory offences – they are only susceptible of a certain method of marking'; 'experience in the law may vary but knowledge of the law should be fairly constant . . . a depute is taking a decision principally on legal grounds, now the law doesn't change'. They also stress their shared professional backgrounds and the close ties between the comparatively small number of prosecutors in Scotland (less than 230 in 1982): 'there must be a large measure of cohesion because we are all doing the same job and we have a similar background'; 'we all tend to act more or less the same because we are all part of the same history . . . we all tended to get our style of marking from the same communal font of knowledge . . . with senior fiscals, you will find that they have worked in the same offices together'.

Deputes, particularly very new recruits, are not, in fact, given free rein to make decisions in relation to prosecution arguably because of the necessity for routinisation which appears to underlie the whole marking process. Deputes are expected to accept the procurator fiscal's decision as final and may be obliged to consult him regarding certain cases: 'we try to have common practices throughout the office by way of styles and by way of reaction to a particular fact'. One procurator fiscal explained it thus: 'some new fiscals have an overwhelming sense of power . . . you can't be in the fiscal service for two or three weeks and make an informed decision on prosecution . . . so they aren't given carte blanche'.

CONCLUSION

When a fiscal makes decisions relating to the prosecution of crime the wide discretion which he has in law is limited and shaped by a number of factors. These include both the general framework which structures the marking task and the particular organizational style adopted by different fiscal offices. In addition, boundaries to decision-making are set by external factors inherent in the criminal justice process itself, by internal restrictions derived from the nature of the fiscal service and by fiscals' own perceptions of their role as prosecutors. Succeeding chapters will discuss the impact of these factors on particular decisons taken by the fiscal at the pre-trial stage.

4

TO PROSECUTE
OR NOT TO PROSECUTE

> Of all the decisions that have to be made by those with a
> responsibility for the conduct of criminal cases by far the
> most important is the initial one as to whether or not a
> charge should be preferred . . . a wrong decision either way
> can have disastrous consequences. [Royal Commission on
> Criminal Procedure – Evidence from Director of Public
> Prosecutions: 1979]
>   No one else is in a better position to make charging
> decisions which reflect community values as accurately and
> effectively as the prosecutor. [Miller: 1969: 294-5]

INTRODUCTION

IN SCOTLAND NOT ONLY is there an independent legally qualified
prosecutor authorised to decide whether or not to prosecute but that person is
specifically enjoined to weigh up the merits of a prosecution on grounds other
than strictly legal criteria. The standard text on Scottish criminal procedure sets
down the criteria regarded as relevant in considering whether or not to prosecute:

  (i) Whether the facts disclosed in the information constitute either a
      crime according to the Common Law of Scotland, or a contravention
      of an Act of Parliament which extends to that country;
 (ii) Whether there is sufficient evidence in support of these facts to justify
      the institution of criminal proceedings;
(iii) Whether the act or omission charged is of sufficient importance to be
      made the subject of a criminal prosecution;
 (iv) Whether there is any reason to suspect that the information is inspired
      by malice or ill-will on the part of the informant towards the person
      charged;
  (v) Whether there is sufficient excuse for the conduct of the accused
      person to warrant the abandonment of proceedings against him;
 (vi) Whether the case is more suitable for trial in the civil court, in respect
      that the facts raise a question of civil right. [Renton and Brown:
      1972: 19]

Where the fiscal has decided initially not to proceed the option to re-open a case is always available except where there is a statutory time-bar on the institution of proceedings.[1] This is particularly useful where the fiscal decides to *no pro* a case (not to proceed) for evidential reasons and is then presented with information concerning similar offences since the later offences may corroborate the earlier one. This rule, known as '*the rule in Moorov*' (1930 JC 68), applies only when the incidents are closely linked in time and the accused is charged with all the offences.

Fiscals themselves stress that the option not to proceed is regarded by them as a legitimate and sometimes preferable alternative to prosecution: 'if there's no sound reason for taking a case then I wouldn't take it'. Yet an examination of annual statistics produced by Crown Office over the last ten years gives the average figure for no proceedings cases as only 8 per cent and this is supported by figures from our Census. Since this covers all cases where proceedings are abandoned and not merely decisions at the marking stage, it is clear that the option not to proceed is seldom exercised. Why is the apparently wide discretion not to proceed so rarely invoked?

In some jurisdictions the prosecutor exercises such a close supervision over the work of the police that no case gets to the reporting stage unless it is a certain candidate for the institution of criminal proceedings. In such countries the police and other reporting agencies are in effect acting under instructions from the prosecutor both with regard to offences which are not to be pursued and particular crimes which are to be prosecuted vigorously. These guidelines will pre-empt any subsequent sifting process by prosecutors following the receipt of reports. It is true that the Lord Advocate may from time to time issue instructions to local chief constables regarding the reporting of crimes[2] and the police may be required to institute investigations upon the call of a public prosecutor.[3] However, close involvement in police investigations is unusual among prosecutors in Scotland except in exceptional cases such as murder. While fiscals like to maintain close contact with local police: 'I am a great believer in being very much involved with them. I arrange weekly meetings with police chiefs to discuss mutual problems'; 'I think that the closest possible liaison between police and prosecutor should be encouraged', it is only in rare instances[4] that national or local guidelines have been established concerning offences which should *not* be reported to the fiscal: 'I haven't asked them not to report anything – I don't find we get a lot of trifling stuff'; 'if there was one area in which I was always going to say no proceedings I think one would be going back to the police and saying one didn't want that kind of offence reported. But we don't really have any sweeping policy.'

[1] However if a fiscal tells a suspect that no proceedings will be taken the court may hold that the fiscal has barred himself from subsequently attempting to prosecute the suspect for the offence in question. See Thom *v*. H.M. Adv. 1976 SLT 232.

[2] Section 33 Criminal Justice (Scotland) Act 1949.

[3] Section 17 Police (Scotland) Act 1967.

[4] Nationally there appear to be operational speed limits which are not identical with the limits set by statute but these were not uniform at the time the research was carried out.

Fiscals accept that the police are themselves selective in reporting cases: 'if the incident is de minimis [trivial] then it is unlikely to be reported by the police'; 'I would be very sceptical that the police report everything to us – they don't function that way – I wouldn't want to be pestered by a whole lot of cases where there isn't enough evidence'. At the same time, fiscals are quick to stress that: 'we are in no way the vehicles of the police'; 'I resent very much the attitude that we are simply the legal arm of the police'. Indeed some feel uneasy about selective reporting on the part of the police: 'I would be very apprehensive if the police were taking into their hands what they considered was going to prove'. But in general they do not wish to impose policies on the police themselves: 'I don't think you should encourage the police not to investigate a particular offence – it might cause antagonism between public and police – it's their duty to report to the procurator fiscal'. Though no fiscals expressed it directly, there may also be a certain reluctance to interfere with internal police organisation.

In essence then, the fiscal reacts to reports sent in by the police and the other agencies which prepare cases for him. While some fiscals are concerned about the limited amount of information contained in these reports, it is generally accepted that even if more information were available to the fiscal at the marking stage it would probably not fundamentally alter the way in which fiscals deal with the vast majority of reports received. In spite of the apparent latitude which prosecutors in Scotland have in deciding whether to prosecute, fiscals themselves stress that their discretion is in fact circumscribed: 'the fiscal's instruction is if there is sufficient evidence to warrant a prosecution then you prosecute unless you have special reasons for not doing so . . . our discretion is so very limited . . . I am very conscious of this, coming out of the Reporter's service because the Reporter's discretion is much wider'.[1] The idea that the prosecutor is there to prosecute is fundamental to the fiscal's definition of his function: 'in most cases not to proceed would be out of the question.' Yet such assumptions are not the prerequisite of prosecutors universally. In other jurisdictions, such as the Netherlands, the prosecutor is more likely not to prosecute in the majority of cases.

ARGUMENTS IN FAVOUR OF PROSECUTION

The fact that particular acts or omissions are officially labelled criminal does not mean that prosecution is mandatory in all cases since in some jurisdictions, such as Scotland, the prosecutor has the legal authority not to proceed. However, Scottish prosecutors generally present cogent arguments in favour of prosecution in the vast majority of cases. Essentially, these revolve round fiscals' notions of the function and purpose of the criminal law and their role as upholders of that law. Most adopt a very traditional view which accepts that crimes and offences at both Common Law and under statute should be enforced:

[1] See p. 48 in Chapter 3.

'as long as it's the law it's not for me to make the law and to alter the law although I might wish to see some of it changed'.

Prosecutors affirm that their major concern is to safeguard the public interest, a concern which encompasses their understanding of the likely effect that conviction and sentence may have both on those harmed and on the wrongdoer. Thus even where an offence appears to be of little moment the fiscal usually regards it as his duty to prosecute because of the harm or potential harm to the public: 'why make it an offence not to have insurance when driving? Because you could cripple somebody and they would have no compensation . . . why prosecute for not having an offside mirror? Because the driver could reverse and knock down a child.' The presumption is that the threat of prosecution will act as a deterrent in such circumstances.

Punishment, then, is generally regarded by fiscals as a valuable component of the criminal justice process, largely because of its capacity to deter future crime: 'a fine somehow or other stops most shoplifters . . . nine out of ten people you will never see again . . . I'm not sure that failing to prosecute would have the same effect'. The perceived public desire for retribution is also seen as important: 'we have got to go very gradually and slowly with public opinion, it is very high on retribution . . . it is not yet ready for a system where we could mark a serious assault no pro because there was an unhappy love life' as is the need to see that justice is done on behalf of the victim: 'not enough attention is paid to the right of the victim to some sort of retribution'.

It would be untrue, however, to suggest that this emphasis on deterrence and retribution as the justifications for prosecution excludes other considerations. While many fiscals feel that the criminal justice system should not make allowances for personal weaknesses: 'lots of people suffer from depression but they don't go round stealing from shops'; 'I don't think it's right to say this man may well have come up and assaulted this passerby in the street but really he has been deprived and society is to blame', others consider that such factors are important but that it is only by bringing such people before the courts that fiscals can do anything for them: 'there are certain people who will come repeatedly to the attention of the police. What are you to do for them? Often through drink . . . they're not looking after themselves, they're needing a bit of caring, they go away for ten days, get dried out, cleaned up and given food and warm clothing. If we took no action you might find these people would die an awful lot sooner'; 'we deliberately take prosecutions to try to help people because often it is the only way to help someone . . . by bringing him before the court and forcing an agency to take him on . . . for example, we took a prosecution recently for the specific purpose of enabling the appropriate authorities to get the accused back under their wing under medical care'. Generally fiscals are reluctant to involve medical or social work agencies except indirectly through the medium of the court: 'we put everyone through the court even if they have a mental history and make a point of bringing it to the attention of the court in the hope that perhaps some social work backup is provided. It's not really our function to provide social work; we are here as prosecutors.'

There are other factors which in the fiscal's eyes militate against a no
proceedings decision. It appears to some to deny the public open nature of
criminal justice: 'under the present system, the offender is seen to be dealt with
in open court . . . everything can be seen to be done fairly . . . otherwise there is
always the suggestion that bureaucrats are hounding people'. Indeed there may
be positive advantages for the accused in airing the matter publicly: 'one
occasionally takes proceedings against an accused person knowing full well that
if it goes to trial it will not prove purely to bring out the facts in public . . . in
the best interests of the accused – the whole thing is very public, all the town
can see what happened'. In addition, while fiscals stress that the matter of
accountability is not generally a significant factor in considering whether or
not to proceed, there is the possibility that their decisions may be questioned
by members of the public or the complainer. Thus: 'you've got to be able to
justify your decision when a member of the public writes to his or her MP.
Your discretion has got to be very carefully used because you just don't know
what's going to come along afterwards.'

A decision not to prosecute may also be regarded as unsatisfactory by
other agencies within the criminal justice process itself: 'one or two police
officers have expressed annoyance . . . not in very strong words but you can
tell by the way they look at you that they're not very happy about it'. A police
officer told us: 'I think no pro cases are one of the most frustrating aspects of
police work. The due process of law is not being invoked in these cases . . . the
fiscal is the judge and jury which seems to be basically wrong.' Again, other
reporting agencies may feel that cases reported by them should go ahead: 'one
has to be mindful when you are dealing with a case reported from another
government department that if you mark such a case no pro the odds are that
that department will squeal to Crown Office. This doesn't mean that the
standards we employ in these cases should be any different from any other type
of case but it would be foolish to say there aren't pressures.'

NO PROCEEDINGS CASES

The decision not to prosecute, therefore, is at odds with the whole ethos of
prosecutorial decision-making in Scotland. It is only resorted to in those rare
instances where a case falls outside the fiscal's definition of *real* crime. This
section deals with those unusual features of a case, a kind of checklist of appropriate cues, which may cause the fiscal not to proceed. While fiscals stress the
individual nature of the no pro decision, specific aspects of cases, certain
categories of offences and particular types of accused persons appear to invite a
no pro decision by Scottish prosecutors.

Legal weaknesses

All fiscals accept that there may be sound legal reasons for not proceeding:
'the decision not to prosecute is most often exercised simply because there is
insufficient evidence'. In about one-third of no pro cases covered by our Census
insufficient evidence was given as the sole reason or one of several reasons for

not proceeding. Most fiscals regard such weeding out as a straightforward exercise: 'obviously the easiest ones to no pro are the ones where there is just insufficient evidence – lack of corroboration,[1] for example – the assault case where only the victim speaks to the assault and the accused doesn't make an incriminating reply to the police or in a housebreaking where the accused may make an admission of guilt but there is no corroboration of that admission or Section 6(1) of the Road Traffic Act, drunk driving, where a policeman has made a mistake in procedure'.

However, fiscals admit that there might be differences of opinion regarding the strength of a particular case. One experienced fiscal told us: 'I have had deputes coming to me and saying "I haven't got enough evidence" and I have said to them "in my view there is enough" and I would quote law to them, law that they didn't know'. A fairly new depute suggested that evidential requirements might be stretched in certain instances: 'it may well be a case where there may be just enough evidence . . . I will proceed because of the effect it has on the person although he may well not in the end be convicted'.

The availability of legal aid to accused persons in all courts[2] may have an impact on the fiscal's assessment of the likelihood of securing a conviction. While it may be stoutly denied by some that such developments have altered the strength of evidence required before a case will be prosecuted: 'I don't think my standard has changed in ten years. I would hate to think that. I always thought sufficiency of evidence was important and the fact that there's much more legal aid nowadays shouldn't have changed our standards', others do accept that such changes have made an impact: 'because of the increase in the provision of criminal legal aid for accused persons there is no point in my going ahead with a case where I may have insufficient evidence'. Some police officers also feel that this is so: 'the level of evidence which is being sought today is very much greater, or appears to be to us than what it was in our previous experience. Fiscals are looking for stonewall cases.' Not surprisingly, however, defence agents argue that cases which they regard as weak are not weeded out often enough by the fiscal. As one defence agent explained: 'I took about five careless driving cases to trial in a row and won them all. I say won them all, I did not, I really contributed nothing, the evidence was never there. This is a criticism of the fiscal for bad marking.'

Trivial matters

Apart from insufficient or unsatisfactory evidence the major reason for a no pro decision and the one which was given in about one-sixth of all no pro cases covered by our Census is based on the principle *de minimis non curat lex*,

---

[1] 'The essential idea of corroboration is that the testimony of one witness, whether direct to the actual commission of the crime, or indirect to some circumstance implicating the accused in the commission of the crime, is enforced by testimony, direct or indirect, of some other witness so that there are concurrent testimonies . . . each pointing to the accused as the person by whom the crime was committed.' [Sheehan: 1975: 121]

[2] Since 1975 legal aid has been available in all criminal courts – see Chapter 6 for further discussion.

that the law is not concerned with trivialities. This appears to be associated with the distinction between crimes *mala in se* and crimes *mala prohibita*. Gordon explains the difference thus:

> the view that all breaches of the criminal law are formally equal is not held by the only modern Scottish textbook on the subject. The criminal law is regarded as divisible into two sections; one deals with the crimes – (mala in se; literally evil in itself) like murder, robbery and rape, while the other (mala prohibita) is concerned with what are commonly called public welfare offences created by statute, being at best only technical crimes. [Gordon: 1978: 15]

One fiscal described the distinction in this way: 'you have to draw a line between criminals with a capital C, a sixteen year old who vandalises property and breaks into people's houses, and criminals with a small c, the persistent drunk and incapable offender who contravenes the Licensing (Scotland) Act'.

While the vast majority of reports to the fiscal are concerned with minor statutory offences, criminal procedure which governs the processing of cases is, essentially, geared towards the moral and legal condemnation of serious crime. Some fiscals feel that the prosecution of what they regard as trivial cases might minimise the public opprobrium which should attach to serious crimes: 'there is a danger of mixing serious cases with trivia not so much that things aren't being done properly but that some people think that they are not being done properly'. Several fiscals use the term 'rubbish' to cover those offences which appear to them not to merit the full weight of prosecution yet which are tedious and time-consuming to process: 'there is nothing more frustrating than doing a trial which takes a long time involving what really is the most trivial of offences. It certainly can get you down. You feel that you are using all your skill to prosecute something that really is not worth very much.'

In most offices there are no explicit rules about what constitutes a trivial offence and fiscals find it hard to define in abstract terms what the word denotes to them. However, they are able to give numerous examples from which it is possible to discern distinct categories. The great majority of fiscals consider that certain road traffic offences merit the label trivial. These range from breaches of Construction and Use Regulations[1] (dirty number plates, horns out of order) to Vehicle Excise Act infringements. The most common is careless driving.[2] 'I am not inclined to prosecute simply because there has been a bump unless I can find apart from the collision that there has been an act of carelessness of a fairly material degree'; 'if a person has not been convicted before on a road traffic offence, if nobody has been injured, if there are no other charges, it is very likely that we will not take proceedings'. It is considered that such cases can be quite adequately dealt with in other ways: 'if it is just a small

---

[1] Section 40(1) Road Traffic Act 1972 under which 'the Secretary of State may make regulations generally as to the use of motor vehicles and trailers on roads, their construction and equipment and the conditions under which they may be used'.

[2] Section 3 Road Traffic Act 1972.

bump between two cars it should just be left to the insurance companies and drivers to sort it out'.

In adopting this attitude to careless driving fiscals feel they are echoing the public's approach: 'I think more and more people are realising that the careless driver isn't criminal'; 'we feel we are reacting to the public attitude as represented to us by the bench and by local solicitors and by the verdicts we have been getting in some of the trials'. Some fiscal offices have gone so far as to virtually decriminalize Section 3 offences which conform to the pattern described above: 'I have a policy on Section 3 within this office. The policy is not to take minimal careless driving and the way the policy works is that if two drivers are at fault and they require one driver to prove the case against the other there is just no way it would be taken on'.

Other cases where the *de minimis* principle is applied include minor breaches of the peace where again no personal injury results, and reports of vagrancy or loitering. Fiscals seem to think that occasionally the police are somewhat overzealous in the execution of their duty: 'I get quite a plethora of breach of the peace cases which involve only the police. For example, I got a case in recently where a police panda car manned by a somewhat over-vigilant twosome passed a crowd of youths one of whom was heard to say "Cheerio pigs!" He was immediately arrested for a breach of the peace and was detained overnight. In my opinion that was *not* a breach of the peace – I therefore marked it no pro'; 'you've got the trivia, for example, under the Vagrancy Act . . . it seems to me that when a police officer finds a person on the top of a roof or something like that . . . that's trivia which appears to me as not in the public interest to prosecute, certainly not when one considers the cost involved in prosecution'.

While most fiscals consider that the application of the *de minimis* principle is justified in the kinds of situations already described, there are some who have reservations. The problem of defining trivial in an objective, universally acceptable way was raised by several fiscals: 'in deciding whether a thing is trivial or not, you have to take a lot of things into consideration. It may be trivial to you, just looking at it, it may not be trivial to the parties concerned'; 'trivial matters can have dire consequences, serious defects in a car can have dire consequences'.

There is also an uneasy feeling among some Scottish prosecutors that failure to prosecute trivial cases provides a simple, but possibly unethical, way for fiscals to cut down on their workload: 'a lazy fiscal will apply the *de minimis* rule more liberally than a conscientious fiscal'. Generally the practice is regarded with some distaste: 'I tend to take the view that it's sad there's pressure on the court and on the court depute but I don't think that's an excuse for not prosecuting if it's a crime. "We're far too busy, we can't be bothered prosecuting people for urinating in the streets", as far as I'm concerned that's not the point.' But it is accepted by some as a necessary, if somewhat unsatisfactory, compromise between expediency and a true definition of trivial. The concept of trivial is therefore a relative one: 'you may find that people who think that the road traffic stuff is of no moment are the people in the very busy offices who are not saying that this is unimportant, but that it is unimportant in relation to the quality and volume of the other stuff that they have got to deal with with limited resources'; 'I think the problem is that most of our courts are unfortunately becoming overloaded and therefore we are marking some cases no proceedings . . . the less serious road traffic offences – a vehicle parked on the public road without insurance – anything which is really trivial – it is an attempt to cut down the rubbish – we know the court can't cope with it'. Indeed, one office has been obliged to apply the principle blanket fashion to certain offences because of pressure of work: 'you get set guidelines . . . there are certain cases that we take up and others that we no pro . . . it's to do with lack of police manpower and of time to do reports . . . if you were to take up every case the court would be packed out'. Conversely some fiscals consider that the district court might lose its *raison d'etre* if trivial cases were not prosecuted: 'if you start marking any case no pro on the *de minimis* principle, you'd be left with no cases at all in the district court'.[1]

The accused's personal characteristics: General impact

Criminal lawyers traditionally regard themselves as being concerned with the conduct of an accused person rather than his personal characteristics. In assessing the nature of an offence, then, the fiscal's primary focus should be on the criminal act or omission. Generally speaking the prosecutor does not take the circumstances of the alleged offender into account in deciding whether to prosecute: 'we see things very legally . . . we only think about corroboration or whether there is a crime . . . we don't really think about the family'. Focusing on the accused person's characteristics as an excuse for the commission of a criminal offence is regarded by some as a difficult matter to justify given the fiscal's duty to uphold justice: 'there may be cases where a particular prosecutor may feel that he should not prosecute for considerations other than purely legal ones but it's something that would need to be very, very carefully watched. It's very difficult to treat everybody equally.' To such fiscals, personal circumstances are regarded as relevant to sentencing but *not* to prosecution: 'often I see there is material which would affect my decision but basically it is mitigatory for the court, it is not for me'.

Not all fiscals share this circumscribed view of their role as prosecutors however. A few quite avowedly adopt a less restrictive approach, which takes the personal characteristics of the accused into account when considering whether or not to prosecute: 'I would like to think of myself as a more lenient fiscal in the sense that I hope to exercise a wider discretion in appropriate cases than some of my colleagues . . . I do feel in view of the importance of one's decision and the repercussions of proceeding there is perhaps more need for fiscals to look at certain cases a bit more closely. There are certain possibilities for wider, more generous and sometimes more humane approaches'; 'we should have a more compassionate attitude towards accused persons'.

---

[1] See Chapter 5 for fiscals' views of the district court and its role in relation to the processing of minor offences.

The personal circumstances or characteristics of persons accused of any offence may encourage a no pro decision. In our Census one-sixth of all no pro cases were regarded as mental health or social work matters where prosecution was not seen as appropriate. Thus those persons who are so obviously mentally disturbed as not to be able to exercise control over their actions are generally not prosecuted but may be committed directly into psychiatric care under the Mental Health (Scotland) Act 1960.[1] There is also a grey area between a psychiatric condition which actually prevents a person from forming *mens rea*, the intention to commit a particular criminal act, and a mental illness which does not have this effect. The criminal law tries to maintain a clear distinction between the two. Recent caselaw, however, shows that judges differ in their interpretation of the concept of legal responsibility.[2]

Fiscals too vary in their assessment of the weight which they feel should be given to mental instability in deciding whether or not to prosecute. The menopausal woman may be regarded by some fiscals as capable of exercising only limited responsibility over her actions, particularly when subject to stress: 'A. was menopausal, had been taking treatment for depression . . . she was charged with assaulting a fifteen year old girl . . . the background to it was that her daughter had run away from home supposedly with this girl and had not returned. The accused was in a very bad state of acute hysteria. I was certainly not willing to prosecute that woman . . . it would probably put her over the edge.' Similarly the person who has suffered bereavement under difficult circumstances may be regarded as temporarily unbalanced: 'the accused was charged with a domestic assault . . . there was a history of some mental deficiency and his child had been killed a few weeks before. . . I took all that into account. I didn't prosecute the man.' However, it is clear from our examination of marking that fiscals may choose to prosecute although there are indications of mental instability, for instance where an accused charged with a minor assault has slashed his wrists in the police cell and shown signs of mental imbalance and in a case involving malicious damage to police property where the offender had a history of psychiatric illness.

It should be noted that the fiscal may not always be aware of an accused's mental history when marking a report. While the police complaint may state that the accused is receiving treatment for a psychiatric illness: 'where I get a case reported there may be an indication that the accused has been to see a doctor or has gone into hospital for some treatment so I get in touch with the psychiatrist or doctor', it is important to note that information which might suggest unusual circumstances is not always immediately available to the fiscal in the initial report, for example: 'we had a case the other week. It looked absolutely routine . . . a minor assault and breach of the peace, but it transpired that the chap had, some years ago, had a plea of insanity in bar of trial at a

[1] A recent study looks in detail at the interface between criminal justice and mental health in Scotland: Chiswick, McClintock and McIsaac: *Discretion in Arrest and Prosecution: The Problem of the Mentally Abnormal Offender*: AUP: 1982.

[2] Contrast Brennan *v*. H.M. Adv. 1977 JC 38 and H.M. Adv. *v*. Aitken 1975 SLT (Notes) 86. See also G. H. Gordon: *Criminal Law*: Chapters 10–12.

F

murder.' Generally, the first indication the fiscal will have of any medical or psychiatric history will come not from the police but from the accused person through his solicitor: 'it is quite common when an elderly person steals a food item, to have representations from doctors or solicitors saying that this person is of good character and it was an isolated incident'; 'I had a case where it was brought to my notice by a psychiatrist from Harley Street that if proceedings were taken he felt certain the accused would kill herself'.

Occasionally it appears that fiscals will take note of the effect that a prosecution may have on an accused person's present standing or future prospects. It sometimes seems that conduct committed by a person who has a good reputation in the community may be regarded as a one-off incident for which there is probably some reasonable excuse. So, where students committed a theft it was regarded as a prank and prosecution was deemed unnecessary: 'these people are going to be professionals . . . for a little prank they have theft on their record. I wasn't prepared to take them to court.' Similarly: 'some apparently worthy citizen is charged with some minor sexual offence . . . prosecution might mean the end of his job, his career, his position in the local community'. Again, where a teacher was reported for being drunk and incapable, the fiscal decided not to proceed because the offence was so out of character. It is felt by some fiscals that the shock of being apprehended by the police will be enough to ensure that generally law-abiding citizens will not offend again: 'a baker giving short weight . . . if we had prosecuted him he would have lost his business . . . I ended up giving him an official warning'; 'some young lads took some wild birds' eggs . . . they were not bad lads really, and it was decided to send warning letters to them . . . to act as some kind of sanction'. It is interesting to compare the kind of detailed knowledge that a fiscal in a closely-knit rural community may have about the inhabitants with that available to prosecutors in large city offices. This may lead the former to take personal considerations into account more frequently. Figures from the Census support this contention since the percentage of no proceedings case recorded by each fiscal office was in inverse proportion to the number of cases received so that the smaller offices appeared to make use of the option more frequently.

Personal characteristics and particular offences

Although fiscal offices do vary in their use of the no pro option, it is possible to specify certain situations where the combination of a particular offence and particular accused persons may cause fiscals to consider not prosecuting. One of the examples most frequently mentioned is the person accused of shoplifting, whose conduct may be excused because of age[1] or mental state:

[1] In a study undertaken by the Essex police, the vast majority of old age pensioners apprehended had committed a theft from a shop and the police chose not to prosecute in 88 per cent of these cases. The report explained its rationale thus:

> Elderly offenders pose special problems for decision-makers. When some elderly people commit criminal offences, they are displaying

'in a minor shoplifting, if you have a single article or a very trivial amount and the accused is suffering from some kind of disability or pain, you may want to exercise discretion and not proceed'; 'I look out for menopausal females who are acting completely out of character. I would also try to get the social work department to deal with an old person that you feel has got economic problems and steals food'; 'there is an age below which proceedings cannot be taken; why not a top limit too?'

Nevertheless, there is some scepticism on the part of certain fiscals about a psychiatric explanation of shoplifting even where the offence appears to be an isolated incident: 'I think you have to be very careful about shoplifters . . . there are a few that appeal on emotional grounds as being people who need some kind of help. The majority in my view are just thieves. When you say it's a first offence, it's the first time that person has been caught; it's the first time that person has been reported.' In fact: 'very often a decision on whether to prosecute or not is resolved because of evidence to the effect that the accused was only watched because she had been suspected of shoplifting for a long time'.

Fiscals are also aware of the kinds of criticisms that may be made where it appears that there is a high no pro rate in cases, like shoplifting, where middle-class people are more likely to be apprehended. Some see a danger in stressing what they regard as the perceived incongruity of an offence committed by a prominent member of the local community: 'a woman of substantial means, acquainted with the Lord Chief Justice of England who had served as a magistrate in England . . . it seemed clear to me that her shoplifting must be an aberration but I still marked it for prosecution because I felt if it came out that she had these connections then I would become subject to criticism'. It is considered that in such cases it would be fairer to have the matter decided in open court: 'our attitude would be to put that shoplifter through the court . . . if she is receiving treatment for nerves then that can be explained to the court'. Therefore it is not surprising that, except in a few offices where there is a clearly defined policy of not prosecuting old age pensioners accused of stealing small items of food for the first time, most shoplifting cases are prosecuted.

Other cases where fiscals may consider the option of not proceeding are those involving domestic disputes, usually between husband and wife. While this offence category is probably the one which produces the greatest variety of responses from prosecutors, there seems to be a general feeling that many women who have been the victims of assaults perpetrated by their husbands will be unwilling to give evidence in court and will even ask the fiscal not to proceed: 'wife assault is always a little bit difficult because what happens with

---

evidence of distress not connected with the offence. There is also
evidence to suggest that, on a few occasions, elderly offenders
over-react to the situation and have even been known to commit
suicide after being accused of some quite minor offence. [Markham:
1980: 97]

a lot of them is that initially the complaint is made and later the wife wants to withdraw it'.[1] The fact that some fiscals anticipate problems in proving such offences affects decision-making in wife assault cases. Such incidents appear not to be regarded in the same light as the general run of offences involving personal violence but are treated very much as *sui generis*. It is interesting to note that although there is no separate classification in official criminal statistics for domestic assaults, police, fiscals and social workers make a clear distinction.

Some fiscals see their role in such cases not so much as prosecutors but rather as mediators between husband and wife. They regard themselves as having a public duty to uphold the institution of marriage and should be wary of threatening it by their actions:[2] 'we regularly interview wives, exercise discretion and decide whether or not to drop the charges. We consider what effect a prosecution would have on that marriage . . . if you've a wife coming along saying "everything is solved, we're back together again" we might consider dropping it'; 'I would be, as a rule, prepared to concede to a request by a wife not to proceed provided I had seen the wife and seen the husband in the presence of the wife . . . if there had been a genuine reconciliation, the injury was not excessive, there had been no previous convictions and some indication of sorrow and an assurance that it wouldn't happen again'. Such fiscals consider that prosecution is a counterproductive measure in such cases: 'it does no good to bring such cases before the courts. When the man is fined, it is the family who are penalised.'

Assaults in the domestic sphere are regarded by some fiscals as matters with which the criminal law could not and should not cope: 'why prosecute when obviously in many cases it's a drinking problem, the kind of thing where social work aid would be preferable'; 'all you can do is try and involve the social work department. I find out if they know anything about the family and what their views are and whether they think they can use the report as an actual lever to make the couple see sense.' (Seeing sense was apparently defined by the fiscal as continuing with the marriage.) Another approach is to regard the husband's conduct as excusable, given certain conditions: 'there have been cases where I felt the husband acted in a way you would expect a normal person to react . . . perhaps finding his wife with another man, provided he did not go beyond reasonable assault'. A few fiscals expressed a sense of irritation with the victim in wife assault cases, regarding her as a frivolous, vacillating complainant: 'the wives come up before the trial and ask me to drop proceedings. I do no pro it but I always read the Riot Act to them'; 'sometimes there's a history of falling out, bringing in the police and then not going ahead because someone won't give evidence . . . we take the view that if a woman

[1] Although a recent research study suggests that this claim is unjustified. In only 6 per cent of domestic violence cases surveyed did the wife ask for charges to be dropped, and always after a considerable court delay. [Dobash & Dobash: 1979: 222]

[2] It is interesting to note that even one serious assault by either spouse on the other may be grounds for a successful divorce action in Scotland – see Divorce (Scotland) Act 1977.

takes a man back after she's had trouble with him, she can't expect to call the police just when it suits her'.

On the other hand, many fiscals regard domestic assaults as offences which should be prosecuted, whether or not the victim is prepared to co-operate: 'domestic assaults must be taken seriously . . . there are a considerable number of cases where the wife does not wish us to continue . . . very seldom do we let that influence us . . . the wife is not necessarily her own best adviser in these matters'; 'every wife beater, in my view, is a potential murderer . . . one has to think of one's self-protection [the repercussions on the fiscal where a history of unprosecuted wife assaults culminates in a fatal attack]'. Thus most fiscals tend to agree that, in spite of the reasons for such incidents, proceedings are necessary to underline the serious nature of the offence: 'the court has the authority, it has more effect than simple social work . . . it brings people to their senses'.

To sum up, then, domestic assault cases are treated in very different ways by Scottish prosecutors: 'this is one where you will get all the diversity you can hope for because there are fiscals who will have the husband and wife in and lecture them, there will be people who will no pro, send warning letters or get the police to warn them. There will be people who say "look, you created a situation in which you needed the help of the police; if you have got anything to say in mitigation, come and tell the sheriff". It is one where your judgment has to be based on speculation . . . quite apart from anything else most of us are in the situation of being husbands or wives. That is the area where you find the biggest variety in fiscal approach.'

While domestic assaults provide perhaps the clearest example of the effect which personal factors may have on the fiscal's decision, there are other types of offences which also cause concern and may prompt the fiscal to exercise his discretion not to proceed. For example, quarrels between neighbours are not always regarded as suitable cases for prosecution: 'these are a couple of neighbours involved in a fight over a boundary fence . . . sometimes by taking it to the court we are just setting them at one another's throats again . . . you use your judgment as to whether or not it's worth proceeding'. There may be problems concerning the veracity of the complainants: 'stairhead brawls[1] are probably one of the most difficult types to deal with . . . there's a great deal of difficulty getting a conviction . . . it's usually seen that the other parties are equally to blame'.

Generally, the criminal courts are not seen as being the solution to such problems: 'the only way they can resolve these squabbles is to settle their own differences. You cannot get the courts or the police to settle it though the local authorities try to re-house people when they are not compatible.' Even judges may regard such matters as unsuitable for prosecution: 'in a longstanding feud between neighbours, there was criticism from the bench for this case coming to court . . . we were told we should just let matters go unless there are

[1] Disputes between neighbours living in the same tenement and sharing access to their individual dwellings by means of a common stair.

exceptional circumstances, injury caused or specific complaints to MPs'. The
fiscal may feel he can deal with the matter satisfactorily without actually
prosecuting: 'in a case involving disputes between neighbours last year I wrote
to the head of each particular household and told them that this was stupid and
to behave themselves, but if they came to my notice again, I would prosecute
them. That letter went out to both families and I have not heard any more
about them.' On the other hand, where the accused's conduct constitutes a
continuous breach of the peace, the fiscal may regard it as his duty to proceed:
'if it's a breach of the peace . . . a continuing occurrence, for example, playing
a record-player loudly at night and shouting and swearing when someone
says "will you turn it down?", my instinct would be to prosecute'.

Many fiscals have a similar attitude towards habitual prosecutions under
Section 70 of the Licensing (Scotland) Act 1903, the offence of being drunk
and incapable: 'I only take them because the police say they receive complaints
from the public about a person lying drunk in the street. Although it was their
own act which put them into that condition, they are ill and they should not
just be chucked into a police cell.'

The prosecution of cases involving minor sexual offences against children
is also fraught with difficulties for the prosecution. Fiscals stress that they have
to be aware both of the possible traumatic effect upon the child victim of an
appearance in court and the need to ensure that there will not be a repetition
of such conduct on the accused's part: 'you have got the public interest to
consider. The accused is part of the public but equally so are the children. It's
so easy just to say "proceed and let it all be tested in court and then you
will get the answer" but, so far as one can, one has got to look at the thing very
carefully.' However, account may also be taken of the reactions of the victims'
parents to a no proceedings decision: 'this is a case of indecent exposure to
some young seven or eight year old girls. I am inclined not to prosecute
because of a psychiatric report on the accused. The only thing that is worrying
me is the attitude of the parents of the young girls if they learn that this young
chap is not punished in some way.'

To sum up then, this review of no proceedings cases shows that the criteria
which may ground a decision to drop proceedings are not easily defined. They
may relate to different interpretations of what constitutes sufficient evidence,
what is defined as trivial or to what extent a person's actions may be excused
because of his or her personal circumstances. However, the decision whether
or not to prosecute may also depend on factors which are not within the
fiscal's control such as the resources available for dealing with accused persons
outwith the criminal justice system.

ALTERNATIVES TO PROSECUTION

Existing procedures

One of the reasons why fiscals may decide not to proceed in only a limited
number of cases is because there is little or no scope for dealing with criminal

matters except through prosecution in the criminal courts: 'there is a lack of alternatives. The rule of law is particularly inflexible in this country and although we tend to sit back smugly and think we have got one of the best systems of law in the world in fact we are gradually being left behind by other countries.' A committee on alternatives to prosecution in Scotland was established in July 1977 under the chairmanship of Lord Stewart:

> to consider the effect on the criminal courts and the
> prosecution system of the volume of minor offences at
> present dealt with by summary prosecution and whether
> some other process might be devised to deal with such
> offences while maintaining essential safeguards for accused
> persons.

At present the only formal alternative available to the prosecutor[1] is the administering of a warning either by the police on his instructions, by the fiscal personally or by means of a warning letter.[2] Some fiscals make use of a warning letter in most no proceedings cases and feel that the threat to re-activate the first offence if the accused offends again works well as a deterrent: 'they're generally given a warning letter, it's a strictly termed letter . . . "we're not going to take proceedings against you but if you're brought to our attention again we'll put the two offences together and prosecute".' Other fiscals, however, do not find the warning device very useful. There are ethical and legal diffi-culties in imputing a criminal offence to a person without any admission or finding of guilt: 'one has got to be careful that you don't say they have com-mitted an offence because it has not been proved according to the requirement of law'; 'this fiscal does not use warning letters and that is a matter of policy. He thinks there's something strange about saying "we are not saying you have committed an offence but do not do it again".'[3] There is also an uneasy feeling among some Scottish prosecutors that such actions, particularly if the warnings are made verbally by the fiscal to the accused, may appear as empty paternalistic gestures more suitable to a bygone age: 'one has got to try and avoid sounding pompous and superior, as though you are ticking off some naughty child'.

In addition fiscals express concern that some more positive intervention is required: 'I am frequently stymied in certain cases because on the one hand something has to be done and yet on the other hand the step of formal court proceedings seems out of proportion'. Accused persons may be regarded as disturbed, ill or in need of help and support rather than criminal prosecution: 'when I first got involved in the fiscal office at X I was appalled at the human

---

[1] The fixed penalty system which offers an alternative to prosecution is not admin-istered by the fiscal service but by the police.

[2] Except in the case of arrangements governing the prosecution of personnel at foreign bases in the UK. See the Visiting Forces Act 1952.

[3] Since the time when this research was carried out, Crown Office has advised fiscals that if they choose to use the warning in a particular case they will be regarded as having decided not to take court proceedings in respect of that case.

remains that were being dragged before the court for no purpose'. Prosecution for trivial matters may be seen as counterproductive: 'it worries me that the bloke who comes up for a minor Road Traffic Offence sees a Common Law criminal, a bad type, being disposed of in a way that he thinks is less harsh than the way in which he is disposed of, that makes people begin to lose their respect for the law'.

Occasionally fiscals may refer a case to medical or social work agencies: 'in a few cases with psychiatric overtones I have arranged that the person consult his GP with a view to arranging out-patient treatment'; 'within the category of no pro there is the informal referral to the Social Work Department, the informal referral to the drink experts at X Hospital'. Some fiscals refer cases to the local Police Community Involvement Branch:[1] 'a father was accused of assaulting his 14-year-old daughter because she was staying out at night and being deliberately disobedient . . . I referred the case to the CIB'. Such arrangements are more commonplace in the small rural fiscal offices where the assumption of such a role by the prosecutor may be more acceptable and where his intimate knowledge of the local community will underlie any no pro decision. In these areas it appears that many criminal incidents are in any case settled informally by the local inhabitants without recourse to the police or the fiscal: 'it's rather like a large village where people do tend to sort things out for themselves. They only call for the police because they cannot sort it out . . . in a community like this the less formality the better . . . we seem to be able to find a solution to most things.'

Nevertheless most fiscals are reluctant, even if they have reservations about the applicability of existing procedures to all cases, to develop alternative ways of dealing with accused persons without legal authority for such measures: 'our hands are tied by the lack of alternatives – we are really looking for something with the authority of the law behind it'. While those who emphasize their right to make decisions on each individual case do not relish the idea of introducing blanket no pro categories and formal diversionary procedures: 'this is part of the possible disadvantage of Crown Office taking the umbrella control over all prosecutors . . . people are treated on a conveyor belt system rather than as persons'; 'I am against direction by the Lord Advocate in respect of general discretion . . . it is pursuit of the unobtainable', the majority of fiscals are willing to explore the possibility of more formal diversionary schemes: 'there are new thoughts abroad fairly recently on diversion – but we need formal schemes'. Such alternatives, however, should not be introduced merely to cut down on existing caseloads: 'I would like to see some worthwhile alternative . . . what worries me is that far too many people are saying "let's have alternatives to prosecution because the present structure cannot stand the strain". Let worthwhile alternatives spring up themselves and not spring from a desire to alleviate the pressure on the courts.'

---

[1] The *Community Involvement Branch* (CIB) is responsible for crime prevention work, contacts with schools, implementation of juvenile liaison schemes and special projects in the local community.

Possibilities for the future

Of the different diversionary schemes currently under discussion, such as detoxification centres, social work supervision, or on-the-spot fines, an extension of the fixed penalty system[1] appears to generate the most support for a variety of reasons: 'anything where people instantly acknowledge their guilt is appropriate for an instant imposition of penalty. You can see the justice allied to the act from a layman's point of view without any of the abstruse stuff you sometimes get from lawyers'; 'there's probably a future for fixed penalties to cut down on the number of cases going through. If there was a fixed penalty then we might find that the volume of speeding, red lights and double white line charges would go right down'; 'a fixed penalty system for speeding, driving without insurance or MOT and all offences under construction and use regulations would probably have a fairer application throughout the country because at the moment you get people fined different amounts by different sheriffs for the same offence and that's not right'.

There is a divergence of opinion, however, over the particular offences which should be included in such a scheme and on the personnel who should administer it. Most fiscals are anxious to ensure that such a move would not increase the discretion which the police may exercise. In law the police are the servants of the fiscal so too great an extension of their powers would naturally be viewed with some concern: 'if you have a fixed penalty system then what the police say becomes the law. I think it would give the police responsibilities and functions which are really our province'; 'what worries me about the fixed penalty is how do you work it and at what levels . . . obviously you can't work it for careless driving, people going through a red light, these are subjective things . . . they're bound to vary in seriousness. I've always been a wee bit chary about the possibility that a policeman on the spot fixes a fine.' On the other hand, some fiscals do not see their role as the administrators of an expanded fixed penalty system: 'personally I don't think it is our function to deal with that . . . I don't think it's necessarily a part of the system of prosecution at all'.

While fiscals see the need for change in this area, then, they are reluctant to alter either the existing balance of power between themselves and the police or their own traditional working practices: 'one way possibly to deal with it would be for these cases to be reported here to the fiscal office as they are at present and we could assess the case . . . it's better to maintain the sort of principle that we already have in our system . . . things are simply reported to the fiscal and the decision is made here concerning prosecution or diversion'.

There is one area where it appears that many fiscals would be very willing to relinquish control and that is the difficult problem of the persistent drunken offender: 'winos coming before the court . . . being brutalized . . . I don't want to be dealing with the poor down-and-out drunk in court . . . they should be taken to some sort of centre and dried out for the night'; 'I don't see any point

---

[1] At the present time, its operation extends predominantly to cases of illegal parking only. See p. 135 et seq.

in prosecuting poor old drunks who don't do a great deal of harm to anyone but themselves'. Scottish prosecutors do not, however, place a great deal of faith in the diversion of such offenders to detoxification centres:[1] 'there might be an argument for having an enforced period in some sort of institution where they could be dried out . . . but it might be just a waste of money . . . these people will always present a problem no matter what you do . . .'; 'the drunk and incapable offenders I get have been drunk and incapable for a long time and will be drunk and incapable for a long time. As far as I can see the only thing they really don't like is going to prison because they will not get drunk and they won't get any sympathy. I don't think they want to stop drinking, I don't think they see drink as a problem and I don't think they could respond to treatment'; 'I don't think anybody should force people to go and attend a drying-out unit . . . it's a restriction of their liberty'. A cynical view is that the fine acts as its own drying-out mechanism: 'that's less for the offender to get drunk on'.

The role of social work agencies

The criminal justice process in Scotland, although it no longer has its own probation officers, is empowered to call upon local authority social work departments to provide background information on convicted persons in the form of social enquiry reports[2] and to supervise offenders on probation. Teams of court social workers and the office of court liaison officer ensure that a degree of continuity is maintained in the relationship between court personnel and social workers and that interested social workers build up an expertise in court work and work with offenders generally. However, in supplying evidence to the court and in writing social enquiry reports social workers develop relationships with court personnel rather than fiscal staff.

At present it appears that there is little contact between fiscals and social workers at the marking stage and that the court is the only forum where they meet. The major stumbling-block to such overtures seems to stem from an uncertainty on both sides about the role of the social worker in criminal matters and the powers and resources available to social work departments in such cases allied to a certain unease on the fiscals' part about the value of social work in the criminal context. Most fiscals admit that they are very uncertain about the nature of social work generally: 'I am rather ignorant of what they do . . . I know of course what they do in respect of their direct connections with the court, where they're asked for an SER [Social enquiry report] but I

---

[1] Under Section 5 Criminal Justice (Scotland) Act 1980:

> where a constable has power to arrest a person without a warrant for any offence and the constable has reasonable grounds for suspecting that that person is drunk, the constable may, if he thinks fit, take him to any place designated by the Secretary of State for the purposes of this Section as a place suitable for the care of drunken persons.

[2] See *Social Enquiry Reports in Scotland:* J. Curran and G. Chambers: HMSO: 1982.

have very little knowledge of what the other departments do'; 'I'm ignorant of how much involvement they have with a case . . . I have a lack of knowledge of how precisely they work. Perhaps if we knew how they worked we would more readily refer cases to them'.

Except in cases of non-accidental injury to children,[1] there is no formal referral though fiscals can and occasionally do consult social work departments: 'I have sometimes written to the social work department in domestic assault cases to see if they can offer any assistance . . . I don't know if they follow it up because they don't reply to my letters so how effective it is I don't know'; 'I think our only direct contact is through the social work liaison officer who attends court . . . options are open to us to refer specific cases to the social work department but these would be pretty rare'. Social workers too agree that there is little contact: 'I've probably only been once to the fiscal office and I've been on the phone a few times but I don't know the fiscal'; 'the fiscal's job is to prosecute, my job is to provide the court with the necessary information'.

While few fiscals actually articulate what they regard as the legitimate role of the social worker *vis-à-vis* accused persons, three possible functions can be discerned. The first and more traditional notion stresses the idea of social workers as information gatherers presenting background information on accused persons. Some fiscals would like such material to be available to them when they are making decisions regarding prosecution: 'we're totally dependent upon the police to know the full facts . . . I think in a number of common law cases a background can make such a difference . . . I would like to see what is virtually a social enquiry report . . . if there's a social worker involved with the family already I think it would be preferable to know what the social worker thinks of the family set-up'; 'the Reporter gets a social background report before he decides whether to proceed . . . why shouldn't I? . . . for example in domestic issues, the elderly, mentally impaired people, . . . where there are special circumstances, physical or mental, which the law technically does not recognise'.

However, some fiscals do not regard such a suggestion as either legitimate or worth pursuing: 'I just don't know how people would react to that. For example in a wife-assault case the accused and his wife would regard it as a domestic incident involving themselves and they might be rather angry if some well intentioned social worker knocked on the door one day and said "the procurator fiscal has asked me to come along and get some information on you".' Social workers also can see difficulties in fulfilling such functions: 'if we were going to provide the fiscal with background information at the time of prosecution you are asking people to accept a new mode, a new concept for which this country isn't ready'. Other fiscals are critical of the information currently provided to the court by social workers: 'I have not been impressed by very many of the social workers I have met nor their reports . . . some of

[1] Various Crown Office Circulars provide fiscals with guidelines for liaison in such cases and National Health Service Circulars covering procedure in cases of suspected non-accidental injury to children are distributed to police, fiscals, Reporters, health boards and social work departments.

the reports have pretty fatuous comments which bear no relation at all to the crime . . . it is only the older social workers who make a sensible recommendation'; 'I have a certain mistrust of social work departments . . . I think social work reports are on the whole trite and superficial'.

The second function which social work agencies can be regarded as fulfilling or having the potential to fulfil is in providing assistance to an accused person. Clearly they already do so in relation to convicted persons placed on probation but they might also, according to some fiscals, provide supervision as an alternative to prosecution. The aim of this help in the fiscal's eyes would be to obviate the need for prosecution by providing the kind of support and control which might normally form the basis of a probation order. Many fiscals would be willing to channel certain kinds of offenders away from the criminal justice process and into the hands of another agency, provided that agency share the fiscal's assessment of the goals appropriate to a diversionary programme.[1] With regard to the generic social work department[2] introduced by recent legislation, however, fiscals do not feel that such shared interests exist at present: 'I think their aims sometimes do conflict with ours . . . some social workers have perhaps somewhat unusual ideas about prosecution and are not terribly helpful'; 'I don't think the social worker's attitude is along the same lines as my own . . . I don't trust the average social worker . . . I would be frightened they would reveal certain information to their clients'. The absence of shared objectives is also noted by social workers: 'really we're starting from two entirely different standpoints – we're client-centred, fiscals seem to be centred on some protection of the public good, they always seem to err on the side of safety'.

Many of those fiscals who have been prosecutors since before 1968 when the Social Work (Scotland) Act introduced the concept of generic social work consider that the demise of the probation service as a separate entity has encouraged this lack of confidence: 'I think that the Social Work (Scotland) Act was a disaster, it wrecked a very good probation service. We've got the situation now where we have no probation officers. We have social workers and the two are very different.' According to these critics of social work the old probation service was an arm of the criminal justice system working for the court and so probation officers were much more willing to accept the legitimacy of prosecution in most cases and the need for deterrents: 'the probation service accepted the fiscal's role as prosecutor . . . social workers do not . . . they have different philosophies'. Social workers are aware of these criticisms: 'if we were to introduce probation officers tomorrow fiscals would know exactly what they were whereas they have never accepted social work as a generic service'. It appears that fiscals are very much aware of their responsibilities to protect

---

[1] Such programmes have been extensively developed in the United States and Canada. See *The Dilemma of Diversion: Resource Materials on Adult Pre-Trial Intervention Programs: US Dept. of Justice: 1975* and *Studies on Diversion: Law Reform Commission of Canada: 1975.*

[2] Where a single worker and through him the social work department provide a comprehensive service to the whole family.

the public from the results of possible future offending by persons against whom proceedings are dropped. The social work department is regarded as having a legitimate role in helping such people only if in so doing it is also able to prevent the commission of future criminal acts by persons referred to its care. Social workers must therefore be able to act as controllers of as well as helpmeets for their clients. Fiscals express doubts about their ability to do so: 'you've got social workers who're not experienced in life themselves . . . a degree in social work doesn't give them control'.

One fiscal gave an interesting example of differences in approach between the social work department and the fiscal office: 'we had a custody case the other day, a man who was going to Glasgow for treatment for sexual and drink problems, who had his case stolen on a train and approached the police. The police put him in a room and started their enquiry about the bag, and the man for some reason thought he'd been locked in and went berserk. We got the report in the morning that he'd maliciously damaged police property. He did break a door, but it's not really a crime as such, there's something behind it that caused him to do that. So I phoned up the social work department. I spoke to the head worker, and said "look, if you can get the man some money, if you can get him somewhere to stay and take him on to Glasgow to his treatment centre, we'll drop this and let you do that". In the event the social work department weren't forthcoming. They couldn't promise me they would be able to actually give this man money and accommodation in which case I had to think of the public. This man let loose without money or accommodation. I could see him doing something else to get back into "clink" for the night, so in the end he was prosecuted and sent home. They weren't able to give me the answer that I wanted or the help I wanted . . . whether that was because they genuinely couldn't do it or they were being obstructive I don't know.' According to the social workers involved they had been willing to offer help to: 'arrange for the accused to see a social worker, direct him to the right agency who could provide him with money, put him in touch with the Homeless Officer' but the fiscal had considered that 'these arrangements offered insufficient safeguards' and was unwilling to relinquish responsibility to the social work department.

There is a strong feeling among Scottish prosecutors that social workers choose to ignore the general public interest in favour of their client's needs exclusively: 'social workers tend to focus on the problems of the accused and pay no attention whatsoever to the problems of the complainer . . . it all goes back to this question of do-gooding . . . I don't really approve of it'; 'I think social workers treat everyone alike . . . they assume that everyone is entitled to their help whereas fiscals have to draw a line between persons in need of some help and criminals with a capital C'. Some social workers may not feel able or willing to adopt an authoritarian stance towards their clients: 'I think that as social workers we have to be very careful about when we go to the fiscal because prosecution may be extremely detrimental to the work you're doing with a client'; 'many fiscals are very blinkered in their attitudes. I would love to be able to get them to understand that there are sociological reasons for crime. Most people involved in the criminal justice process have a very calvinistic approach to offenders.'

Some fiscals are not critical of social workers themselves but feel that social work departments could not cope with more cases than they already have: 'I think if they had the time they would do a very good job . . . they have the theoretical ability . . . but they are so badly understaffed . . . it's a question of resources and nothing else'; 'the options are open to us to refer specific cases to the social work department but referrals would be pretty rare because of our appreciation that they are overworked and there aren't the facilities available'. Fiscals too work under considerable pressure and may have no time to devote to what are generally regarded as marginal activities: 'I have got no communication with the social work department and the reason for this is . . . simply that fiscals just have not got the time to go round and discuss cases . . . this goes back to the amount of work we have to do . . . you've less and less time to indulge in what are termed *frills*'.

The third and by far the most radical involvement which a social worker might have with the fiscal relates directly to the making of the decision whether to prosecute or not. Obviously both information supplied by a social work department on an accused person and the availability of a positive alternative to prosecution in the form of social work referral affects the fiscal's decision. But at present this decision still remains entirely in the prosecutor's hands, he is not compelled to take such factors into account and the welfare of the accused person is not his concern. Even those few fiscals who favour closer links with social work agencies at the stage preceding prosecution stress that such links should not impose any direct pressure on the fiscal to make particular decisions: 'I think we could have a relationship with the social work department at the pre-trial stage provided there was a formal scheme . . . we are talking about the relatively minor criminal cases where there are special circumstances . . . cases where help is needed . . . working with the social work department would be very worthwhile but with the fiscal having the final decision . . . no doubt taking into consideration what the social worker thinks but not under any circumstances allowing the social workers to think they can sway that decision'.

The onus is placed very squarely on the social work department to approach the fiscal with any matters which might be regarded in social work terms as relevant to the prosecution decision: 'they have to come to me with the details about what they call their clients and I call the accused . . . I feel the approach properly has to come from them'. But the assessment of the status which such information should have in the decision whether or not to prosecute and the stage at which the relevant factors should be considered are the fiscal's alone: 'the social work department got in touch with me on one occasion . . . they indicated that the person wasn't very well and I said "well, that's fine . . . we will hear from a doctor at some stage in the proceedings" and that was the end of it . . . the doctor's report was taken into consideration by the court'.

This sense of distance and an unwillingness to regard the social worker as a fellow professional with his own area of competence which might have important implications for prosecutorial decision-making is in contrast to the close relations which have developed in some areas between the Reporter and the fiscal: 'we have an understanding with the Reporter . . . but there is a certain unease between us and the social work departments . . . they approach us rather less than they should do'. Social workers also note this unease and relate it to a difference in professional standing between themselves and the fiscal: 'as long as the fiscal has the powers that I see him having at present and as long as social workers have a low status, we can never get any closer professionally'; 'we never have much cause to believe that we could be involved in his decision-making – we could not question his professional ability'.

CONCLUSION

The fact that fiscals are not in law required to prosecute all alleged offences does not appear to influence decision-making at the marking stage in the vast majority of cases. Scottish prosecutors seem to regard the option not to prosecute which, in theory, is always available to them, as a marginal issue with little relevance to the processing of most criminal matters. Those cases where proceedings are not brought are regarded by fiscals as inappropriate for prosecution because they are defined as legally untenable or too trivial or because of unusual characteristics associated with the alleged offence of offender. Such cases often fall into identifiable categories, for instance careless driving or wife assault. Nevertheless, it is clear that fiscals vary considerably in their exercise of the no pro option and do not necessarily deal with similar types of offences or accused persons in the same way. For all fiscals the emphasis is on prosecution. While this may be in part a reflection of the lack of alternatives available to prosecutors it is largely a product of the particular orientation of the criminal justice process in Scotland towards court proceedings.

5

THE FORUM
FOR A CRIMINAL CASE

INTRODUCTION

THIS CHAPTER ANALYSES the discretion which is afforded in law to the
Scottish public prosecutor to select the appropriate forum for trial in certain
criminal cases and discusses how such discretion is exercised in practice. In
Scotland there are two distinct modes of criminal procedure: *summary* where a
sheriff or lay justices adjudicate and *solemn* where a high court judge or sheriff
determines the legal issues and a jury of fifteen lay people decides matters of
fact. Four courts exercise criminal jurisdiction, the High Court of Justiciary,
the sheriff and jury court, the sheriff summary court and the district court.[1]
All Common Law offences can be tried either on summary or solemn procedure
with the exception of murder, rape, treason, incest, deforcement of messengers
and breach of duty by magistrates which can only be prosecuted in the high
court. There is therefore:

> no rigorous classification of crimes which may be tried
> without a jury, and it is not necessary that there should be
> one, because under our system of public prosecution, the
> discretion of determining whether the crimes reported to
> them should or should not be tried summarily is vested, in
> the first instance, in the Crown Office. [Clark and Bendall
> *v*. Stuart (1886) 1 White 191, Lord McLaren at 209]

In the case of statutory offences the relevant Acts which create these
prescribe the appropriate form of procedure as with certain offences under the
Road Traffic Act 1972 which can only be tried summarily. At Common Law
the district court can only fine up to £200 and imprison for a maximum of
60 days; the sheriff court can impose a fine on summary procedure of up to
£1,000 and imprison for a maximum of 3 months; the sheriff when hearing
cases on solemn procedure can impose an unlimited fine and a maximum of
2 years in prison and the high court has unlimited sentencing powers. In relation
to the district court district justices are specifically barred from hearing certain

[1] See Diagram 6 *Jurisdiction of the Scottish Criminal Courts* p. 81.

Diagram 6 Jurisdiction of the Scottish Criminal Courts

Jurisdiction   Sentencing Powers

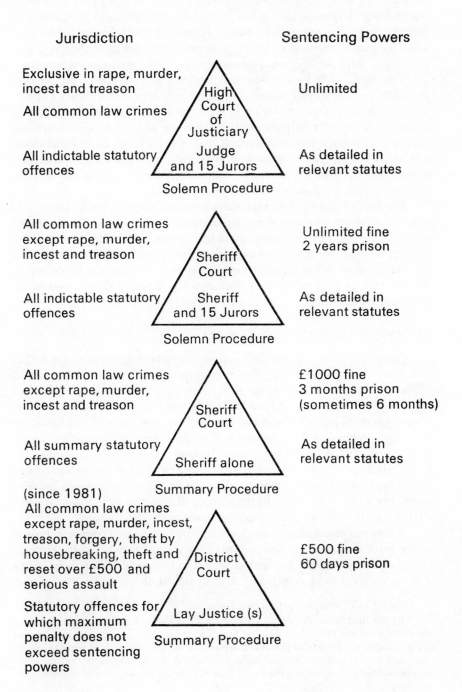

Exclusive in rape, murder, incest and treason

All common law crimes

High Court of Justiciary

Unlimited

All indictable statutory offences

Judge and 15 Jurors

As detailed in relevant statutes

Solemn Procedure

All common law crimes except rape, murder, incest and treason

Sheriff Court

Unlimited fine 2 years prison

All indictable statutory offences

Sheriff and 15 Jurors

As detailed in relevant statutes

Solemn Procedure

All common law crimes except rape, murder, incest and treason

Sheriff Court

£1000 fine 3 months prison (sometimes 6 months)

All summary statutory offences

Sheriff alone

As detailed in relevant statutes

Summary Procedure

(since 1981) All common law crimes except rape, murder, incest, treason, forgery, theft by housebreaking, theft and reset over £500 and serious assault

District Court

£500 fine 60 days prison

Statutory offences for which maximum penalty does not exceed sentencing powers

Lay Justice (s)

Summary Procedure

G

types of cases, such as assaults where a weapon is used, and are given exclusive jurisdiction in other cases. Thus by choosing a particular charge the fiscal may bring a case within the jurisdiction of a particular court though the same set of circumstances if prosecuted under a different charge would be heard in a different court. For example an offence concerned with obscene publications might be prosecuted in the district court under the Burgh Police (Scotland) Act 1892 or in the sheriff court as the common law crime of shameless indecency.

Therefore, while his decisions are regulated to some extent by statutory provisions and are subject in some instances to the approval of crown counsel, the Scottish prosecutor exercises a key role in selecting the court of trial. In examining this aspect of prosecutorial discretion which provides the central focus of this chapter, it is clear that the criteria upon which the fiscal draws in making such decisions are influenced by his views about more general matters such as the nature of serious crime, sentencing policies and the role of a lay judiciary within the Scottish criminal justice system.

The first section of this chapter discusses in detail that small minority of cases where the fiscal makes the initial choice in favour of solemn procedure, subject to the approval of crown counsel. In making such a choice the fiscal is in effect helping to define what constitutes serious crime. The second section looks at the other end of the spectrum in examining the fiscal's notion of trivial offences and the part which he considers a lay judiciary should play in the processing of such cases.

CHOOSING SOLEMN PROCEDURE[1]

Courts exercising solemn jurisdiction in Scotland hear about 4,000 cases each year, less than 2 per cent of all persons proceeded against for crimes and offences. Solemn procedure, as the name suggests, is reserved for more serious criminal cases and corresponds to trial on indictment in the English criminal justice system. A jury of fifteen lay people determines issues of fact following the judge's rulings on legal matters and decides whether the accused's guilt has been established by the prosecution beyond reasonable doubt. Unlike the position in England and Wales there is no right of election in Scotland so that the accused cannot when charged with certain offences choose to be tried summarily or on indictment. In the absence of statutory restrictions on jurisdiction it is the fiscal not the accused who makes the initial choice.

Where he decides that a case merits trial by jury he will prepare a petition setting forth the name, age and address of the accused person and the criminal charge or charges against him and present it to the sheriff for a judicial examination, which is held in private.[2] The sheriff, at the fiscal's request, either

---

[1] See Diagram 7 *Steps in Solemn Procedure* p. 83.

[2] At the time when the research was carried out the option open to the sheriff to examine the accused, called the judicial examination, and to the accused to emit a declaration in reply was never exercised so that at first appearance the accused normally remained silent. Since then Section 6 of the Criminal Justice (Scotland) Act 1980 has revived the practice of judicial examination permitting the fiscal to ask the accused certain types of questions. See also p. 131.

Diagram 7 Steps in Solemn Procedure

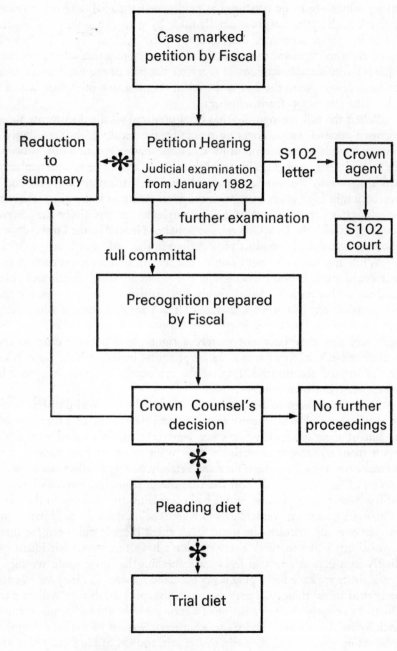

* Opportunity for plea negotiation

commits the accused for further examination, allowing the prosecution more time to investigate the case, or commits him for trial. The latter step is known as full committal. The fiscal then prepares the precognition containing all the available evidence including witness statements, productions (documents and articles which are to be produced as evidence at the trial) and other relevant material. Such statements are generally made by witnesses to the fiscal in person and each separate account is described as a precognition. The fiscal, however, has no right to interview the accused. It is worth noting that solemn procedure requires a considerable amount of work on the part of the fiscal which would not be necessary were the case to be taken on summary procedure where the police take statements from witnesses.

When the full precognition has been prepared all the documents are sent to crown counsel with a covering report by the fiscal which increasingly has come to include an expression of his recommendation regarding the processing of a case. Crown counsel decide what the disposal should be in a particular case, their instructions are binding on fiscals and they themselves appear for the prosecution in high court cases with the fiscal acting as instructing solicitor to the advocates depute. Cases of great complexity or sensitivity may involve consultation with the Law Officers, the Solicitor General or the Lord Advocate, who may occasionally conduct prosecutions in the high court.

While this study did not examine the way in which crown counsel make their decisions, it is possible to gauge the extent to which fiscals feel able to influence such decisions. Some fiscals are adamant that: 'one doesn't make recommendations to Crown Office. As far as I am concerned if I have kept a man on petition I will not justify my actions to Crown Office.' But most fiscals feel that they have not merely a right but a positive duty to make recommendations: 'we now as a matter of course include within our notes our conclusions and recommendations on the evidence'; 'you usually drop a hint and express your own opinion'.

Most fiscals seem to be fairly satisfied that the eventual decision reached by crown counsel with regard to the appropriate form of procedure takes account of their suggestions: 'it's my view that crown counsel very seldom depart from our recommendation'; 'they want to know your views – if you can make out a good case then they are certainly willing to take your views into account'. One experienced fiscal felt that the situation had improved over the last few years: 'in days gone by we had complaints that nobody in the Crown Office even read what you said'. Even where the local fiscal and crown counsel disagree over a particular case some fiscals think there is still room for further negotiation: 'I like to think that you don't have to accept their instructions blindly in a case where you feel that something has gone quite wrong . . . several times we have had a ping pong back and forward . . . they are not absolutely deaf to anything you may say . . . although I think they will be a little reluctant to change their instructions'; 'I thought it should be Section 1 [causing death by reckless driving] and it came back as a Section 3 [careless driving] and I phoned up about it and they said that crown counsel had in fact swithered for a long time over the particular case but if the fiscal thought it should be a

Section 1 then go ahead with the Section 1'. Other fiscals feel that it is useful to bring to crown counsel's attention local factors which may be of importance, particularly in deciding whether a case should be taken in the high court or in the sheriff court: 'in a spate of horrible house-breakings recently I asked very strongly that this matter be treated by the high court and crown counsel certainly went along with that'.

Choosing the appropriate form of procedure is an important prosecutorial decision even though it is subject to review. Yet the standard texts on Scottish criminal procedure offer few guidelines to assist fiscals in deciding the form of procedure most appropriate in a particular case. Writers mention a variety of factors which the fiscal may take into account in deciding the appropriate form of procedure – the gravity of the offence, previous record (if any) of the accused person, the sentencing policy of the judge and the justification for the increased public expense, inconvenience and length of time entailed in solemn procedure. However 'there are no definite pre-determined rules applicable and apart from the above considerations, the matter depends on the circumstances of each case and the way in which the individual procurator fiscal chooses to exercise his discretion.' [Sheehan: 1975: 138]

In spite of the absence of formal rules most fiscals consider that rules of thumb do exist and indeed some fiscals appear to have assimilated these criteria to such an extent that description of them becomes unnecessary: 'it's an easy decision . . . it more or less decides itself'. The majority are able to produce a checklist of factors relating to the criminal incident, the accused person, the processing of criminal cases generally and wider public policy considerations: 'I don't think there is any hard and fast policy but there are obvious guidelines'. Relevant criteria include whether the incident is perceived as serious, what previous convictions (if any) are recorded against the accused, the expense and time entailed in taking a case on solemn procedure, the sentence deemed appropriate for a particular offence and public feeling about certain types of crime.

Seriousness

The major factor in deciding to put a case on petition appears to be the seriousness of the offence. In our Census this was given as the main reason in almost 50 per cent of reports where the fiscal chose to prosecute on indictment. Fiscals distinguish broadly between offences against the person and offences against property and apply different criteria on the basis of this distinction. The assessment of seriousness in either case can be a complex matter, depending to a great extent on individual judgment: 'severe injury[1] – that is purely a subjective term because what I think is severe is not necessarily what someone else would think of as severe. If for example A was in a pub and there was a fight and he picked up a bottle and hit someone on the body with it, I would charge that as a summary complaint, but where a member of the public is attacked with a

[1] The choice of the charge *assault to severe injury* generally indicates that the case will be taken on solemn procedure.

weapon and receives an injury requiring more than five stitches then I would put him on petition.'

In offences against the person the result of a particular assault for the victim is regarded as important: 'a fractured limb, a head injury where there is a fractured skull or any question of permanent disfigurement should be serious enough to merit petition', but it is certainly not the sole criterion in assessing the serious nature of such an offence. The particular circumstances surrounding the criminal incident may be equally or sometimes more important and the carrying of or using an offensive weapon may be a key aspect: 'there is one area that I regard as very serious and that is the offensive weapon. The air rifle, knife, chain – all of these things which can in fact do terrible damage ... you are very close to murder if you have got an offensive weapon in your hand'; 'if there is a weapon involved, I start from the point that it should be a petition'. It appears that even a minor assault, if inflicted by a weapon, may be dealt with on petition: 'we had a recent case of a boy at a disco – he did not approve of the change of record and he went round to the kitchen, produced a fourteen inch long blade carving knife and went for the disc jockey. The injury was not very bad although the motive was.'[1]

So far as crimes against property are concerned reference is generally made to the amount stolen or an objective valuation of goods so that thefts over £1,000 are normally put on petition. This is usually applied independently of any subjective knowledge on the part of the accused as to the value of the items stolen since: 'when someone steals something they are hoping it is something valuable'. Occasionally, however, the fiscal is prepared to think again: 'the amount is sometimes the most flexible. We sometimes decide to take something which seems to be a big amount on summary procedure. We had one once where somebody stole what looked just like a box of tricks but turned out to be an enormously valuable computer. But (a) it was immediately recovered, and (b) he had not a clue what he had stolen so it was in fact put on summary.' On the other hand, an accused may be charged with the theft of small amounts only but the number of charges may suggest a course of conduct meriting trial by jury: 'I put a quite modest case on petition because the accused keeps on using other people's DHSS allowance books. Now we are going to have to pull her up.'

Previous record

For both categories of crime, offences against the person and offences against property, there are other factors which the fiscal takes into account in making the initial choice of procedure and such cues may either add weight

---

[1] According to Scottish criminal law motive is not recognised as relevant in establishing guilt or innocence but the idea of general intention to do harm has a long history. Hume uses the expression 'dole' which he describes as 'that corrupt and evil intention, which is essential to the guilt of any crime . . . and indicates a corrupt and malignant disposition, a heart contemptuous of order and regardless of social duty'. [Hume: 1797: 21] In fact there is little doubt that motive is taken into account by the judge in sentencing so that it is of importance to the fiscal in determining the forum for a criminal case – see Cawthorne *v.* H.M. Adv. 1968 JC 32 and Smart *v.* H.M. Adv. 1975 SLT 65.

to the heinous nature of a crime already defined by the fiscal as serious or counteract the impression in the fiscal's mind that a particular offence is not serious enough to merit petition. Thus in our Census the accused's previous record determined the choice of procedure for 25 per cent of the relevant reports. The previous record of the accused is an important one: 'criminals of long standing may only steal something worth £2 but they have got such form that it might have a salutory effect to put them on petition'; 'you can look down the list of previous convictions and if they are approaching a sentence which is in excess of six months then it is probably time they were going on petition'. The fact that the accused held a position of trust particularly in the public service – for example, as a postman or a policeman – could also cause the fiscal to favour solemn procedure: 'if somebody is a public employee, for example a postman stealing mail, that really is a serious breach of the public trust and has to be treated more seriously than if the accused had been an ordinary punter'.

Procedural matters

The fiscal of course must always bear in mind the nature of Scottish criminal procedure when deciding whether to place an accused on petition:

> there is an important distinction between solemn and
> summary criminal jurisdiction which strikes one at the
> outset. In summary procedure there is no petition for
> warrant to apprehend, and no judicial examination and
> committal. The absence of a preliminary petition materially
> affects the procedure. It necessitates fuller information before
> proceedings are begun, because the prosecutor knows that
> he has to go to trial upon the charge as stated in his
> complaint. It also calls for careful study, because the
> facility and rapidity of summary process may readily lead
> to hasty prosecution and careless drafting. [Renton and
> Brown: 1972: 84]

The fiscal has authority to put an accused person on petition initially and then reduce the case to a summary matter before full committal without obtaining crown counsel's consent. Therefore: 'petition may be used as a convenience – by that I mean that the police have reported to me the likelihood of other charges or they report something which may be a serious matter and which I want to look into a bit more'; 'a petition gives you time to think so that there is no great difficulty in dealing with it at first instance'. The fiscal's choice of petition is subject to crown counsel's agreement so that his initial judgment is subject to review: 'I don't take the ultimate responsibility – if I go into the grey area of borderline cases which may or may not merit petition then I am likely to take the view that it should go on petition and it is for crown counsel to reduce it'. On the other hand, pressure of work and expense may militate against petition: 'it may be the start of a long series of paper work and at the end of the day the accused may still only get six months or less';[1] 'it sometimes has to be decided in relation to the volume of work which the court can cope with'.

Fiscals also note that they have to bear in mind the unpredictable nature of jury verdicts: 'it's pot-luck with juries, they can let a person off for the most ludicrous of reasons. A judge will look at the case and say "he's guilty", or "not guilty" whereas a jury can let a person off not because they don't think he did it but because they feel sorry for him'; 'you know how a sheriff would look at it but what about a jury?' This may encourage Scottish prosecutors where they have a choice to opt for summary procedure since 'there's too many imponderables from a sheriff and jury for comfort.'

Sentencing goals

The assessment of seriousness, the weight to be given to an accused's previous record and procedural matters are not judgments made in a vacuum. There is an underlying rationale which informs such decisions, the goal towards which the fiscal seems to be striving. In theory fiscals have no part to play in either determining or even recommending sentence since their involvement ends with conviction or acquittal. However, the sentencing structure is such that the selection of a particular form of procedure sets limits on the sentencing powers of judges. There seems little doubt, then, that the fiscal in his choice of procedure is making a conscious calculation of what he considers the appropriate sentence for the particular criminal incident in the event of a guilty verdict: 'I must look at it in the light of the sentence he is likely to receive'; 'you decide in the light of the known facts, all known facts, what an appropriate sentence should be for X at the end of the day'. This may require a familiarity with individual judges' sentencing policies particularly in the case of sheriffs (who may sit summarily or with a jury) since there is little point in going to the trouble and expense of a jury trial when a sheriff would have meted out the same sentence had the case been heard on summary procedure: 'you see, you have got to know your sheriff – I know my sheriff and he is quite capable of going up to the limit of summary complaint. So he is quite prepared to give a bloke six months if he has got several convictions for theft – that isn't the time to go on petition'; 'I would probably not put on petition a youngster who committed a fairly serious offence because in my experience the sheriff here would send him to Borstal and he could do that without a jury trial'.

However, both the fiscal in prosecuting and the judge in sentencing have to consider matters of public policy which may relate to local feeling: 'it depends on what is happening in the district – a couple of years ago I was concerned about reports of mugging in X and we had offenders, none of them had any previous convictions at all, who attacked an old man completely unprovoked. They went straight on petition. I certainly acted out of a desire to prevent this sort of crime from expanding'; 'there was a multiple assault on police officers in an area of this sheriffdom that has a high record of assaults on

[1] In certain circumstances a custodial sentence of up to six months may be imposed by a sheriff sitting without a jury and therefore there would be little point in taking such a case under solemn procedure.

police officers and difficulty in policing. That merits a petition to clean up the town.' There may also be matters of national concern to take into account: 'one would be foolish to say that one wasn't aware of the public outcry in DHSS cases – more and more are reported now than ten years ago'; 'over the years there have been campaigns to stamp out particular types of assault – for example, razor slashing – it is policy to try to get rid of that sort of crime'.

A concerted effort by police, prosecutor and judge to clamp down on particular types of crime is regarded as a legitimate response to public pressure. Fiscals have fairly convinced views that stiffer sentences are valuable as deterrents. This is so in spite of the fact that the public attitude to particular offences may very well change over time: 'there are cases which in days gone by could well have been taken as breaches of the peace but now are treated as serious matters . . . a wee drunk wandered into the GPO and put a bit of paper across saying "give me some money or I will blow the place up". The girl looked at it and got a fright – it was regarded as extremely serious because of the Northern Ireland situation and bombs being planted.'[1] Scottish prosecutors are also aware of this shift in public attitudes: 'times and fashions change – housebreaking is a serious, serious matter for the person who has been offended against but a housebreaking is just a housebreaking . . . if a person is apprehended having broken into a house with intent to steal, 9 times out of 10 his case will be dealt with on summary procedure'.

In making the initial decision regarding the appropriate form of procedure, therefore, the fiscal cannot refer to a uniform set of criteria. He must rely on his own judgment which may well be based on an assimilation of practices adopted in the office where his career in the fiscal service began: 'who knows what is standard – this is one of the difficulties that fiscals have in taking cases on indictment as opposed to summary procedure. We don't really have clear guidance on this apart from what we pick up in our early years . . . it should be more or less the same in all offices but some people are working with a different understanding of the concept of seriousness from others. I like to think that I only take cases on indictment that really do merit indictment. My criteria are as follows: is this a crime which is likely to be disposed of or should in the public interest be disposed of by imprisonment? If so, are the sheriff's powers whatever they happen to be at summary level enough or does it have to go on indictment?'

CHOOSING THE DISTRICT COURT[2]

There are two courts exercising summary jurisdiction in Scotland: the sheriff court and the district court.[3] In general a sheriff, who is appointed by

[1] Section 5 of the Criminal Law Act 1977 makes specific provision for bomb hoax offences.

[2] See Diagram 8 *Steps in Summary Procedure* p. 90.

[3] Only the district court in Glasgow has a stipendiary magistrates' court presided over by a full-time legally qualified stipendiary magistrate with the same powers as a sheriff sitting summarily.

Diagram 8 Steps in Summary Procedure

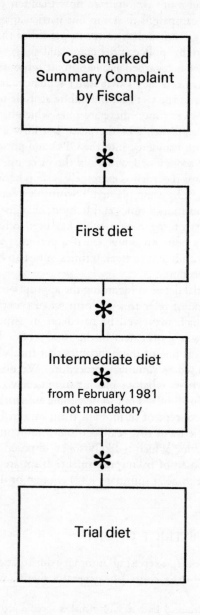

Case marked
Summary Complaint
by Fiscal

*

First diet

*

Intermediate diet
*
from February 1981
not mandatory

*

Trial diet

* Opportunity for plea negotiation

the Crown and must be an advocate or solicitor of at least ten years' standing, can hear and determine all summary criminal cases committed within his sheriff court district. District justices, however, who are lay people usually appointed by the Secretary of State on the recommendation of local justices' committees and who preside over district courts serving local authority areas, have only limited jurisdiction. Their powers are much less than the jurisdiction granted to lay magistrates in England and Wales. At the time when the research was carried out, cases of forgery, theft by housebreaking, theft or reset of an amount exceeding £25, theft or reset under £25 where the accused had already been convicted of a similar offence, assault resulting in a fractured limb, assault to the danger of life, assault by stabbing and assault with intent to ravish could not be tried in the district court.[1] In addition no prosecutions of children under 16 can be brought in the District Court.[2]

The maximum penalties available on summary conviction are also different in the two types of court. A sheriff in summary cases can impose a fine of up to £1,000 or a maximum custodial sentence of three or in some instances six months; district justices can sentence a person convicted by them to a maximum prison term of sixty days or set a maximum fine of £200. Although exclusive jurisdiction may be granted to a particular court by statute,[3] and occasionally the Lord Advocate issues a direction stating that certain offences should be prosecuted in one summary court rather than the other, as with minor criminal incidents taking place at football matches which must be tried in the sheriff summary court, the choice of court is generally at the discretion of the fiscal. This section considers in detail the factors which influence the fiscal in choosing one summary court rather than the other, focusing mainly on his attitudes towards the district court and how these affect selection.

Until 1975 the fiscal service presented cases in the sheriff court only since solicitors employed by the local authority dealt with all the business of the burgh, justice of the peace and stipendiary magistrates' courts. One fiscal recalls that time: 'the local authorities had their own prosecutors. These chaps were private practitioners doing this as a little sideline . . . some of their procedures were absolutely disastrous . . . but because of the local arrangements no one seemed to appeal.' In Glasgow and Edinburgh the burgh courts were manned by full-time professional staff. One fiscal who had been a burgh prosecutor in Glasgow described it thus: 'these courts were autonomous. The burgh prosecutor could make his decisions without reference to any higher authority. We had a large room, and there were normally three prosecutors

---

[1] Section 285 Criminal Procedure (Scotland) Act 1975. Since Section 7 of the Criminal Justice (Scotland) Act 1980 came into force it has been competent for the district court to try cases of theft, reset, falsehood, fraud or wilful imposition, breach of trust or embezzlement where the amount does not exceed £200 including instances where an accused has been previously convicted of a similar offence and any statutory offence for which the maximum penalty does not exceed 60 days imprisonment, a fine of £200 or both.

[2] Section 31(1) Social Work (Scotland) Act 1968.

[3] For example the Road Traffic Act 1972 confers exclusive jurisdiction on the sheriff summary court in certain offences, such as careless driving; conversely, offences under the Burgh (Police) Scotland Act 1892 are invariably prosecuted in the district court.

working in that room and when cases came in we frequently consulted one another.'

The District Courts (Scotland) Act 1975 not only abolished the old burgh and justice of the peace courts and replaced them with a system of district courts but also gave the power of prosecuting cases in the new courts to the district procurator fiscal.[1] This entailed additional work for the fiscal in areas with which he had hitherto been unfamiliar, as one procurator fiscal explained: 'there are such things as the Burgh Police (Scotland) Act, the Licensing Act and I had gone almost 18 years and I'd never heard of these because these had all been dealt with in the burgh court'. Thus the fiscal now has to decide which court is the appropriate forum for those cases which may be tried in either summary court.

Some fiscal offices have separate arrangements for dealing with district court work. The police will send reports to the fiscal staff in the district court office direct, selecting these cases on the basis of the legislative provisions already discussed. Most fiscals do not consider that this limits their own discretion: 'on the whole the police reporting cases to the district courts is convenient to us. In general I think that the division can be very simple . . . If there is any doubt there is a revision by a depute . . . I don't think it infringes our discretion at all'; 'the police primarily decide which ones go to which court. They report the cases they consider to be appropriate for the district court but with the fiscal looking at a particular case he may decide it was more appropriate in the other court and he does an interchange. If it is sent to the wrong court then the fiscal will correct it.' However, it was mentioned that it is not always easy to send a case back to a different court: 'the district court starts at 10 o'clock and the sheriff summary court at 2 o'clock. It very often happens that by the time the fiscal in the sheriff court looks at a case it is too late to send it back to the district court' and that the police do make mistakes: 'they make errors of discretion and they make errors of simple law'. But the advantages of streamlining in the processing of these cases appear to outweigh such reservations.

Older fiscals who recall the days when the burgh and justice of the peace (JP) courts were under the control of the local authority feel that the extension of the fiscal's jurisdiction to include the district courts: 'was a sensible reform, the cosy, cosy days of the burgh prosecutor are by and gone. I feel to a certain extent we have stolen their thunder . . . it was a disturbance of their ways . . . they were terribly important people.' As in the days of the burgh and JP courts the bench is assisted by a legally qualified clerk employed by the local authority.

The district courts, then, can in certain cases provide a forum for trial which is both cheaper and arguably more democratic than the sheriff court since its judges are lay people selected from the local community[2] who provide

---

[1] See *Lay Justice: some preliminary observations* [Scolag Bulletin: June 1980: 80–2] which offers a preview of a research project on the district courts in Scotland currently being carried out by Dr. J. McManus and Z. Bankowski.

[2] 'Anyone may put forward a nominee for appointment by writing to the Secretary of the [local] advisory committee [which] consists of local people who are able to consider

their services without payment. However it appears that by no means all cases falling within the jurisdiction of the district court are in fact tried in that court. In our Census 78 per cent of all cases triable in either summary court were prosecuted in the district court, the vast majority involving only one charge against an accused person cited to appear. The report of a Working Party on the Lay Summary Courts published in 1972 presents a guide to those considerations which may make it desirable to reserve cases to the sheriff summary court:

1.   that the offence is of a nature that is likely to give rise to difficult questions of law;

2.   that the offence is of a nature that is likely to give rise to complexity in proof;

3.   that mental disorder is involved;

4.   that . . . those offenders who appear likely to become persistent criminals might be prosecuted before the sheriff court;

5.   that where the nature of the offence was one of high emotional content or controversy the possibility of a miscarriage of justice would be reduced if it was tried by a judge who, because of his legal training and judicial experience is likely to be more detached. [Working Party on Lay Summary Courts: 1972: 22–3]

In discussing with fiscals those criteria which influence them in choosing the court of trial for summary cases it is clear that selection is determined to a large extent by their assessment of the quality of lay justice as administered in Scotland. While the factors outlined by the Working Party are clearly relevant, they must be located within this broader framework.

Some fiscals are totally opposed to the idea of lay people administering justice: 'I am not in favour of lay magistrates at all. I don't think the system works . . . it is an absurd system'; 'the composition of the district court is undoubtedly against the public interest because you have lay persons sitting on the bench . . . I supported the district courts at the last change of government but now I feel it was wrong.' The essence of such sweeping condemnation appears to be the non-legal, non-professional nature of lay justice.[1] Such fiscals consider that: 'all prosecutors much prefer the legally qualified judge'. Since the introduction of legal aid for district court cases and comprehensive duty solicitor schemes covering all summary courts, lay justices may be faced with legally qualified counsel for both prosecution and defence.

In fact very few fiscals question the value of a legally qualified bench as the best forum for the trial of all criminal matters. Occasionally fiscals comment

---

the suitability of candidates and recommend them or not . . . In addition district and islands councils may nominate up to one quarter of their members to serve *ex officio* as justices for their area.' [Handbook for newly appointed justices of the peace: 1978: 5]

[1] The irony inherent in this criticism has been noted in recent writings which suggest that the pressure to professionalise and create 'specialised non-specialists' is antithetical to the whole notion of lay justice. [Christie: 1978]

favourably on the district courts: 'one of the best forums for prosecutions because it gives a very very fair judgment'; 'in the laycourts A will be convicted if the lay magistrates want to convict . . . I'd rather be tried by a court prepared to exercise that amount of discretion and not in the professional courts where a person will be found guilty according to the evidence'. Such remarks are, however, rare. Several fiscals spoke of their initial efforts to make use of the full jurisdictional powers of the district court and their subsequent disillusionment: 'I was very keen on taking away from the sheriff court the trivial rubbish, particularly trivial Common Law rubbish because I was anxious that justices shouldn't just sit and deal with simple statutory offences, drunk and incapable, urinating in the street, all the very low quality work. I wanted them to feel that they had something to contribute to the community but subsequently I had to reconsider my split of work.'

While some Scottish prosecutors are against the notion of lay justice in principle, the majority of fiscals are more selective in their criticism and specify particular aspects of the district courts and the local bench which disturb them.

Lack of legal knowledge

The most common reason given is a lack of legal knowledge and expertise on the part of the lay bench: 'quite a number of justices do very little to acquaint themselves with even the rudiments of the law'; 'the justices I have seen in action display a basic misunderstanding about the law and about the evidence'; 'the procedural errors they all make which can well be fatal to convictions in many cases are appalling'. For instance: 'when Justice X heard the first witness speak to the act of shoplifting he was about to convict the accused and was then told by the district clerk that the accused had the right to cross-examination'; 'I don't think that lay justices know what the term "proof beyond reasonable doubt" means.[1] You frequently in district courts get expressions like "I'll hold you guilty but I'll give you the benefit of the doubt in this case and fine you" – it sounds dreadful.' It is admitted that justices have the services of a legally qualified clerk[2] to give them advice on points of law but these officials themselves do not always appear to the fiscal to be sufficiently knowledgeable: 'where lay justice might fall down is in the quality of advice given by the clerks'; 'the district court clerks are not very well tuned up in criminal law'. Fiscals find it tedious to have to reiterate what they consider simple points of law: 'in the district court you have to go into the law in great detail'. Such misgivings may determine whether a case will be sent to the district court: 'we might feel that there are evidential complexities or something which they might not be able to cope with terribly well and we would want a sheriff to deal with this although on the face of the actual offence it is district court material'.

---

[1] It is interesting to note that the reasonable doubt concept in criminal law is accepted by theoreticians and practitioners alike as a notoriously difficult one. [See Eggleston: 1978; Williams: 1979]

[2] 'It is the clerk's duty by statute to advise the justices, either at their request or on his own initiative on matters of law, practice and procedure.' [Justices' Handbook: 1978: 27]

Absence of professional approach

In addition, the fact that lay justices are not qualified lawyers means that in fiscals' eyes they lack not only legal expertise but also a professional approach to their work. Fiscals suggest that this deficiency shows itself in a number of ways. For example, they think that justices are easily led both by clerks of court: 'there's a suspicion that the legal assessors have authority over the lay magistrate ... you're never sure whether the assessor is telling the magistrate what to do or he is just simply advising',[1] and solicitors representing the defence: 'an inexperienced justice is capable of being influenced too greatly by a persuasive defending solicitor'.

Although justices must sign an undertaking to complete a course of basic instruction in court duties it is felt by some fiscals that the lay bench lacks the mental self-discipline and objectivity which lawyers acquire as part of their professional training:[2] 'if only lay justices were trained with as much rigour as Children's Hearings members, but they are undisciplined and have an inability to dominate proceedings which a professional really does not like in court'; 'lay magistrates have not had any inbuilt prejudices ironed out by training for the bench – a sheriff has controlled that by legal training'; 'at a recent trial under the Licensing (Scotland) Act against a local publican for dispensing drink to persons under 18, the Crown case was proved beyond a doubt but Justice X went on to say "I am in this trade myself and I am going to give you the benefit of the doubt and find you not guilty" '.

Without the common thread of legal reasoning to guide them, fiscals do not always comprehend the rationale behind justices' verdicts: 'I find it very difficult sometimes to understand how a particular justice came to a particular decision'; 'I much prefer the sheriff court because you know that if you have a decision on the law, it's going to be very rarely that you disagree with it but justices seem to take different views from us, for example, from what we consider is a breach of the peace'; 'justices sometimes come to decisions that we think completely wrong in law – for instance, a recent wife assault case which was quite clear in which there was evidence and where even the accused admitted that he had hit her. The justice found it not proven and there's just no explaining that kind of thing.'

Organisation of lay justice

Many fiscals are critical of the way in which the district courts are adminstered. Local authorities are responsible for the district courts in their areas though they are assisted by justices' committees and can seek advice on training and organisation from the Central Advisory Committee on Justices of the

---

[1] Though according to the handbook for newly appointed justices 'the clerk takes no part in deliberations on conviction or sentence'. [Justices' Handbook: 1978: 27]

[2] It should be noted that no justice should sit on the bench in the district court until he has completed training in accordance with a scheme made by the Secretary of State and set out in Appendix 1 of the *Handbook for Newly Appointed Justices*.

Peace. Since the 1975 Act the practice of having a bench of three, a multiple bench, has been encouraged. The 1972 Working Party pointed out that:

> there is a long-standing tradition in Scotland of criminal charges being heard by a judge sitting alone [unlike] England and Wales where successive Lord Chancellors have taken the view that three is the best number of justices to try a case. The great virtue that is attached to the plural bench is that it is a built-in method of ironing out the prejudices that everyone entertains . . . it is more likely to reach a balanced decision. [Working Party on the Lay Summary Courts: 1972: 39–40][1]

Fiscals, however, do not, in general, welcome this development: 'the multiple bench removes from the justices individually the necessary precision of mind . . . they mull over things . . . if you are sitting on your own I think you have got to concentrate more and you have got to make your *own* mind up. There are one or two good justices who, when they take charge of the thing, just proceed themselves and they don't care about the people sitting on either side'; 'a multiple bench is really difficult for the legal assessor to control and advise'; 'it not only takes a lot of time but there can be divergent opinions on a particular case from the start'. Mention was made of lack of experience because justices do not sit regularly, in contrast to the former burgh court: 'my burgh court experience was of one magistrate sitting with an assessor and new bailies[2] being introduced from time to time . . . the bailie was a fairly practised magistrate before very long. The new system introduces justices to a bench who may have very little opportunity of sitting on the bench whether they like it or not and, as a result, their experience must be particularly thin.'

Selection of justices

The kind of people selected for the bench are not always considered suitable by fiscals: 'people who are unwilling to take decisions end up on the bench'; 'they get confused, their principles tend to be ten years out of date'. There appears to be a certain amount of agreement among fiscals that a lay justice should be a member of the same community as the alleged offenders who appear before him: 'they theoretically are the people who are closer to the victims of the crimes – shouting and swearing in the street, the fracas at the bus stop, the old man who is urinating outside the pub at 11 o'clock at night, it tends to be his own type, his own community who are the victims, the bloke who sprays some gang slogan on an underpass in the housing estate . . .'; 'these people are in touch, in daily contact with the members of the public who they are sifting through the court . . . I think the lay court has this connection with

---

[1] Multiple benches are not at all uncommon in solemn procedure where benches of several judges may be summoned to deal with a particularly difficult point which has arisen during the course of a trial.

[2] This was the name given to the lay judge presiding over the former burgh court who always sat alone.

the people who are going through, they understand the social problems of a particular area'.

Such local knowledge on the part of lay justices is sometimes favourably contrasted with the sheriffs' lack of contact with people appearing in the criminal courts: 'it will only be the fewest of sheriffs who will have seen perhaps a breach of the peace. There is a classic case of an infamous sheriff who was famous for his disposals and he thought he would get to know what X was like on a Friday because there was so many cases of breach of the peace so what he did on a Friday was when the 10 o'clock pub closing was still in operation he went down to X main street in his bowler and his other garb and stayed there from about 9.30 to 9.50 p.m. and, of course, the place was deserted and he just thought "oh well, there is nothing happening here, I'll just go away home", so I think that showed a total lack of understanding that the trouble would only start after the pubs came out – from 10.30 to 12 there would be trouble.' Nevertheless it is also felt that a middleclass, more educated bench might be better able to cope with the complexities of criminal trials: 'in X the justices tend to be more professional than working class . . . it makes a difference in the assimilation of evidence and in making submissions or having a debate with them'.

In addition some fiscals question the motives of justices: 'most of them want to sit not in order to get experience but for the benefit of sitting up there like Allah'; 'they are not there because they want to administer justice for the good of the public, they are there for their own selfish ends, they are masochistic or they have got strong feelings of being self-important'.[1] However, the claim that justices nominated from councillors generally tend to favour members of their wards is not supported by fiscals. In one fiscaldom, there were teething problems in the early days: 'I've been subjected to political pressure . . . some bailie trying to influence the scheme of things but there was no question of corruption'. In fact, one fiscal pointed to justices' scrupulousness in this regard: 'one justice decided to absent himself and said "I'm not taking the case. I know this man." '

Sentencing decisions made by lay justices

Although fiscals, unlike prosecutors in some other jurisdictions,[2] have no direct part to play in determining sentence, they certainly have an interest in the disposals meted out to convicted persons. Many are highly critical of district court sentencing decisions. There is a feeling among some fiscals that justices are too soft: 'our district court tends to be very lenient . . . I mean they give them good advice, admonish them, send them away, sentence deferred . . . crooks just smile at that . . . I've heard them talking about it'; 'justices forget about inflation as far as their fines are concerned and they're terrified of putting people in prison'. This influences the kinds of cases that fiscals send to the district court. For example: 'a man who had come up before them for punching

---

[1] It should be remembered that, while lay justices are reimbursed for travelling and other expenses, they are not paid for their services.

[2] As in South Africa and the United States where the prosecution is required to recommend an appropriate sentence.

H

somebody in the face at a disco would get fined £5 and further down the
queue a man would come up before them for not having an MOT certificate
and they could fine him £30. Now I asked them why were they doing this
and they said "Well, he has got a car, he can afford to pay a fine, whereas a guy
involved in a punch-up, he might not have much money, he may be on the
'bru' so he can't afford to pay a fine". I seriously had to reconsider my split of
work to the district court. I am not going to have people fined £30 for not
having an MOT certificate'; 'when I came here first of all the type of assault
where a man is knocked to the ground and kicked when he is lying defenceless
was a matter (there being no serious injury) perfectly within the scope of the
district court, but they seem to have been unable to appreciate the potential
seriousness of that assault. Imposing £5 fines . . . I feel the public interest is not
being properly served. I have had to take these cases in the sheriff court.'

One of the major criticisms is the variation in the sentencing practices of
lay justices: 'sometimes we get a good day, a realistic day, sometimes we
don't . . . there is too much variety throughout the length and breadth of
Scotland with the justices'; 'the district court can be hit or miss . . . it just
depends who's on the bench, it depends on their social attitudes sometimes on
their political views'; 'if there was simply one justice there would be some
consistency in sentencing but with the vast number of justices they obviously
have their own views. It may be difficult for someone to understand why he
was fined £5 for committing an offence similar to his neighbour and his
neighbour was fined £50 the following week.' While it should be noted that
sheriffs also vary in their sentencing policies, it is felt by fiscals that individual
sheriffs are more predictable and consistent: 'with the sheriff you get perhaps
an even flow of justice – you can probably predict what he's going to do'.

Not all fiscals feel that justices' sentencing decisions are wrong or err on
the side of leniency: 'some breaches of the peace will be dealt with more
severely in the district court simply because the justices are local residents'; 'I
think the lay magistrate is liable to penalise an accused according to the man in
the street's principles. I don't think it does any harm to have a human element
in fairly minor crime'; 'justices may take a very commonsense, down-to-earth
view of things . . . you sometimes get the situation that the penalties in the
district court are more realistic than in the sheriff court'. However most
Scottish prosecutors feel: 'far more confident that the judge in the sheriff court
will arrive at the correct sentence rather than the lay justice in the district
court'.

Widening the jurisdiction of the district courts

At the time when this research was carried out the matter of giving lay
justices the power to hear a broader spectrum of offences was being debated.
Most fiscals considered that the district court's jurisdiction should not be
widened in spite of the beneficial effects such a redistribution of business might
have on the sheriff's caseload: 'I do not think there is room for the extension of
the powers of the district court. I only think it could be exercised when the
justices are properly appraised of how to conduct cases'; 'only very minor

offences should go to the district courts because we know the justices are not going to be strict and sensible'. The recommended solutions were rather to syphon off the very minor cases by marking them for no proceedings or to appoint more stipendiaries: 'I'd be loathe to extend their powers . . . I'd rather see an extension of stipendiary magistrates'.

A few fiscals did, however, feel that lay jurisdiction should be widened to cover more offences: 'minor traffic offences, speeding offences, television licence cases . . . second offence shoplifting, thefts of greater value, even minor housebreakings because when we look at the sheriff's sentences very often they are within the existing powers of the district courts'. But a more senior depute admitted that: 'while there's no reason why they couldn't give more work to the justices, it is really a matter of politics'. That political decision having now been made,[1] it will be instructive to see how fiscals *manage* cases under the new legislation which widens the jurisdiction of the district courts. Unless the views represented in this chapter have changed dramatically, it may be that fiscals will continue not to make full use of the lay courts and will send only those cases which they consider suitable for lay judgment to the district courts thus circumventing the intention of the Act to substantially increase district court caseloads.

CONCLUSION

The nature of Scottish criminal law and procedure, then, provides the fiscal with an opportunity to exercise considerable discretion in determining the appropriate forum for a criminal case. While the vast majority of accused persons are tried before courts of summary jurisdiction, our analysis of the small number which the fiscal decides to place on petition is informative since it illustrates not only how prosecutors define what constitutes serious crime but also the part fiscals play in determining sentence. At the other end of the scale our examination of the attitudes adopted by legally qualified prosecutors towards the lay judiciary suggests that such evaluations are critical to the distribution of business between summary courts.

[1] See Section 7 Criminal Justice (Scotland) Act 1980.

6

AVOIDING TRIAL:
THE NEGOTIATION OF GUILTY
PLEAS

> If the adversary system is defined with only the trial in
> mind, we are blinding ourselves to the realities of a system
> of decision that is predominantly pretrial in character.
> Under such circumstances, adjudication does not define the
> adversary system, but is instead the outcome of a failure of
> pretrial negotiations. [Skolnick: 1967: 69–70]
>   The vast majority of convictions are not the result of
> any form of trial in open court, but are the result of pleas of
> guilty by defendants, and therefore it is the manner in which
> these guilty pleas are 'decided' upon by the defendant in
> the pretrial stages that ought to be seen as the single most
> important aspect of decision-making in the penal process,
> although typically one of the most under-researched and
> complex of all. [Bottomley: 1973: 105]

INTRODUCTION

THE EXPRESSION PLEA NEGOTIATION has become a familiar one to
readers of criminal justice literature in recent years and writers in both the United
States and Britain have put forward opposing views about the ethics and
efficacy of negotiated pleas. Before considering in more detail the conclusions
of these studies and comparing their findings with the situation in Scotland it
is important to have a clear understanding of the wide variety of informal and
formal arrangements which are covered by the term plea negotiation. At its
most basic, it involves any exchange between prosecution and defence which
endeavours to make adjustments resulting in trial-avoidance, 'the exchange of
official concessions for a defendant's act of self-conviction'. [Alschuler: 1979: 3]
Some writers have likened it to:

> a buying and selling transaction in a market that has no
> fixed prices – the defence counsel is a buyer seeking as low

a price, charge or sentence as possible. The prosecutor is a
seller seeking as high a price, charge or sentence as possible
within the constraints imposed by criminal statute and his
sense of equity. [Nagel and Neef: 1976: 1020]

In most Common Law jurisdictions these exchanges may take place at
any time before the conclusion of a trial. Adjustment may be concerned with
the reduction of certain charges, the dismissal of certain charges where the
accused is charged on several counts or the exclusion/inclusion of information
about the criminal incident or accused person in return for an admission of
guilt. In addition, some criminal justice systems permit negotiations to take
place directly with the judge over sentencing, so that a guilty plea will be
entered on the understanding that the judge will agree to a particular sentence.[1]
Negotiations are generally carried out informally in the prosecutor's office or
within the court building but may also take place in open court. The expression
plea negotiation, then, may be misleading since it suggests a unified, coherent
concept which seldom reflects the enormous diversity of such arrangements.

It is clear that decisions made by prosecutors in the course of plea negotiations have much in common with those matters relating directly to marking
which have been discussed in preceding chapters. Indeed, like the decision
whether or not to prosecute:

the negotiated plea is only one of a series of discretionary
decisions that characterise the administration of criminal
justice. From the initial decision of whether to investigate a
crime to the final decision of whether to revoke a parole,
the entire administrative process rests upon discretionary
choices, formally recognised or not, of men who must fit
law to cases. [Newman: 1966: 76–7]

These decisions are usually made in private, are not based on strict guidelines and are not open to public scrutiny or judicial review. In the following
discussion consideration will first be given to research on plea negotiation in
the United States and Britain and available literature on the practice in Scotland.
Then the findings of our own research will be discussed, including the various
kinds of charge manipulation and similar procedural devices used to effect a
guilty plea in Scotland, the different arrangements adopted by prosecutors and
defence agents to avoid a trial and the perceived benefits of such practices to
prosecution, defence and accused persons.

BACKGROUND

While it is certainly unwise to 'look too readily and reflectively across the
Atlantic for authoritative explanations of plea bargaining since the researcher

---

[1] There is no authority for such sentence bargaining in Scotland: 'the judge does not
and may not take part in these discussions, he will have no knowledge thereof until the
plea is tendered in court nor will the parties have any prior intimation of the judge's views'.
[Sheehan: 1975: 120]

is not comparing like with like', it is, nevertheless, useful to consider what extensive research in the United States has to say about the practice of plea negotiation. [Thomas: 1978: 170] The practice did not occur with any frequency until well into the nineteenth century since court records show that before 1850 most cases went to trial. But by 1967 it was estimated that 'about 90 per cent of all convictions in American state courts were the result of guilty pleas' [President's Commission on Law Enforcement and Administration of Justice: 1967: 9] and that a large proportion of accused persons pleaded guilty following negotiations between prosecution and defence. Several reasons have been given for this dramatic change but the principal factors appear to be the proliferation of new statutory offences contributing to a marked increase in the number of persons prosecuted and a desire stemming from the trend towards individualization in the criminal justice process to mitigate the constraints imposed by mandatory sentences. It has been said that effective plea negotiation:

> provides for a sound allocation of judicial resources, does
> not use up the time of police officers or witnesses, often
> saves the victim from the potentially embarrassing publicity
> of a trial, provides criminal justice officials with needed
> flexibility and lets the defendant participate in the decision
> making process. [Nardulli: 1978: 218]

Indeed several decisions of the Supreme Court have confirmed that the practice 'properly administered, is to be encouraged'. [Santobello v. NY 404 US 257, 260, 1971] Nevertheless many writers are highly critical of the guilty plea system as it operates in the United States:

> the practice of plea bargaining forfeits the benefits of formal,
> public adjudication; it eliminates the protections for
> individuals provided by the adversary system and substitutes
> administrative for judicial determination of guilt; it removes
> the check on law enforcement authorities afforded by
> exclusionary rules; and distorts sentencing decisions by
> introducing the normal correctional criteria. This
> nullification of constitutional values should not continue
> without careful examination. [Harvard Law Review: 1970:
> 1407]

Some critics have advocated its total abolition and certain states have gone so far as to prohibit the practice absolutely (Alaska) or for particular groups of offenders (Oregon) or selected types of offences (Arizona). Both the American Bar Association and the National Advisory Commission on Criminal Justice Standards and Goals have established standards for plea bargaining 'to move the process closer to the formality of the judicial process while retaining the flexibility which makes the process important to case disposition'. [Felkenes: 1976: 135]

However, a recent issue of an American legal journal devoted entirely to plea bargaining[1] suggests that there is still a need for research to uncover the nature of plea negotiation and its impact on the criminal process:

> there appears to be a distinctive shift in discussions about plea bargaining and trials that reflects less a shift in values of those who have been thinking and writing about the issue and more the development of new data about how criminal courts in fact operate. [Casper: 1979: 571]

According to these commentators, blanket condemnation of plea negotiation ignores the realities of the criminal justice process which is essentially geared to non-adversarial solutions. Emphasis on due process notions[2] obscures the co-alignment which exists and must exist between the defence and the prosecution to ensure the smooth functioning of the system.

The criminal process is:

> dominated by an elite of actors (the judge, prosecutor, and defence counsel). These actors enjoy a virtual monopoly of power – to initiate and dismiss charges, to sentence, to rule on legal motions, to raise legal motions – and share certain common interests (to expeditiously dispose of their caseload) as well as a common orientation to their clientele (most believe that most defendants are guilty of something). This state of affairs leads to the development of a dispositional strategy – reflective of the interests of the courtroom elite – that emphasises the expeditious handling of cases. [Nardulli: 1978: 219]

Nevertheless according to recent research plea negotiations themselves are not the cause of injustice in particular cases. Such grievances are rather the result of extra-legal factors such as difficulties encountered by the defence in gaining access to all available information on a case and the need for co-operation between the defence and the prosecution at all stages of the criminal process. Instead of simply advocating the abolition of plea negotiation some writers go so far as to recommend a fundamental re-allocation of responsibility for the conduct of the case from counsel to judge possibly along the lines of the Continental inquisitorial system. [Church: 1979: 524]

Plea negotiation in the United States, then, has provoked a great deal of discussion and controversy. However, it is only recently that the subject has excited comment in England and Wales: 'in Britain today very little is known of the informal bargaining processes which go on between prosecution and defence with regard to a negotiated plea of guilty'. [Thomas: 1969: 68] During

---

[1] *Law and Society* Winter 1979.

[2] Where a concern for individual freedom demands strict adherence to formal procedures and necessitates that the prosecution be able and be called upon to prove its case in open court. See H. L. Packer: *The Limits of the Criminal Sanction*: Stanford: 1969.

an enquiry concerning the outcome of jury trials in the Birmingham Crown Court researchers discovered that:

> over 70 per cent of a sample of defendants who changed
> their plea from not guilty to guilty claimed to have pleaded
> guilty either because of pressure from their own barrister,
> or else because they had been involved in some form of
> negotiated settlement of plea. [Baldwin & McConville:
> 1978: 545]

While the study reiterated the benefits to be derived from negotiated pleas which are presented by American commentators also, the researchers had strong reservations about the justice of such practices. Many accused persons felt that information favourable to their case had not been fully presented, victims were distressed by the apparent excessive leniency resulting from some negotiated pleas and legal practitioners considered that the involvement of the judge in private case conferences could not be defended. Indeed, the court of appeal in the leading case of R v. Turner [1970] 2 AER 280 stressed the importance of justice being administered in open court and emphasised that private discussions over pleas should take place only when really necessary, for example 'where counsel for the defence wished to tell the judge that the accused had not got long to live, a fact of which he [the accused] was and should remain ignorant'. However, it is clear from a stream of recent cases that this decision has not inhibited negotiations with regard to pleas either between defence and prosecution or involving the judge.[1]

Plea negotiations in Scotland deserve special consideration in this study because they provide a valuable insight into prosecutorial decision-making. Preceding chapters have discussed the way in which fiscals make decisions at the marking stage. While arrangements concerning pleas are generally negotiated at a later stage, plea negotiation and marking in the Scottish context share similar characteristics. As with marking there are no rigid guidelines determining which cases merit negotiation.[2] In fact the standard text on Scottish criminal procedure does not even mention the practice except that it is indicated that the prosecutor may accept a *partial plea*.[3] Another authority states that:

> it has long been an accepted feature of Scottish criminal
> procedure that before the start of the trial the prosecution
> and defence (if the accused is legally represented) will
> frequently have a brief discussion of the case in an effort to
> find if any plea of guilty will be given, each party seeking
> to know if the other is prepared to make any concessions.
> [Sheehan: 1975: 120]

---

[1] For a useful review see Baldwin & McConville: *Preserving the Good Face of Justice: Some Recent Plea Bargain Cases* (1978) New Law Journal 872–4.

[2] 'There is no statutory authority for plea adjustment.' [Thomson: 1975: 97]

[3] The term partial plea denotes that the fiscal will dismiss certain charges in return for a plea of guilty to certain others.

No details are given about the content of such negotiations, the forms which these negotiations take and the role of trial-avoidance arrangements in the criminal justice process. Yet such decisions are not only of profound importance to the processing of criminal cases but also emphasise the wide latitude of discretion which a fiscal has. Like decisions regarding prosecution, the negotiation of pleas is essentially an informal, private matter so that there is little caselaw on the subject or public awareness of the prevalence of such arrangements. There are no published figures on the degree to which pleas are negotiated in Scotland but it is clear from statistics collected routinely by Crown Office that in about a third of all solemn cases and a tenth of all summary cases the accused changes his plea from one of not guilty at first appearance to a guilty plea at a later stage. Such reversals are not necessarily the result of negotiations between prosecution and defence but it is likely that such arrangements are a major factor in many cases. Furthermore these figures do not include those cases where arrangements are made before first appearance in the summary court or first diet in the solemn court.[1] It will become clear from the discussion which follows that negotiations may take place from the earliest stages of the process.[2] While there is little available information on plea negotiation, then, it is a topic which excites considerable comment and controversy both within the fiscal service itself, among defence agents and from the police. Many of the same criticisms which have been made of the American system of guilty pleas have also been applied to Scotland.

Crown Office has responded to such criticisms by issuing several circulars briefing fiscals on plea negotiations. Thus fiscals have been enjoined to consult a senior fiscal and/or the marking depute, the person who originally endorsed the prosecution, before concluding any agreement which involves the acceptance of a partial plea and they have also been exhorted to encourage defence agents to negotiate pleas at an early stage. Nevertheless, no guidelines have been issued which definitively attempt to regulate trial-avoidance arrangements and, as later sections of this chapter show, different fiscals and different offices adopt different approaches to plea negotiation in the same way as they do towards decisions at the marking stage.

In the discussion which follows, three basic questions are asked about plea negotiation: What does plea negotiation mean in the Scottish context? How is it structured and managed? Why is it considered a useful device? The next section therefore describes the different forms which plea negotiation may take so that the reader will have a better understanding of the basis on which pleas are negotiated.

[1] In solemn proceedings the accused is not asked how he pleads until the first diet held shortly before the trial but there is a procedure authorised by Section 102 of the Criminal Procedure (Scotland) Act 1975 as amended by Section 16 Criminal Justice (Scotland) Act 1980 under which the accused himself or his solicitor can write to the Crown Agent at any stage before service of the indictment indicating his intention to plead guilty to some or all of the charges libelled in the petition. If the solicitor offers a partial plea only the fiscal involved must brief crown counsel and give his recommendations.

[2] The introduction of intermediate diets in summary cases under Section 15 of the Criminal Justice (Scotland) Act 1980 is designed to facilitate negotiations before the trial diet.

FORMS OF PLEA NEGOTIATION IN SCOTLAND

In Scotland trial-avoidance arrangements generally focus on the particular charge or charges, *charge bargaining*, which may be invoked in relation to a particular criminal incident. That is to say, so called *sentence bargaining*, requiring the active or passive participation of the judge, is not a feature of the Scottish criminal justice system though the fiscal exerts some control indirectly over sentencing both by his choice of charge and by his selection of procedure and court. In addition the fiscal may influence disposition by his verbal utterances or omissions in summing up. The Scottish prosecutor, unlike his English counterpart, is 'the master of the instance' and as such is not bound to adhere to the particular charges or style of charging libelled by the police in their report of a criminal incident. While framing charges at Common Law the fiscal must take into account such factors as the results of the criminal act or omission, the accused's intention and the weight to be attached to the evidence. However, an amendment of charges may be the result of negotiation between prosecution and defence particularly in Common Law offences. Such adjustments vary considerably and may range from major amendments to a complaint or petition to arrangements affecting only the verbal utterances by fiscal or defence. The modes of charge bargaining in Scotland are as follows:

Reduction of charge

The fiscal is offered a plea of guilty to a lesser charge than that originally specified on the complaint or petition. Thus, for instance, a criminal assault could be libelled as any one of the following charges at Common Law: attempted murder, assault to the danger of life, assault to severe injury or simple assault. Reduction is particularly apposite where a degree of uncertainty or ambiguity may be attached to a particular event or where witnesses may prove unreliable: 'in a typical public house brawl witnesses have drink taken – I have to consider to what extent a sober man in the witness box could remember what had happened when he was drunk'; 'an accused was charged with quite a serious assault – he'd driven a lorry on to the pavement at his co-habitee but the evidence wasn't very good – a question of the co-habitee not coming up to scratch – so we traded a bit and he got off with simple assault'. For the fiscal reduction of a charge in return for a plea of guilty to a lesser charge will at least ensure that the accused is convicted. For the defence agent, a reduced charge may mean a less severe penalty for his client.

Alternative charges

The fiscal is offered a plea of guilty to an alternative charge. The nature of Scottish criminal law is such that certain charges go in tandem so that an accused person can be charged with one particular charge or the other. Thus a breach of the peace charge may be substituted for one of assault or a plea to reset may be accepted instead of the original charge of theft. While strictly speaking such adjustments result in an alternative rather than a reduced charge being accepted by the defence, this is generally done with the intention that the accused will incur a lesser penalty upon conviction for the alternative. At the time when we conducted our research it was fairly common practice for fiscals to cite the alternatives of reckless driving[1] and careless driving[2] and here there was clearly room for negotiation with the defence since the statutory penalties varied.[3]

Deletion of charges

The fiscal is offered a plea of guilty to some charges but not to others. This adjustment can entail the deletion of any charges or combination of charges on a complaint or petition, subject to the need to retain certain charges for evidential purposes discussed in more detail later in this chapter. It is particularly applicable where a complaint specifies several road traffic offences or where the accused is charged on several counts for the same offence type, for example, where an accused was charged with six charges of possession of a controlled drug his defence agent offered to plead to five charges. In another case charges under Section 3 (careless driving) Section 25 (failure to stop after an accident) and Section 6(1) (drunk driving) of the Road Traffic Act 1972 were specified on the complaint and pleas of guilty to Section 3 and Section 25 only were accepted. One defence agent informed us that: 'where one gets a combination of charges of breach of the peace and assault it may be that the fiscal is prepared to desert the charge of breach of the peace and accept the plea of guilty to the assault'.

Amendment in the wording of charges

The fiscal is offered a plea of guilty to all charges provided that he delete certain portions of the charge or charges. This type of negotiation can only occur with Common Law charges where the style of the charge is not regulated by statute. It is particularly common in assault or breach of the peace charges, for example: 'take the typical public house brawl where a man has been assaulted in a number of ways – punched, kicked, knocked to the ground, head stood upon. An agent may approach me and say "my client admits the charge but says that he did not stand on the man's head". I might well take part of the charge out'; 'it may well be that there is a charge of assault which says "that you did punch and kick, you did strike him repeatedly" and you can maybe get "repeatedly" taken out'; 'the accused had been charged with cursing and swearing and brandishing a tri-coloured flag at a Celtic-Rangers match and the fiscal deleted "cursing and swearing" '. In theft cases, also, an accused may refuse to plead to the theft of certain items, for instance: 'very often you get a charge of theft, which charges the man with breaking into a shop and stealing a whole list of things. I had a case like this, my client insisted that he had only stolen confectionery but not 4,000 cigarettes.' The impact of such changes on sentencing will be discussed later in this chapter. While it is clear

---

[1] Section 2 Road Traffic Act 1972.   [2] Section 3 Road Traffic Act 1972.
[3] Section 2 offences can be tried under solemn procedure with a maximum penalty of 2 years imprisonment or an unlimited fine; Section 3 offences can only be tried summarily.

that, strictly speaking, the charge remains the same, it is, of course, the defence agent's intention to reduce sentence in this way or at least to encourage his client to think that this will be the result.

Amendments to fiscal's motion for sentence

The fiscal is offered a plea of guilty to the complaint as libelled on the understanding that he supports in his closing speech to the court the defence agent's plea in mitigation. One defence agent explained this arrangement as follows: 'I may be prepared to say something in mitigation which does not really change what is libelled but may make a big difference to the consequences of what is libelled in terms of sentence and the fiscal may be prepared to agree'. He gave an example of a charge of culpable homicide where: 'this particular woman died of an injury which should not normally have killed a person. She sustained a broken nose in this assault and blood from her nose fell back into her throat and she choked. The fiscal will be prepared to make it clear to the court that but for that she wouldn't have died. He will say this by agreement.'

OFFENCES APPROPRIATE FOR PLEA NEGOTIATION

While such amendments are applicable across the whole spectrum of crimes and offences, there are particular offences or combinations of offences which typify the general run of cases where trial-avoidance arrangements are made.

Road traffic cases

The majority of multiple charge complaints are concerned with road traffic offences. About one third of all reports covered by our Census specified more than one charge and most of these involved one or more road traffic offences. Such complaints lend themselves particularly well to plea negotiation as one defence agent explained: 'where there are multiple road traffic charges – the police have gone round and checked everything and *thrown the book* – you may get anything up to a dozen charges in which case you say to the fiscal "I will give you a plea of guilty to the main ones, say drunk driving" [Section 5(1) Road Traffic Act 1972] and he will say "I'll drop no insurance, [Section 143(1)] no MOT" ' [Section 44(1)]; 'construction and use offences – you get a whole string of these and the defence agent says "we will plead guilty to charges 1, 2 and 3 if you will drop charge 4" '.

Violence against the person and breach of the peace

Charges in these categories may relate to ambiguous incidents where it is often difficult to obtain reliable evidence or be certain either of the exact sequence of events or the degree to which the accused may be implicated. A defence agent described this instance: 'I had a client on indictment – a very serious assault with a glass beer mug. He had made an awful mess of two brothers in a hotel doorway, and when a third chap tried to intervene my client took a swipe at him. But there was nobody who would confirm what this third boy was saying . . . so that was dropped.' Since these are Common Law charges there may be room for amendments to the wording in the way already discussed: 'on a charge of assault you could maybe get "repeatedly" taken out and maybe "with a weapon" taken out or "severe injury" or "permanent disfigurement" '. In fact several agents see these amendments as the most usual form of plea negotiation: 'adjusting pleas so far as I am concerned, normally covers the situation where you are deleting parts of a charge. A primary example is the wording in breach of the peace.'

Series of theft or fraud charges

A complaint with a run of similar charges may lend itself to plea negotiation, for example, a fraud case: 'the accused decided to leave and had no money to do so. So they financed their departure by bouncing a series of cheques round the whole country which added up to a few hundred pounds. They pled guilty to all of the charges except two which are the most minor.' The same is true of multiple thefts, where it may sometimes happen that the accused will be charged with all the housebreakings which took place in a particular area on a certain day. Fiscals themselves have suggested to us that shopkeepers may sometimes include in their list of stolen goods all recent losses which may in fact also cover items mislaid or possibly taken by shop staff.

These offence types, then, are regarded by prosecution and defence as affording particularly useful opportunities for the successful negotiation of pleas. In the next section consideration will be given to the variety of ways in which such negotiations are managed at different stages in the criminal process and to those factors, such as the patterns of negotiation within particular fiscal offices and the relationship between particular fiscals and particular defence agents, which help to structure trial-avoidance arrangements.

MANAGING PLEA NEGOTIATIONS

General framework

The phrase plea negotiation is slightly misleading when one comes to look at the way in which such arrangements are made in the Scottish context. Firstly, it may give a false impression of a formal procedure which bears no relation to the generally informal manner of such communications. The absence of strict guidelines regulating negotiations has already been noted but should be emphasised again here. Secondly, it may present a picture of the two sides coming together to discuss cases whereas overtures are almost always made by one party (the defence) with the other party (the prosecution) having, in theory at least, an absolute right of veto. Thirdly, it may confuse the reader in that the term plea negotiation encompasses a wide variety of arrangements, ranging from the relatively structured to the very informal.

There are, however, certain general factors which have a considerable impact on the management of plea negotiations and may help to structure what might otherwise be a very haphazard affair. In relation to each individual case, for instance, the nature of the charges may allow more or less leeway for negotiations. Similarly, the timing of trial-avoidance arrangements will depend to some extent on whether the accused is in custody or at liberty and upon whether the case will be tried on solemn or summary procedure. But it also appears that methods of negotiating depend on matters external to specific cases, such as the degree of pressure on the prosecution and/or the defence to deal with large numbers of cases in a short time, the organisation of work within both fiscals' and solicitors' offices and the extent to which fiscals and defence agents trust each other to play fair. These factors will now be discussed in more detail.

At the marking stage

Clearly the possibility of an agreement being reached between prosecution and defence is a matter for consideration by both sides right from the service of a complaint. In fact, for the fiscal it may be a factor in deciding what charges should be brought initially: 'I find I am putting in the odd extra charge which, on the basis of available evidence, would never prove but it gives a basis for plea negotiation'; 'it's possible for a fiscal looking at the original charge when he's marking it to say to himself with a view to possible bargaining "I'll shove the extra charge in" . . . I've always tended to put in more charges than necessary'; 'a case of assault with intent to ravish I might charge on a higher plane, i.e. attempted rape, with the thought that I might get a plea to the next down'.

Most fiscals do, however, distinguish between charges entered on a complaint for evidential reasons and charges put in purely as bargaining counters. The rules of evidence[1] very strictly define what constitutes relevant information in a criminal case so that the prosecution can be barred from leading evidence relating to matters outside the scope of the charges libelled. For example, under the Road Traffic Act 1972 it is necessary to prove a moving road traffic offence to justify a breathalyser test on a person charged with drunken driving: 'let's assume a situation where a pedestrian sees an accused person driving a car which hits a wall, the police are summoned to the locus and a breath test is positive. The case is marked careless driving (Section 3) and drunken driving (Section 6(1)). I would retain the Section 3 in the pretty sure knowledge I would not get a conviction on that charge and I would put the charge in to spare us the necessity of proving a moving road traffic offence to justify taking a sample.' Similarly a charge of resisting arrest under Section 41 Police (Scotland) Act 1967 should be accompanied by evidence giving good grounds for apprehension by the police, such as a breach of the peace charge: 'the classic pitfall is to accept a plea of not guilty to breach of the peace because if you drop that there's no grounds for the resisting arrest charge'.

Another reason for wanting to retain charges which may not stand up in court is to show a course of conduct: 'it does help you to lead certain evidence to bolster the main charge – for example a publican charged with selling drinks after hours . . . the defence was that it was the tenth anniversary of the pub

---

[1] See Walker and Walker: *The Law of Evidence in Scotland:* 1964; Sheriff I. D. McPhail. *Research Paper on the Law of Evidence in Scotland:* Scottish Law Commission: 1979.

opening – the police had actually watched the locus two nights running but we only charged the second night – we were stuck in not being able to lead evidence to prove that it was not a single incident', or to satisfy witnesses or the complainer: 'the charge on the complaint is the fiscal's responsibility and he is the one who has to defend it in court, for example a police assault as part of a sequence of events – I knew it wouldn't prove in court but it's part of what happened . . . the policeman should be able to tell the court what happened'.

In fact virtually all fiscals positively disapprove of including charges as bargaining counters only: 'I don't approve of including charges if there isn't evidence to support them'; 'if we are doing our job every case that goes into court should prove 100 per cent . . . so one has to be ruthless when one is marking initially'. Nevertheless, such extra charges, which are usually minor in nature, do allow manoeuvre for negotiation and Scottish prosecutors admit this: 'for evidential reasons sometimes we have got to put things down on a complaint that we cannot prove . . . a lot of plea bargaining is facing up to the inevitable'; 'I would put in a charge in order to be able to lead evidence. I frequently put a note on the back of the papers that there really is insufficient evidence and if a plea is offered, to accept it.'

In the larger offices where cases are usually marked by one fiscal and prosecuted in court by another some indication as to the acceptability of certain pleas may be given by the marking depute: 'I regularly mark and encourage the deputes to mark "if plea to alternative charge or second charge tendered, accept" '; 'in a theft I maybe mark the papers "take a plea to reset if offered" '. Such comments may be very helpful to the hard-pressed trial depute: 'there's usually something marked on the papers giving instructions because the person who dealt with it originally has a better chance to read through the statements in the summary. I tend not to have the time especially in custody cases.'

Timing

'Criticisms of plea adjustment [relate] to timing rather than the practice [itself].' [Thomson: 1975: 97] It is generally the case that defence agents decide when the time has come for overtures to be made to the prosecution: 'we fiscals don't initiate discussions. I don't feel it appropriate for me to approach a solicitor and suggest some form of reduced plea'; 'I don't consider the onus is on fiscals to go looking for pleas. It would demean our necessarily reasonably austere stance in the matter.' Occasionally the fiscal may make the first move according to some defence agents: 'if fiscal X had a trial with a number of witnesses before he cited them he would phone to check if we were going ahead with it'; 'it's not unknown particularly in cases on petition for a fiscal to come to us and suggest such and such a plea. I've already had a hint from the X office in a case charged as murder that a plea of guilty to culpable homicide will be acceptable.' But the fiscal is generally happier to wait for the defence to make the first move. This gives him the more advantageous position since a fiscal is then faced with someone who is prepared to 'treat', to negotiate with him.

Such moves from the defence can come at any stage: 'plea negotiation takes place at practically any stage even sometimes before a complaint goes out'. Ideally fiscals would wish defence agents to approach them before court appearance. A plea negotiated at this stage obviates the need for preparation of trial papers, obtaining full statements from the police or calling witnesses, though an accused person is entitled to change his plea without cause shown where he has pleaded guilty under a Section 102 letter.[1] There is little doubt that negotiations concluded at this stage tend to favour the prosecution since discussions generally take place in the relative calm of the fiscal office and not in a busy courtroom where the fiscal may be under considerable pressure to reduce the number of cases going to trial. The prosecution will always have a police summary of the evidence and possibly may have had direct contact with the police officers involved in the case whereas the defence agent may only have a copy of the complaint or petition and a statement from the accused. He will have no idea how the prosecution witnesses will stand up in court or what the strength of the Crown case is. He may have had no time to look into the matter fully and he may only see his client for the first time at the pleading diet or first diet: 'virtually all solicitors arrange for their client to come and discuss the case beforehand . . . unfortunately experience shows that the accused rarely comes until the night before or the morning itself'. Professional ethics bar the defence agent from approaching the fiscal before he has consulted his client: 'if it's possible I would approach the fiscal before the first call, but my instructions from the accused are of paramount importance'.

It is not surprising, therefore, that most defence agents would prefer to wait until they have more information before tendering a partial plea. The defence case will not only depend on the nature of the evidence which can be produced to negative the Crown case but also may rest upon any legal flaws in the prosecution evidence which may invalidate the proceedings: 'I always like to try and negotiate from a position of strength . . . in terms of there being something wrong with the complaint . . . it is amazing the number of times that the statute has been put in wrongly by the fiscal in a complaint'; 'under the 1976 Licensing Act it provides that the fiscal must give notice fourteen days before the trial that containers contained what they said they contained – now fiscals have repeatedly failed to give that notice and I have no qualms about using that. I would be failing in my duty if I did not use a technicality like that, I could be sued for professional negligence.' The defence agent may therefore need time to establish to his own satisfaction that there is some failure to comply with the requirements of Scottish criminal procedure.

Efforts have been made by Crown Office to encourage both fiscals and defence agents to negotiate at an early stage. A note to this effect was published in the Scots Law Times and the Journal of the Law Society of Scotland in the spring of 1980.[2] Defence agents were advised that:

> the Lord Advocate has instructed procurators fiscal that it is
> part of their duties to meet defence solicitors for the purpose

[1] See footnote 1, p. 105.
[2] Scots Law Times: February 15, 1980: 42. Journal of the Law Society of Scotland: Vol. 25, No. 4 April 1980: 132.

of: (a) discussing the evidence available to the Crown,
(b) arranging minutes of admission in respect of evidence
which is not to be contested, and (c) giving to defence
solicitors copies of statements of witnesses whose evidence
is regarded as formal, or technical.

Such arrangements it was hoped would mean that:

solicitors will avail themselves of the opportunity to meet
the procurators fiscal for this purpose and that as a result
some witnesses may be excused attendance and that, in
particular, last minute pleas of guilty, which so disturb the
planning of court business and greatly annoy those cited
needlessly as witnesses, will be considerably reduced.

A circular was sent to all fiscal offices prior to this publication advising
them to encourage early negotiations. However, it appears from a follow-up
study carried out by us in the autumn of 1980 that neither fiscals nor defence
agents could see any marked increase in the number of guilty pleas negotiated
pre-court or pre-trial. There did appear to have been a change in relation to
the disclosure of information which is something which may encourage early
negotiation. It appears that fiscals are now more willing to allow defence
agents to see papers relating to the case as recommended by Crown Office.
This may, over time, encourage defence agents to approach fiscals at an early
stage and thus obviate the need for court proceedings.

In custody cases particularly negotiations can rarely be conducted before
the pleading diet except as very much last minute affairs since the duty solicitor[1]
only sees his client in the cells immediately before the case is called: 'negotiation
usually takes place in the corridor of the court, it takes a matter of seconds.
The defence agent will say "will you accept a plea to such and such or will you
delete such and such?" you can say yes or no'; 'where individuals are appearing
from custody there will only be room for a quick attempt at negotiation
before the court begins'.

Defence agents also claim that accused persons held in custody prefer not
to plead guilty at first appearance: 'at first appearance people generally are
afraid they are going to be kept in custody and so they plead not guilty in the
hope of obtaining bail no matter how stone-walled the case may happen to
be . . . at that time the duty solicitor will have insufficient information really
to question them any further on the matter'. Timing of negotiations in custody
cases will also be affected by the fact that the duty solicitor's involvement
ceases after first appearance and no defence case can be constructed until legal
aid has been granted to an accused and he has obtained an agent to act on his

---

[1] All sheriff and district courts maintain a list of solicitors who are prepared to act in
criminal cases. These solicitors work a rota system taking it in turn to act on behalf of
accused persons appearing in custody before the court for the first time. Such solicitors are
known as duty solicitors because the accused has no choice and must accept the solicitor
who for the time being is on duty. See C. N. Stoddart: *The Law and Practice of Legal Aid in
Scotland*: Greens; 1979.

I

behalf: 'you can't investigate the case, you can't pay for an investigating agent
to get you precognitions so you can't move as a solicitor until you know that
the accused has asked for legal aid'.

In both custody and cited cases the balance of power will shift depending
to a considerable extent on the time at which negotiations take place. Agents,
while deploring the practice of tendering late pleas: 'you want to do it before
the trial so that it doesn't cost everyone a lot of money' nevertheless admit that
negotiating at a late stage may work to their advantage, the fiscal allocated to
take the trial may be inexperienced and have had little time to read all the cases
set down for the trial. In the hurly-burly of a busy courtroom snap decisions
have to be made and the trial depute may be anxious to reduce the number of
trials: 'the best time to make an offer of a plea is at 9.55 on the morning of the
trial or even better at 2.30 in the afternoon'.[1] Many fiscals certainly consider
that the defence tender partial pleas at the last minute for selfish reasons: 'there
are two out of the eight defence agents who normally do court work here who
would not make much effort to negotiate a plea because they would rather go
ahead with the trial in order to get the money'; 'agents on legal aid get paid for
appearing in court. A full day's legal aid fee would be paid where people
change their plea in court.'

Most fiscals are keenly aware of the problems faced by the trial depute
when offered a plea directly before or even during a trial: 'the case is down for
trial, the accused pleads not guilty then before the trial while other business is
going on the defence will try and negotiate'. Since there may be very little
time for the fiscal to consider those factors which will determine the acceptability or otherwise of a plea such hasty negotiations are regarded by the prosecution as potential traps for the unwary fiscal. This is particularly so where
some of the cases may have been marked by another fiscal: 'you've got to be
wary – and look at the series of charges and say "somebody who took this up
must have thought that there was sufficient evidence". I tend to libel everything,
otherwise charges which are left may be incompetent.' The younger more
inexperienced deputes generally know that it is easy to make a mistake and
possibly drop the more serious charge in the heat of the moment: 'you find
as an inexperienced fiscal that agents try to talk you into pleas which are really
not acceptable. In relation to one particular charge I wasn't aware of the relative
penalties – they both seemed similar to me and afterwards I was really annoyed
with myself for accepting the plea to the less serious charge.'

When a fiscal is offered a plea actually in court there is generally no time
to follow the advice given in Crown Office circulars and consult the marking
depute or a more senior colleague: 'the depute in court is offered a plea . . . how
can he discuss it with a senior?'; 'you would just be walking into the court and
all of a sudden a horde of black gowned gentlemen appear upon the scene all
trying to negotiate at one time'; 'it's a matter of practicalities . . . you might
not get a senior colleague or the person who marked it might not be in the
office . . . it's a spur of the moment decision when you're in court'. While it

---

[1] Courts generally begin sitting at 10 a.m. and 2.30 p.m.

may be possible for the fiscal to ask for an adjournment and allow himself time to consult with a senior most fiscals prefer to make a decision there and then. The decision to negotiate pleas appears to be regarded as an important aspect of professional competence: 'the procurator fiscal leaves us pretty well to ourselves when it comes to the trial – he trusts us'; 'my deputes have the widest possible discretion in the matter of plea negotiation'.

Variations between fiscal offices

While it is certainly true that the patterns of negotiation described above occur in all fiscal offices, it is clear from this research that offices vary both in the degree to which defence and prosecution are prepared to co-operate in order to negotiate pleas successfully and in the timing of such arrangements. The question of trust, which appears to be the crucial element in ensuring satisfactory negotiations, will be discussed in a later section. The present discussion focuses on other factors which have an important bearing on plea negotiation and which result in a variety of arrangements in different offices.

The ratio of custody to cited cases will certainly have an impact on patterns of plea negotiation. It has already been noted[1] that the larger urban offices tend to have a higher proportion of custody cases than the smaller rural ones. This inevitably means that plea negotiation will be more likely to occur in such offices after the pleading or first diet. The procurator fiscal in one urban office described the situation thus: 'we get very few pleas of guilty in summary cases before the first diet and most of them go out for trial. Fifty per cent will go to trial, 30 per cent will intimate their pleas in advance, the other 20 per cent will negotiate in court on the day.' The sheer volume of cases may change the nature of plea negotiation in large fiscal offices: 'in X the fiscal may have to deal with maybe 150 cases at one court sitting. He will have very little time to whip through the papers whereas here in a small rural office plea negotiation is a leisurely affair . . . you have ample time to think about it.'

An important factor in plea negotiation is the sentence which an accused person is likely to receive upon conviction for a particular offence.[2] Prediction of the probable sentence is, according to fiscals, much more difficult in city areas where the court is served by a large number of sheriffs on a rota system. Conversely fiscals in small offices appearing before the same sheriff find it relatively easy to forecast sentence: 'we're lucky here because we've always got the same sheriff – we're usually pretty certain what's going to happen'; 'our sheriff is predictable . . . it is possible within reasonably close limits to forecast what he is going to do'.

The division of labour[3] which is an inevitable consequence of bigger caseloads in the larger fiscal offices may also be an important factor in nego- tiations: 'it is difficult in X to find out who is dealing with the case'. There is pressure upon both fiscal and defence agent to process cases as quickly as possible. A defence agent explained: 'too often papers are passed round the office from one to another and you get the trial papers two days beforehand. You don't

---

[1] See p. 35.   [2] See p. 88 et seq.   [3] See p. 41.

have time to look at them until the night before and you think "I have to do something about negotiating a plea".'

There are in addition the difficulties encountered in maintaining super-vision over young and inexperienced deputes, which may be considerably easier in a smaller office. New deputes may not be prepared to negotiate at all because of the fear of accepting an unsatisfactory plea: 'if you're a new depute they'll tend to start off with ridiculous offers so I started by saying no to everything'; 'if you are inexperienced agents will try and talk you into pleas which are really not acceptable'. This vulnerability is more apparent in the larger offices where it may be difficult to contact a senior or more experienced depute to obtain advice.

There also appears to be considerably more hostility towards agents in the busy urban areas than in quieter rural locations. Fiscals draw a distinction between the specialist criminal lawyers who tend to practise in the cities and solicitors who handle all types of legal work, suggesting that the former are less trustworthy and more likely to spring unpleasant surprises: 'there's a big difference between those who specialise in criminal law and those who are in general practice . . . I'm less likely to trust the former'. Fiscals in urban areas have some harsh criticisms to make of defence agents' professional behaviour: 'solicitors in X are extremely reluctant to advise a client to plead guilty. The premise that they use is that it's not part of their duty but that's a very debatable point – a number of cases here go to trial that don't need to go to trial.'

Efforts have been made to counteract the problems associated with heavy caseloads, a higher proportion of custody cases, inexperienced deputes and lack of contact with defence agents which may hamper negotiations at an early stage in larger offices. For example, in Glasgow the post of Registry Allocated Depute, the RAD, has been established to streamline the negotiation of pleas in summary cases. An experienced fiscal deals with all negotiations in summary cases up to the actual trial. Thus defence agents know that there is a central point to which they can refer if they wish to negotiate: 'defence lawyers have good reason to believe that here permanently is someone they can come and talk to . . . there are quite a number of lawyers who negotiate pleas well in advance so much so that the diet can be cleared and the case brought forward for sentence to be passed by means of a joint minute of acceleration'.[1] This arrangement may also forestall unsatisfactory agreements by less experienced deputes: 'if the RAD refuses a plea he will mark the papers that he has done so and the depute must then go ahead to trial'. In the larger offices, also, it is generally the case that certain experienced fiscals are given the task of handling negotiations with regard to solemn cases pre-trial. Nevertheless, there is still the problem faced by all fiscals of the plea which is offered either immediately before or even sometimes during the trial. Such situations do not allow the time to consult with others although: 'we are trying to direct the attenton of a

[1] 'It shall be competent for the court, on a joint application in writing by the parties, to discharge a diet fixed in a summary prosecution and fix in lieu thereof an earlier diet.' [Renton and Brown: 1972: 230] See also Section 314 Criminal Procedure (Scotland) Act 1975 as amended by Section 11 Criminal Justice (Scotland) Act 1980.

great number of inexperienced fiscals coming into the service to the fact that they should seek guidance from a senior. Prosecution in the public interest implies that it is an informed action – you can't be in the service two or three weeks, make one of these decisions and call it an informed one.'

The importance of trust

While the factors outlined in previous sections have a marked effect on the way in which pleas are negotiated, perhaps the most important single criterion is the nature of the relationship which exists between particular fiscals and particular defence agents. The degree to which either party is prepared to negotiate with the other depends very much on a mutual exchange of respect and understanding. Given the informal nature of plea negotiation and the absence of tangible yardsticks by which to measure the efficacy of negotiation in many instances, this is not perhaps surprising. While it has not been possible in this research to demonstrate the impact of 'trusting relationships' or the lack of them on plea negotiation, fiscals and defence agents consider that, in the absence of trust, trial-avoidance arrangements become virtually impossible.

The development of a good working relationship leading to successful plea negotiation appears to depend on a number of factors. Firstly it is important that the parties have experience and knowledge of each other's working practices. A factor of considerable importance to defence agents is the degree to which the fiscal is prepared to acquaint them with the facts of the Crown case. In some offices it appears that fiscals are more willing to divulge such information than in others as the following remarks by defence agents show: 'we are able to obtain a list of Crown witnesses from the fiscals at X and we are able to discuss the content of those statements made to the police when we're not able to contact witnesses'; 'the fiscal at Y is very ready to be frank about any weaknesses in the Crown case which may be known to him'; 'the fiscals at Z won't let you see the police report and are not keen to negotiate'; 'you get some fiscals who won't give anything away' and from a fiscal: 'the defence is perfectly at liberty to precognosce our witnesses so I don't see why we should give them police statements'. Those fiscals who are prepared to be frank about the Crown case generally expect that the defence will reciprocate by negotiating early and by providing the fiscal with information where relevant: 'some defence agents are quite meticulous at advising you in advance that they intend to negotiate but some of them don't seem to care at all'; 'if the fiscal tells you what is in his statements you will tell him all the cards that you have in your hand . . . if I do suddenly produce a witness or I come upon further evidence which is going to help me one of the first people I go and tell is the fiscal'.

However, in return for co-operation the fiscal demands more than the mere communication of information from the defence agent. He expects that the defence agent will play fair: 'I operate what I call a "cards on the table" policy . . . I tell defence agents what I've got – why keep these things up your sleeve provided it's fair on both sides'; 'if you try to deal fairly with the fiscal and remember that you are all part of the one profession then I don't think you should have difficulties'. Playing fair seems to entail the mutual acceptance of certain rules of the game. The major canon appears to be that the defence agent will not take advantage of the fiscal's goodwill and frankness. There is firstly the danger that defence agents may not be as honest in their dealings with the fiscal as the fiscal is in his negotiations with them: 'the difference between agents is that you might accept from one his version of what happened as given to him by his client while you might not accept it from another one'; 'you would believe what defence agent X told you about his client but you might not always believe what defence agent Y said'; 'some people I don't trust – I wouldn't accept a plea if it was the best plea in the world – unless it was good for me – I fear in the back of my mind that they're not giving me the truth and I'd rather go to court'. Some fiscals also tend to think that reliance by the defence on technicalities, mistakes in the indictment or presentation of evidence, should not be used to undermine the prosecution case in court: 'certain agents take objection on matters that are purely technical to get their clients off . . . you get defence agents whose tactics are really underhand – they go for acquittal at all costs'. Some defence agents agree that: 'where you have a good personal relationship with a fiscal you often do feel you've possibly let him down if you make use of a technicality – the tricks of the trade'.

More fundamentally it is necessary if co-operation is to flourish between fiscal and defence agents over the negotiation of pleas that all parties share a common understanding of their part in the administration of justice. On a philosophical level, fiscals and defence agents express this mutual understanding as follows: 'I think we're both working towards the same end . . . there's no feeling that we don't co-operate'; 'we don't see ourselves as adversaries – we are all answerable to the court to speak the truth'. Fiscals like to stress that, as members of the legal profession, they share with the defence a common code of ethics and have a special allegiance to the court and the demands of justice. On a more practical level, this means that the fiscal expects a fair defence agent not to pursue hopeless cases and to negotiate with the prosecution at an early stage: 'good agents will usually phone up . . . they ask for information, we usually oblige them because they say "I'm wanting to have enough evidence to present to my client to get him to plead guilty" '. Conversely, where a fiscal has a bad opinion of defence agents any adverse comments are not based on the agents' lack of legal expertise but rather their insistence on pursuing a case in the face of the evidence: 'there are agents in X who will never plead guilty to the whole lot. They will simply want to take out some charges so that they can turn to their client and say "look, I've got you off with this charge" even if the client has already said "look, I'll be pleading to everything" and that's shocking and you get to know which ones these people are and if one of them approaches me with that type of plea then my reaction is "no, it's a plea as libelled or not at all".' While fiscals agree that: 'every accused has the right to make the Crown prove its case' and go to trial, they feel strongly that the pursuit of some cases borders on the unethical: 'a lot of agents don't really provide a very great service for their clients'. It should be noted, however, that some defence agents feel equally strongly that cases should be pursued in the client's interest and that evidence can quite legitimately be withheld from the prosecution to be used in the course of the trial. One co-operative defence agent admitted: 'I think technically speaking I am not a good defence agent because I go and tell the fiscal if I come upon some fresh evidence favourable to the defence'.

The development of trust is also, to some extent, a product of successful personal interaction between the fiscal and the defence agent: 'the character of the fiscal and the way in which I get on with him makes a tremendous difference and there are certain things which I find very difficult to go and ask a certain fiscal about . . . the one I deal with here is a very understanding person'; 'it is very easy to get a personality clash, in other words you are arguing between each other rather than arguing about the case in front of you . . . there are good and bad agents'. This inevitably means that, particularly where there are no deputes expressly designated to deal with plea negotiations, defence agents will tend to be selective in approaching certain fiscals rather than others with a view to negotiation. While fiscals tend to play down the personal element: 'if you are going to accept a plea you will accept it no matter who it's from'; 'to bargain to any great extent with one solicitor would be bad practice' defence agents insist that this is an important factor: 'I have a tendency to deal with fiscal X, I think agents across the board tend to form an association with one fiscal rather than another'. Such informal relationships may develop more easily in the relatively unstructured and stress-free environment of the small rural office. Each party gets to know what the other's approach will be to the negotiation of particular pleas so that fairly accurate predictions can be made and co-operation can thrive: 'you know with fiscal X what he is prepared to negotiate upon . . . when he was away . . . it was terrible we didn't know who we were going to get'; 'defence agent X used to say "we only have a trial if you and I can't agree or the client won't take advice" we have a discussion on it and decide where the truth lies'.

It is important here to note that factors relating to variations between offices may also have an impact on the development of trust. Time, experience and lack of pressure may also help to contribute to the development of co-operation between fiscal and defence agent: 'there are more trials in office X because it's a busier, more impersonal place and you are dealing with different fiscals, whereas here the same fiscal is available all the time'. It is clear, then, that the successful management of plea negotiation for both prosecution and defence depends to a large extent on factors other than the legal strengths or weaknesses of individual cases. Similarly the attitudes of Scottish prosecutors towards trial-avoidance arrangements reflect wider concerns which reach beyond the management of individual cases, as the next section shows.

WHY NEGOTIATE?

Since Scottish criminal procedure is essentially adversarial in nature involving a contest between the traditional protagonists of prosecution and defence it is important to ask why the negotiation of pleas which depends on co-operation and compromise between prosecutor and defence agent has become such an integral part of the criminal justice process. In this section the reasons given by fiscals and defence agents for their willingness to negotiate are presented and discussed.

The Prosecutor's viewpoint

General attitude to plea negotiation. The image of the fiscal as an impartial prosecutor is hallowed by tradition but may not always be reflected in fiscals' practical aspirations. Some fiscals are quick to point out that they are not: 'in the business of securing convictions'; 'it would give the wrong impression if I said I saw myself as there to secure convictions at all costs because that is clearly not so'. Others, however, admit that they experience a sense of failure when an accused person is acquitted: 'the guy walks free and you know perfectly well that he has done it and that's just appalling'.

Most fiscals would agree that where proceedings have been instituted the prosecutor's implicit assumption in prosecuting is that the accused is guilty of some or all of the charges libelled against him. This makes it difficult for him to regard an acquittal as the correct verdict: 'I think if one has decided to prosecute, one has got to adopt a positive view. The view that if prosecution is appropriate, then conviction is appropriate.'

While the number of accused persons, particularly at summary level, who choose to question this assessment by going to trial remains small, the availability of legal aid in all courts since 1975 appears to have contributed to a substantial increase in the number of trials. Certainly the presence of legally qualified persons on the defence side allows more scope for plea negotiation since most fiscals would not consider negotiating directly with an unrepresented accused: 'I would not deal with the accused. It may happen that one of the police officers will mention to me that the accused is willing to plead to so and so and I will then say to the sheriff "will your Lordship take a plea of guilty to such and such?" but I don't negotiate with the accused.'

Caseload pressures. The major reason for negotiation of pleas offered by fiscals is to cut down on the number of trials, particularly at summary level. Neither the fiscal service nor the sheriff and district court personnel are equipped to deal with the volume of cases which would go to trial if pleas were not negotiated: 'it saves judicial time, fiscal time, defence time and very particularly it saves expense to the state in paying witnesses'; 'it is undoubtedly useful for the court and for the public. If every person who pled not guilty initially went to trial there would be a lot more folks coming into the court as witnesses – at vast expense to the Exchequer.'

While the pressure of heavy caseloads is particularly strong in the busy urban offices, every fiscal office has experienced an increase in the number of reports received. The feeling that they are bound by constraints on time and money which makes them more vulnerable to offers from the defence is strongly expressed by some fiscals: 'it was my intention not to appear to be a person who was prepared to negotiate pleas but the system beats me'; 'I think we have to concede quite often . . . although we are not supposed to. I am being honest about this, other fiscals might not acknowledge it. I am sure we all do it'; 'you should be taking every trial on its merits and negotiating any pleas in that trial on their merit but you cannot help but think of the other ten trials'.

In fact, reactions to the idea of plea negotiation suggest that fiscals have a rather negative unfavourable attitude towards it: 'plea negotiation is a necessary evil'. The idea that justice could be bartered is not at all welcome: 'plea bargaining – I don't like using that word . . . it means you give me something, I'll give you something and it's not quite right'.

Problematic nature of trials.   Nevertheless the very nature of the unpredictable trial process itself appears to encourage plea negotiation. While acquittal rates are still relatively low in Scotland (3.5 per cent of all persons proceeded against in Scottish courts during 1979),[1] theoretically at least the outcome of a trial is never certain. There is the possibility that the prosecution is not in possession of all the facts, for example, and that at the trial the defence will produce new evidence corroborating the accused's account which could tip the balance in favour of an acquittal: 'you might have this case on paper that sounds very good but a solicitor might say to you "the information here is wrong, what I have got doesn't rightly agree with that" and you have got to make up your mind whether you think it'll prove or not'.

It is important to remember that the police summary which the fiscal receives initially may present a very clearcut case but subsequent events or further information may alter the fiscal's first assessment of the gravity of an incident or the culpability of an accused person: 'very often the fiscal marks the papers for prosecution on the police summary without detailed statements from the various witnesses. When he gets the full statements he finds that it is not quite so good'; 'precognition is always a slightly vague thing and you can't really tell how the witnesses will give their evidence; cases that go on and seem good on paper don't always work out that way'. There is also the problem of witnesses who fail to appear: 'the lack of a witness may make a big difference to proving a particular charge' or prove reluctant to give evidence: 'in husband and wife cases you may well have the feeling that you are not going to prove any of it because the wife is not going to speak up so any plea is better than none'.[2]

Juries, too, are unpredictable creatures: 'I do not know how a jury is going to react . . . you could have the best case in the world but the jury will reject the evidence . . . if you had accepted a reduced plea then that person would be behind bars'; 'there are occasions when you get quite cross about the jury and say "why the dickens did they find that person not guilty?" There's too many imponderables for a sheriff and jury trial for comfort. So you always have to have this in mind when you're discussing pleas.'

Sometimes the publicity and trauma which surround the trial of particular crimes may encourage the fiscal to negotiate, for example: 'in sex cases plea negotiation saves victims embarrassment' and in crimes involving loss of

---

[1] See Tables 3 and 6: *Criminal Statistics Scotland 1979:* HMSO: 1981.
[2] But see p. 68 footnote 1.

property the abandonment of a trial in favour of plea negotiation in the early stages ensures that stolen items are returned to their owners promptly.

Pursuit of the just sentence. There are obviously sound reasons from the fiscal's point of view, then, for avoiding trials and negotiating with the defence instead. It would be misleading, however, to conclude that these demands of expediency always dictate what the fiscal's course of action will be. In deciding whether to accept pleas fiscals are also making their own assessment of an accused person's culpability and the punishment appropriate to such conduct. Thus according to fiscals negotiations only take place when: 'a chap will be sufficiently punished by accepting a plea'.

This may seem to be a departure from the traditional model of the fiscal, who, unlike his Continental and North American counterparts, is deemed to play no part in determining sentence. There is little doubt, nevertheless, that in defining the acceptability or otherwise of a negotiated plea the fiscal is weighing the probable sentence which the accused is likely to receive on the complaint or petition as amended by negotiation against the probable sentence on the original charges as libelled. While the fiscal cannot be certain about what the actual sentence will be it appears that most sheriffs are fairly predictable: 'after a number of years with a sheriff you can form a reasonably good conclusion as to what he will do'. Fiscals seek to ensure that the actual punishment will be commensurate with the appropriate one, that amendments following negotiation will not materially affect sentence: 'you get the accused who's up for six charges of housebreaking – minor charges – he's 16 (eligible for Borstal) and he'll say "I'll plead to five, not the sixth". He's going to be sent to Borstal on the five so you let it go'; 'it's a matter of saying to oneself "is this going to make any substantial difference to the disposal"'; 'I would be loathe to say "we'll just forget about that one" unless it was a very trifling charge in relation to the others and taking it out was not going to substantially affect the court sentence which is the ultimate object of the thing'.

The practice of accepting a reduced plea where the likely result will be a much lighter disposal is universally condemned: 'it would be absolutely ridiculous letting X off with carrying an offensive weapon and accepting a plea to breach of the peace'; 'it's a very bad thing to drop a serious charge because there is better evidence on a less serious charge. It makes the public feel that the law, the PF and the police do not protect them.' Fiscals stress that this occurs very rarely: 'very seldom is there a material retreat on a complaint once it has been served'; 'I doubt very much if in the majority of cases an acceptance of a plea which has been reduced affects disposal'.

Cases unsuitable for negotiation. There are certain types of cases which Scottish prosecutors generally regard as inappropriate material for plea negotiation, for example where the accused is alleged to have obstructed or assaulted the police: 'certain charges you won't drop, you won't drop police assault or resisting arrest because there can often be allegations of police mismanagement at the back of it . . . you are just leaving yourself open for there to be a complaint against the police and that's normally very heavily disputed'. Defence agents are very aware of this, as one explained: 'I think the fiscal always consults the police concerned if he's going to drop something – if the police are involved I shouldn't think he'd be keen to drop that'.

Some defence agents even feel that fiscals occasionally refuse to negotiate because the police would be unhappy if the accused were not prosecuted on all charges as libelled by them: 'the fiscal will say things like "this is a police complaint and therefore we must go on otherwise we're letting the police down"'. However, this is emphatically denied by fiscals: 'assaulting the police is a fairly serious crime and for that reason I would be most unlikely to take it out – I would not be thinking I've got to have good relations with the police, that I don't want them to think I'm letting them down – I wouldn't do it for that reason – I think the police appreciate that you are independent'.

On the other hand, where the complainer/victim is a member of the public and not a policeman fiscals differ in their willingness to negotiate pleas which may cause concern to such people. The acceptance of a partial plea may mean that the victim of an alleged assault will not receive the recognition from the court which he may feel he deserves since the charge relating to that particular assault has been dropped. Some fiscals feel strongly that suffering to the victim is only one factor among the many which they must take into account: 'I would be governed by my own assessment of it rather than just by consideration for the victim – the victim can only know one piece of the jigsaw puzzle. You can see all the pieces and therefore properly assess the importance of each piece'; 'if somebody has been assaulted and there is not enough evidence, I simply will not bother about what that person thinks'.

Conversely, some see themselves as championing the victim: 'the only person to speak for the victim is the fiscal who appears in the public interest. It is intolerable – almost contrary to natural justice – that almost the only person who isn't considered in the court is the victim – if that should happen the fault lies fairly and squarely with the prosecutor'; 'you've got to bear in mind the man in the street – he is convinced that that man did it – you've got to bear in mind that the victim wants to be in court, he wants to say "that was the man who did it, I saw him"'. According to these fiscals, the nature of the offence and the relative suffering of the victim *should* be taken into account: 'I take a more serious view of cases where you actually have a victim . . . X knocked off his bicycle or assaulted in some vicious way as against cases where you have no actual damage affecting the public interest'. It may be vital for the victim's reputation that all the evidence be led, particularly in sexual offences: 'the plea offered was to attempted rape and at first I thought that might be a good plea to take because there wasn't a great deal of evidence against him but there were other interests to be taken into account – the victim wouldn't have a chance to clear her name'. Similarly, where stolen property is in issue fiscals will not generally drop charges: 'I will never accept a not guilty plea where property has been recovered. I am not prepared to get involved in disputes as to the ownership of property.'[1]

[1] Since the time when this research was carried out the Criminal Justice (Scotland) Act 1980 has introduced compensation orders. Acceptance of a partial plea could now deprive a victim of the opportunity to apply for such an order.

Some fiscals seem to feel that the trial process has to be invoked and justice be seen to be done in open court where a particular crime is especially offensive to the public: 'I take a hard line depending on the age and personal circumstances. Assault and robbery on an elderly lady, assault on a child, I wouldn't be disposed to accept pleas, reflecting what we consider the public attitude'; 'I always prefer in baby battering, particularly where there are neighbours involved who have gone to the trouble of reporting a case, that the matter be fully ventilated in court so that if the accused is going to get convicted he gets convicted properly and if he is going to be vindicated he will be publicly vindicated'. However, this idea that certain cases require public airing is at odds with the fact that the outcome of most criminal cases is actually determined in private.

In effect plea negotiation reverses the traditional ordering of issues, the establishing of evidence being pre-empted by the determination of sentence. Thus by negotiating pleas the fiscal is aiming for the result which would have been achieved had the accused been found guilty on all the charges as originally libelled while avoiding what he regards as a time-wasting, costly exercise which may not always produce the just result: 'my first criterion is to see that justice is done . . . there is no point in negotiating pleas which are blatantly stupid . . . I cannot conceive that it will ever by completely in the public interest to take a plea to something substantially less than the evidence will stand'; 'every fiscal has to say to himself "is the plea that I negotiate in the public interest?" The interest of society must be protected. So long as I am not taking this plea because it is convenient for me not to go to trial – personal considerations must not come into it.' Plea negotiation is therefore an acceptable part of the prosecutor's job: 'provided the plea offered meets the justice of the situation then by and large it's all right'.

The defence agent's viewpoint

For defence agents the negotiation of pleas is regarded as an integral part of their job shaped by what they consider to be the best interests of their clients: 'my job is to ensure that if there is a question of a plea of not guilty and if they are entitled to an acquittal to do one's best to secure an acquittal. If a plea of guilty is indicated to advise them and perhaps attempt to persuade them to plead guilty . . . then the object is to have the penalty mitigated as far as possible'; 'if the client's attitude is that he is not guilty then the object of the exercise must be to achieve an acquittal. If the client is prepared to admit his guilt and that guilt is less than that alleged in the complaint then the object . . . is to achieve the acceptance of that situation either by the court or fiscal and to achieve a reasonable sentence.' Naturally, an acquittal is regarded as the best result and agents see that as their ultimate target, whether or not they judge the accused guilty: 'although you feel within you that the person is guilty because of the strength of the evidence, if a person maintains his innocence to you then you have got to go ahead and defend him'; 'the defence agent's got to presume that the accused is not guilty . . . if you can get someone off on any grounds you are bound to do it'.

However in many cases the accused will either admit to his agent that he has committed some of the charges libelled against him or has no convincing case which would stand up in court. The latter situation appears to be a fairly common one which requires careful handling by the agent. Usually agents try to persuade the accused to tender a plea of guilty to some charges at least: 'I frequently do have to convince the client and in more specific terms explain exactly what the evidence against him is'; 'if you have no hope of winning the trial you tell the client we can do a much better job by pleading guilty'.

At the same time, defence agents do not consider that they are called upon to determine whether the accused is guilty in law. The onus is on the prosecution to prove its case beyond reasonable doubt: 'I can get a chap who comes in and I say to him "look . . . you're guilty" and he says "but I don't think they can prove it". Now that is something our system entitles him to do.'

Occasionally, a client will refuse to accept advice, in which case some agents will refer him to another solicitor and some will take the case to court: 'if someone came to me and said "I'm guilty but I want you to get me off" I would tell him to go to another solicitor'; 'my view is that you must go to trial if his instructions are "go to trial" because you're his agent'. When a defence agent judges that his client is virtually bound to be convicted in the case against him, he falls back on what he sees as an alternative strategy for securing 'the best result that can possibly be obtained' by negotiation.

The acceptance of a reduced, partial or amended plea by the fiscal or even support from the prosecution in tendering a plea in mitigation may benefit the accused in a variety of ways. If some charges are dropped altogether, this will reduce the number of convictions recorded against the accused and possibly: 'keep your client from having a conviction of a certain type, for example, indecency'. The nature of the criminal process following a guilty plea ensures that only an abbreviated version of the facts is presented to the judge and/or jury: 'it is easier to put a better plea in mitigation following a guilty plea without some nasty evidence being dragged out'.

For plea negotiation to have a beneficial effect from the defence point of view it should result in a more lenient sentence than the accused would have received upon conviction had the case gone to trial. If a charge is substantially reduced, for example, from assault to severe injury to simple assault, this should alter the disposal quite considerably since the accused should only receive the sentence appropriate to the lesser charge. Defence agents also argue that sheriffs look favourably on those who admit guilt: 'there's always the slight bonus to be gained by going cap in hand and pleading guilty'; 'a guilty plea gives you a great plea in mitigation, for example, in assault with intent to ravish . . . it saves the girl embarrassment so the accused is entitled to a bonus from the judge'.[1]

The accused's perspective

Before trying to relate the fiscal's purpose in plea negotiation to the avowed aims of the defence it is necessary to establish the role of the accused person in

---

[1] It is these sentencing concessions on the part of the judge which have generated considerable controversy and conflicting case law in England and Wales – see p. 104.

such arrangements. Defence agents maintain that they always regard themselves as acting on behalf of their clients: 'if you're not consulting your accused then you're not doing your job properly because you're acting as his agent'. Yet the idea of the often inarticulate and certainly legally unqualified accused *instructing* his agent has a rather quaint, unreal ring to it. Defence agents admit that usually accused persons are uncertain of their position and do not have the legal expertise or knowledge of the other key parties in the criminal process, the police, the fiscal and the judge, required for the defence of a criminal charge: '99 per cent of the time clients don't know what's going on'.

The accused, more or less mystified by the legal process, must assume that his agent knows what is best for him. What he does not know is that it may be in the best interests of the agent himself to negotiate a plea. Many solicitors, particularly in busy urban offices, could not possibly represent every client whose case is set down for trial on a particular day: 'there are certain solicitors who through pressure of work in my view force pleas of guilty on their client when they shouldn't do so'. What the accused will probably not be told is that the Scottish criminal justice process could not continue in its present form without the practice of negotiating pleas: 'it persuades an accused to plead guilty, it is an integral part of the system . . . I can't see any alternatives'. And what no defence agent will ever tell his client is that the pay-off, in terms of sentencing, may be non-existent. The accused may think that deletion of a few minor charges will affect the disposal of his case, but both the fiscal and the defence agent may know that it will not. The accused may feel that he has scored some kind of victory, that his side of the story has been accepted, if a partial plea is negotiated. What is not pointed out to him is that at a trial the full sequence of events would be brought out into the open: 'the attitude of most people is to get it over with . . . but it may be against their own interest to rush into something'.

With a negotiated plea, therefore, 'saving the appearances' may be all-important: 'the accused thinks he is getting a better deal . . . different people have different things which they wouldn't like to be thought to have done'; 'it looks good as far as the client is concerned if you can say "if you plead guilty to this, this and this, you'll get off on this and this" '.

The co-alignment of interests

Scottish prosecutors like to say they will only negotiate where it is certain that the prosecution case will collapse in court: 'this was a case where the evidence was not good to go to a jury so that to get the plea it was in our interest to agree to reduce the charge from attempted murder to assault to severe injury'. In such circumstances a *good* defence agent would generally advise his client to go to trial and would not be prepared to negotiate. In such cases it might also be fair to say that no prosecution should have been brought initially. One fiscal explained the low level of plea negotiation in his office on the grounds that such weak cases were weeded out at an early stage: 'very seldom is there a material retreat on a complaint once it has been served. That's probably because in this office anything that's shaky is taken into account at the beginning – it probably accounts for our high no pro rate in the first place.'

Yet it is clear that trial-avoidance arrangements are frequent occurrences although in the vast majority of cases where pleas are negotiated the accused stands to gain very little in material terms. The fiscal and the defence agent, on the other hand, could not function without such arrangements and, increasingly, it appears that new deputes and defence agents very quickly become socialised into accepting these practices as essential to the smooth running of Scottish criminal justice. For example, a recent entrant to the fiscal service asserted: 'in a breach of the peace complaint a tremendous number of agents say "will you drop 'bawl and curse'?" and you do because it doesn't make the slightest difference to the sentence but the client thinks he is getting something out of it' and a senior depute admitted: 'it's a question of the solicitor saving face – he wants his client to get the impression he's doing well by him. He says "you're on five charges – I'll get you off on three" – the client's quite impressed but he and I know that I can't prove those three.'

CONCLUSION

Plea negotiations, then, provide the basis for further insights into the way in which Scottish public prosecutors make decisions. Such trial-avoidance arrangements are generally informal, unstructured and at the discretion of individual fiscals and defence agents. While the timing and content of negotiations may vary, there are constant factors which must be present if prosecution and defence are to agree. These centre around the notion of trust resulting in a co-alignment of interests and co-operation between traditional adversaries.

7

WHICH WAY NOW?

OUR ANALYSIS OF DECISION-MAKING by Scottish prosecutors has centred on the formal and informal constraints which structure the operation of their discretion in the prosecution of crime. This analysis, while concentrating on the fiscal in his contemporary setting, is also indicative of the way in which fiscals will both adapt to and shape future developments in the Scottish criminal justice process. This concluding chapter, therefore, not only selects and synthesises the key issues from Chapters 3–6 but attempts to plot future directions for the Scottish prosecution process at a time of considerable change.

SUMMARY OF RESEARCH FINDINGS

A detailed description of prosecutorial decision-making in Scotland is provided by this study which examines the stage of marking reports concerning alleged criminal incidents. In marking the fiscal determines whether or not a case will be prosecuted, what the charges will be and which mode of procedure and court of trial is appropriate, subject to certain limitations.

Chapter 2 sets the scene with a discussion of prosecution systems in other jurisdictions, a review of the historical development of the fiscal's office and a detailed description of the powers and responsibilities of the Scottish prosecutor today. From this discussion it is clear that, in theory at least, the office of fiscal is accorded considerable autonomy in making decisions regarding prosecution. Such decisions are generally determined in private subject only to the scrutiny of the Lord Advocate and without the restrictions imposed by a detailed criminal code or strict guidelines.

Chapter 3, however, which presents a close examination of marking, reveals a rather different picture. The chapter discusses the way in which this key aspect of the fiscal's work is structured and shows that, while there is considerable variation between one type of fiscal office and another, all fiscals are subject to certain common constraints which set parameters to decision-making nationally. The frameworks of criminal law and procedure are obvious examples but, in addition, we discovered other less predictable factors which shape and limit decisions at the marking stage. Thus, the nature of the criminal justice process, where the police are the providers of information and where there are strong bureaucratic pressures to routinise the handling of cases because of the volume of work, inevitably exerts a strong controlling influence. Similarly, the structure of the fiscal service itself and the fact that Scottish prosecutors hold shared perceptions of what constitutes appropriate working practices for achieving common objectives inevitably restrict individual fiscals' freedom of action.

This general picture is further substantiated in the detailed analysis of the decision whether or not to prosecute presented in Chapter 4 where it is clear that fiscals regard prosecution as the appropriate and generally the only way of dealing with those alleged to have committed crimes. Their exercise of the discretion not to prosecute is only invoked in those comparatively rare cases where their own philosophies of what constitutes crime permit them to re-define an alleged criminal incident as something which either cannot be legally sustained or is too trivial to merit criminal proceedings or can be better dealt with by other agencies. Examples of such cases offered by fiscals include careless driving, domestic disputes, shoplifting and minor road traffic offences. However it would be wrong to conclude that there are blanket policies operating within fiscal offices which determine whether cases may or may not be abandoned before prosecution. In explaining the small number of no proceedings cases fiscals point to the lack of any alternative formal methods for dealing with accused persons, for example an extensive fixed penalty system, a lack which may discourage Scottish public prosecutors from selecting the no pro option. Moreover the relatively autonomous position occupied by the fiscal within the criminal justice process does not apparently lend itself to the development of formal links with caring agencies at the marking stage which might lead to diversionary programmes such as those which have been developed elsewhere.

We also consider in Chapter 5 other decisions made at the marking stage, particularly the fiscal's selection of the appropriate forum for a criminal case. Within certain statutory limitations and subject to crown counsels' approval in petition cases, the Scottish prosecutor decides the court in which an accused person should be tried and the procedure. An examination of this decision tells us more about the goals towards which the fiscal is working in pursuit of what he regards as the just conviction and sentence. While fiscals deny that their remit extends to sentencing, in making decisions regarding court and pro-cedure they are clearly working with their own evaluation of the just sentence and are striving to achieve it. Thus in selecting court and procedure the fiscal draws on his knowledge of judges' sentencing policies. His assessment of the lay judiciary is particularly important in this regard since it is crucial in structuring the flow of cases between the summary courts.

Finally in Chapter 6 we discuss an area of prosecutorial decision-making which is rarely mentioned when the job of a fiscal is being described. Trial-avoidance arrangements, where the prosecution and defence agree that trial proceedings will be waived in return for the reduction or amendment of the charge or charges, play an important role in the Scottish system of criminal justice. Yet they are usually conducted in a very informal, unstructured way in the privacy of the fiscal office or within the court precincts. The form and content of such negotiations vary considerably depending on such factors as the

K

nature of the charges and the status of the case. But perhaps the key factor contributing to the success or failure of these arrangements is the degree of trust which exists between the defence and the prosecution. Although ostensibly operating within an adversary system, it appears that fiscals and defence agents accept that frequently a co-alignment of interests exists between them which encourages recourse to negotiation rather than confrontation. Apart from the philosophical commitment to the interests of justice which they supposedly share they agree that a trial may produce unsatisfactory results for both parties. The prosecutor may lose a case through an acquittal after a considerable expenditure by the state of time and money; the defence agent may be regarded by his client as having failed him if the accused is found guilty on all charges as originally libelled. Plea negotiation is a facet of the fiscal's work where considerable discretion is exercised and decisions relating to trial-avoidance arguably have a more profound impact on the Scottish criminal justice process than the much discussed option not to proceed.

    We are left, then, with a somewhat paradoxical description of the fiscal as operating within certain parameters which considerably restrict the exercise of his much vaunted discretion not to prosecute while being remarkably free to make arrangements with the defence resulting in trial-avoidance. This picture is, of course, incomplete and further research is clearly required to examine what takes place at Crown Office – in particular how crown counsel make decisions – and to analyse how fiscals deal with criminal cases after the marking stage. Given these limitations to our conclusions it is, nevertheless, possible to make some informed speculations about future directions for the Scottish prosecution process.

FUTURE DIRECTIONS FOR THE SCOTTISH PROSECUTOR

    This study has focused primarily on aspects of the Scottish prosecutor's work from a contemporary viewpoint. However, an examination of its historical development demonstrates that the office of fiscal is an evolving rather than a static one which reflects shifts in the criminal justice process as a whole. Thus the growth of Scottish police forces in the nineteenth century affected the investigatorial aspects of the fiscal's work, since the police became the investigators of crime and the fiscal no longer played an active part in obtaining evidence against an accused person.[1] Similarly, the trend towards bureaucratising the criminal justice process which has occurred throughout the twentieth century has had a profound influence on the way in which the Scottish prosecutor makes decisions.[2]

    In attempting to interpret the role of the prosecutor within the administration of justice we examined the nature of his working relationships with others involved in the process of prosecution. We were able to demonstrate that a close interdependence exists between the fiscal and certain other agencies, notably the police. Thus changes which do not relate directly to the prosecutor

[1] See Chapter 2 p. 27.   [2] See Chapter 3 p. 48 et seq.

may nevertheless have an impact upon him. This interdependence is particularly important at the present time given recent statutory innovations and a continuing debate on future directions for the criminal justice process in Scotland. In fact, it is clear that after a period of relative stagnation some important aspects of Scottish criminal justice have been the subject of a re-think with the result that major changes have been made and others are likely to follow. This concluding section will therefore consider these recent legislative changes and also look at other developments which have not yet been enshrined in legislation but which will, if implemented, certainly be influential in re-structuring the role of the Scottish public prosecutor.

There have been two major legislative enactments relating to Scottish criminal law and procedure over the last ten years – the Criminal Procedure (Scotland) Act 1975 and the Criminal Justice (Scotland) Act 1980.[1] The former was never intended to be any more than a consolidating statute. Its importance was in the fact that it gathered together enactments dealing with Scottish procedure contained in sixty-two different Acts dating back to 1587. The 1980 Act, on the other hand, contained some controversial and wide-ranging provisions, derived mainly from the Second Report of the Thomson Committee on criminal procedure in Scotland reporting in 1975. The Committee's remit covered 'trial and pre-trial procedures in Scotland for the prosecution of persons accused of crimes and offences' and its members were 'to report whether, having regard to the prevention of crime on the one hand and to the need for fairness to accused persons on the other, any changes in law or practice are required'. [Thomson: 1975: 1] Although the report stated that the 'existing system of criminal procedure was fundamentally sound and that improvement was all that was needed and not radical change', in its efforts to reduce delays in disposing of criminal business and to secure convictions at an early stage in criminal proceedings the Committee made some far-reaching recommendations. Thus in relation to police powers of detention, for example, the report favoured giving the police the right to detain a person suspected of having committed an offence for up to six hours without charging him and this was implemented in Part I of the 1980 Act. By legitimizing the practice of interviewing suspects without arresting or charging them these provisions not only assist the police but also ensure that the prosecution case will not be undermined by defence submissions that evidence obtained thereby is inadmissible.

Part II, which revived the practice of judicial examination as recommended by the Thomson Committee, had a more direct impact on the fiscal's work. The prosecutor is now entitled to put certain questions to an accused person at the petition hearing and must do so if an extra-judicial admission has been obtained. The procedure, which was common practice during the last century, enables 'the procurator fiscal to ask an accused questions designed to prevent the subsequent fabrication of a false line of defence for example, alibi'. [Thomson: 1975: 43] It is possible that the availability of this device may encourage the

---

[1] The Bail (Scotland) Act 1980 also introduced some important changes but these are only of relevance to bail granting and custody.

fiscal to put certain cases on petition which would previously have been prosecuted on a summary complaint. Section 15 of the 1980 Act also introduced
intermediate diets in summary procedure, which may afford prosecution and
defence more opportunity for the negotiation of pleas.

We have already considered in Chapters 5 and 6 the ways in which the
complainer/victim is regarded by the Scottish prosecutor. The Report of the
Dunpark Committee on reparation by the offender to the victim of crime dealt
with this matter very fully and suggested some radical innovations. The report
noted that the existence of a public prosecutor inevitably affects the status of the
victim in criminal proceedings:

> the transition of the original objective of our criminal law
> [was] from redress for wrongs done to individuals to
> punishment of the wrongdoer with a view to maintaining
> public order. The transition has occurred gradually as a
> result of our system of public prosecution for crime.
> [Dunpark: 1977: 8]

The Dunpark Committee nevertheless considered that there could be 'no
objection in principle to the introduction into our criminal procedure of an
element of compensation for the victim of crime' and recommended that:

> all criminal courts in Scotland should have a discretionary
> power, exercisable by the court when sentencing any
> person . . . to order that person to pay such sum of money
> as seems appropriate . . . as compensation for any personal
> injury, loss or damage sustained as a result of that crime.
> [Dunpark: 1977: 102]

Part IV of the 1980 Act implemented these recommendations which mark
an important transition in Scottish criminal procedure towards a greater
recognition of the victim's rights. For the prosecutor this development may
limit his exercise of discretion in relation to the acceptance of partial pleas
where a complainer seeks compensation. In the longer term the idea that a
third party whose interests may not concur with those of either prosecution or
defence has a role to play in criminal proceedings may have a marked impact on
Scottish criminal justice in general and the fiscal in particular.

While the 1980 Act has attempted to alleviate some of the specific difficulties presented by an increase in the number of trials and protracted criminal
proceedings, it does not deal explicitly with prosecutorial discretion at the
marking stage. Yet as Gordon notes in his commentary on the Act the problems
of delay experienced by the criminal justice process in Scotland could be
alleviated by accepting 'that the prosecution should cut their coat to suit their
cloth, and should prosecute only as many summary cases as the system can
cope with in a reasonable time bearing in mind that many such cases are
relatively trivial'. [Gordon: 1981: xvi] He points out that 'such a reduction
can be achieved administratively by an extended exercise of the discretion not to
prosecute in particular cases, or legislatively by "decriminalising" various

classes of offences, or at least dealing with them outside the court system'. These and other solutions offered for the problems of an overtaxed criminal justice process merit consideration here because they offer an insight into ways in which the fiscal's role may develop in the future.

Decriminalization

It is clear from our research that the exercise of discretion by the Scottish prosecutor over the last decade has been significantly affected by a rise in the level of reported crime.[1] While the reasons for this increase are complex and varied, it appears that the creation by parliament of new statutory offences has been an important contributory factor. According to a recent report by *Justice* the list of distinct and separate criminal offences for England and Wales in 1975 exceeded 7,200.[2] [Justice: 1980] Nearly 3,000 of these offences had been enacted since 1960 and in only about 3,750 was any criminal intent required. While some of this legislation applies only to England and Wales, there has been a trend towards creating more United Kingdom offences and this has had an impact on the nature and level of reported crime in Scotland. Thus statutes as diverse as the Consumer Credit Act 1974, the Sale of Goods Act 1979 and the Companies Act 1980 have all created new offences generally of a relatively minor nature but, if reported,[3] still requiring action by criminal justice agencies. Since in Scotland the public prosecutor has a remit to prosecute virtually all offences, including those matters which in England and Wales are dealt with by government departments, a new offence on the statute book usually means more work for the fiscal.

This may impose an intolerable burden upon the prosecution service, a burden which can only be alleviated by a substantial increase in public expenditure or by cutting back on the number of cases which fiscals are required to process. In the present economic climate it seems unlikely that sufficient additional resources can be made available to meet these demands in full. A reduction in the prosecutor's caseload would appear to offer the more practical solution. Thus over the next few decades parliament, in addition to refraining from the creation of new statutory offences, may actively intervene to reduce by decriminalization the number of crimes already on the statute book.

Many fiscals feel that offence-creating legislation should be curbed: 'there is no doubt that successive governments, particularly since the War, have been overhappy in trying to make criminal offences, and those people who want new laws have just thrown in penalties in order to secure compliance with the law and inevitably there has only been one way to do that and that is to prosecute

[1] See Diagram 1 p. 23.

[2] This figure does not include inchoate offences (attempts) or those created by public local Acts.

[3] The full impact of legislation in certain areas, such as consumer protection, has not been felt by the prosecution service as yet because would-be complainers often fail to report such matters. However, as the Royal Commission on Legal Services in Scotland noted: 'when more and more rights and responsibilities are conferred by statutes, it is natural that we increasingly look for vindication of our rights' [RCLSS: 1980: 20] so that the level of reports received in relation to such offences is unlikely to remain low.

them in court'. They also regard decriminalization as an appropriate step for certain offences such as careless driving: 'I think there is a case for decriminalizing careless driving. There are many situations where somebody commits an error of judgment which we can all commit and will commit inevitably every so often when driving a motor vehicle and by bad luck there is an accident and you are charged. If the insurance cover is there to take care of it all why not decriminalize?' Another category which some Scottish prosecutors regard as a suitable case for decriminalization is being drunk and incapable (Section 70 of the Licensing (Scotland) Act 1903): 'I do not like this offence of being drunk and incapable. We have just got to accept that, although it was their own act which got them into that condition, they are ill and should not be regarded as criminals.'

A move away from offence-creating legislation and active intervention by parliament to decriminalize existing crimes and offences could lead to a significant reduction in the prosecutor's workload. Fiscals would then be left with what they regard as the less routine and more interesting cases which merit the scrutiny of an experienced prosecutor rather than the stroke of an administrative pen. Were the pressures of heavy caseloads to be eased in this way the fiscal would have time to exercise a more creative role in actually initiating criminal investigations[1] and his current dependence on other criminal justice agencies for information, particularly the police, could be reduced. He could, like his counterpart the district attorney in the United States, actively pursue suspected violations of certain offence categories where crime often goes undetected such as fraud and corrupt practices.

Diversion[2]

It is fairly clear from our research that fiscals would welcome relief from many of the routine cases such as speeding and parking with which they are currently deluged: 'many of the cases are run-of-the-mill . . . like drunk and incapable, speeding . . . and don't require much skill at all'. In particular fiscals feel uneasy about treating regulatory offences within the same system as serious crime: 'statutory ones do not involve much moral blame . . . they are not crimes in the sense that assaults are'. This reflects very much the view expressed by other criminal justice agencies and by the public:

> the time has now come for a radical look at the way in
> which society deals with a host of minor offences so that the
> criminal courts would be retained to deal only with matters
> which the man in the street regards as criminal, all other
> contraventions being the subject of a fixed penalty
> procedure. [Justices' Clerks' Society: 1981: 766]

[1] Individual fiscals with an appropriate background in administration or accountancy have been entrusted with investigating suspected fraudulent dealings in conjunction with the CID but this *ad hoc* practice has not been systematised in any way.

[2] See Chapter 4 pp. 67–75.

The option to decriminalize is certainly one way of reducing the level of reported crime and consequential pressures on the criminal justice system, but in so doing it removes the conduct in question from the ambit of penal sanctions altogether. This may not be regarded as a satisfactory solution for certain categories of behaviour over which the state wishes to retain control through the medium of the criminal justice process:

> it might perfectly reasonably be suggested that a particular
> kind of conduct should cease to be an offence and indeed
> this has actually happened in recent years in relation to
> suicide and homosexual acts between consenting adults in
> private. Such a change in status is, however, never likely to
> occur on a "wholesale" scale. [Justices' Clerks' Society:
> 1981: 766]

A more acceptable alternative to the institution of criminal proceedings may lie in the concept of diversion, defined as 'halting or suspending proceedings against a person who has violated [the criminal law] in favour of processing through a non-criminal disposition'. [NCCJSG: 1973: 50]

The Stewart Committee on Alternatives to Prosecution has put forward suggestions for change in this area in its First Report dealing with an extension of the fixed penalty system. It recommended that:

> the procedure should be extended to speeding in excess of a
> prescribed limit by up to 20 mph, failure to comply with
> any of the requirements which relate generally to traffic
> directions and signs and those relating to the remedying of
> defects on motor vehicles . . . offences of using a motor
> vehicle on a road without a current MOT test certificate,
> [certain] provisions of the construction and use regulations.
> [Stewart Committee: 1980: 69–70]

What is probably of particular concern to fiscals is the administration of an extended fixed penalty system and who should be designated as the issuing authority for fixed penalty notices. Our discussion in Chapter 4 suggests considerable ambivalence on the part of the fiscal about the respective roles of the police and the prosecutor in administering an extended fixed penalty procedure. The powers of the police will in effect be greatly extended under the proposed legislation since 'a police constable should be empowered to issue fixed penalty notices [in the majority of cases] and the issue of a fixed penalty should . . . be a matter for the discretion of the individual police officer'. [Stewart Committee: 1980: 47]

The Stewart Committee accepted that there might be a constitutional objection to such extension with critics claiming that the fiscal's power, already eroded by the present fixed penalty system, would be further usurped and the system shade into police prosecution. Nevertheless the Committee maintained that in practice the kinds of offences which would be included in an extended fixed penalty procedure are at present a matter for police discretion anyway since 'the procurator fiscal must depend on police reports when authorising prosecutions in minor motoring offences [and he] seldom hears about the numerous offences which the police do not trouble to bring to his notice'. [Stewart Committee: 1980: 48] The implementation of the Committee's recommendations will certainly have an impact on the number of reports sent to the Scottish prosecutor. In addition formal recognition of the extent to which the police determine whether a criminal incident will actually be prosecuted may, paradoxically, give the fiscal more opportunity to exercise a discretion in relation to cases not subject to a fixed penalty.

Diversion, however, is not merely concerned with ways of exacting penalties without recourse to the traditional court structure. While the Stewart Committee has not so far presented its conclusions on the possibility of diverting accused persons to medical or social work facilities, there have certainly been moves in that direction in the United States. In fact:

> the typical American diversion scheme arranges for the
> re-routing of a proportion of defendants, with the consent
> of the prosecutor, into a programme which provides
> educational help, or a job or vocational training and usually
> some form of personal guidance and counselling. If the
> defendant performs satisfactorily the judge dismisses the
> charges. [NACRO: 1975: 4]

We have already considered the difficulties inherent in creating closer co-operation between the prosecutor and social work agencies, particularly in the absence of a separate probation service. It appears that fiscals are at present reluctant to involve social workers at the prosecution stage and do not perceive social work intervention as legitimate in the context of prosecutorial decision-making. Therefore were formal diversionary schemes involving social work departments to be introduced the fiscal would be required to adapt to a situation where his autonomy and freedom to make decisions might be questioned.

Alternatives to traditional adjudication

Although this study has not focused on the courtwork aspects of the fiscal's job clearly courtroom advocacy is central to the role of the Scottish public prosecutor and his decisions at the pre-court stage anticipate and shape the judicial processing of a criminal case. The fiscal both decides the appropriate forum for a criminal matter (where there is a choice of court or procedure) and is responsible for the conduct of the prosecution case in court. Scottish criminal procedure and the organisation of the criminal courts in Scotland still reflect the traditional mode of adversary proceedings so that the fiscal is required to operate within this framework. While important changes in Scottish criminal procedure have been introduced by the Criminal Justice (Scotland) Act 1980 the adversarial notion of criminal justice remains sacrosanct though ironically, as Chapter 6 demonstrates, it is more honoured in the breach than the observance since prosecution and defence seek, through plea negotiation, to achieve compromise rather than confrontation. Moreover, the reintroduction of the judicial examination where the prosecutor has the right to question an accused person at first appearance is designed, according to its critics, to pre-empt any adversarial engagement. But it remains the case that alternative methods of resolving disputes, at least on the criminal side,[1] have not so far been developed in Scotland.

However, other more radical moves away from traditional modes of criminal procedure are currently under review in many countries. [Abel: 1981: 245] Supporters of alternatives to courts cite the advantages of such ventures in terms of their relatively low cost when compared with traditional institutions, their accessibility, the speed with which they process cases and the increased use which they make of lay participation. Above all they are characterised as likely to offer a better method of resolving disputes than the adversary system which:

> is predicated on the assumption that there are irreconcilable differences between the parties . . . it forces problems into a mould which reduces them to a single dimension . . . it imposes on the parties a definition of the problem and a solution which [may] not correspond to their needs and wishes. [Law Reform Commission of Canada: 1975: 26]

Thus in the United States experiments have begun in more than 100 cities in response to the pressure for informal alternatives to courts. These innovations vary considerably in form and approach, but are all seeking to achieve similar objectives. For instance the Citizen Dispute Settlement Program which began in Columbus Ohio in 1971:

> provides an out of court method of resolving neighbourhood and family disputes through mediation and counselling. Cases are screened and referred by the local prosecutor's office for a hearing within a week after the complaint is filed . . . Law students trained as mediators meet with the disputants . . . the cost per case is about one-fifth of traditional processing. [NCJRS: 1975: 18]

In New York the Institution of Mediation and Conflict Resolution deals with criminal cases referred by the police with the consent of both parties. Interestingly:

> the principal criterion for selection is the perception that the parties' real difficulties may be resolved, rather than the seriousness of the offence . . . allegations as ostensibly grave as rape, robbery, kidnapping and burglary have been found suitable for mediation. [Chinkin and Griffiths: 1980: 7]

---

[1] The Royal Commission on Legal Services in Scotland considered the possibility of establishing small claims tribunals to deal with civil cases presently handled by the sheriff courts but preferred a procedure based on the existing courts. [RCLSS: 1980: 177]

While the main aim of such mediation is to encourage the parties to reach their own solution some schemes insist on a contractual agreement enforceable through the civil courts.

It is largely in the area of civil law that alternative procedures have been introduced into European countries but a few experiments in the criminal field merit consideration. Thus in the Federal Republic of Germany Section 380(1) of the Code of Criminal Procedure provides that reconciliation proceedings must precede the institution of a formal prosecution in 'the case of certain offences – disturbance of the domestic peace, insult, minor intentional or negligent bodily injury, breaches of confidence, the making of threats and property damage'. [Cappelletti: 1978–9: Vol. 2: 117] Such proceedings, *Sühneverfahren*, are presided over by a specially appointed arbitrator, called a *Schiedsmann*, whose job it is to bring about a settlement between the parties so that the victim abandons his right to seek criminal sanctions. The success rate in such cases is reckoned to be about 50 per cent.

In Poland an alternative mode of processing criminal cases exists in the form of the Social Conciliation Commissions which:

> may be broadly defined as bodies of ordinary citizens
> recognised by the law of the country but lacking any legal
> sanctions and acting on a voluntary basis to resolve disputes
> submitted voluntarily to them by other citizens in order to
> bring about social harmony and co-operation within
> communities of neighbours. [Cappelletti: 1978–9: Vol. 2:
> 161]

The Commissions, although in theory subject to the supervision of the state prosecutor, in practice operate independently from the traditional court structure. Their jurisdiction is not precisely defined but appears to include a wide range of criminal and anti-social conduct including 'the infringement of order or quiet at work or in the home, quarrels resulting from communal residence and the neglect of obligations towards one's family or employer'. [Cappelletti: 1978–9: Vol. 2: 163] Both the courts and the prosecutor can submit cases to the SCC or matters may be referred by individual complainers.

While such developments may appear to be very distant prospects for the Scottish criminal justice process it is clear that they reflect trends which the system here is already experiencing such as the need for the victim to play a more active role and the fact that the traditional processing of criminal cases is extremely costly. If alternatives to traditional adjudication were to be introduced in Scotland, the crucial question for the fiscal would be whether or not he would continue to determine the appropriate forum for a criminal case. Were the decision to resort to some form of dispute resolution outwith the traditional court structure to be at the discretion of the public prosecutor he would still retain a large measure of control over the disposal of criminal cases. Otherwise his authority would arguably be weakened and his role as key arbiter seriously diminished.

Public defenders in the Scottish context

This study has emphasised the role of both prosecution and defence in avoiding recourse to a trial through plea negotiation. Indeed the Lord Advocate has instructed fiscals that defence solicitors should be encouraged to approach them at an early stage for the purpose of negotiating pleas and should be given copies of formal or technical witness statements. Nevertheless it is clear from the findings discussed in Chapter 6 that the solicitor representing the defence is not always in the best position to bargain successfully on his client's behalf. He must pursue investigations and arrange for the precognoscing of all witnesses (other than those giving expert evidence) without having access to those resources, such as statements made to the police, which are available to the prosecution. A major criticism of the present system of plea negotiation is the apparent tendency of defence solicitors to drag out proceedings for financial gain. Our research, however, suggests that difficulties experienced by the defence in preparing a case contribute as much to their reluctance to initiate trial-avoidance arrangements as the nature of the criminal legal aid scheme itself where payment is by court appearance.

In any case plea negotiation is not a realistic option where persons are unrepresented. According to the Royal Commission on Legal Services in Scotland which included within its remit existing provisions for legal aid 'although 225,000 people are proceeded against in the summary courts each year, only about 22,000 are awarded legal aid'. [RCLSS: 1980: 102–3] The privilege of being represented by a lawyer under the legal aid scheme depends in all criminal cases on the accused's means and in summary cases there is the additional test of whether it is in the interests of justice.[1] Persons in custody are entitled to the services of a duty solicitor but only at first appearance. If they choose to challenge the Crown case they must apply for legal aid in the usual way. Both duty solicitors and lawyers operating under the criminal legal aid scheme remain private practitioners and the schemes are administered by the Law Society. While this ensures their independence it means that they may not have the same resources available to them as the public prosecutor.

The Commission considered suggestions for change in this area and found that the office of public defender, a salaried state lawyer, might offer a better means of providing legal assistance at public expense to those charged with criminal offences. In Canada, America and Australia such systems are an institutionalized feature of criminal justice and are regarded as acceptable to the judiciary, the legal profession and the general public. Those in favour of the idea note that it combines the concrete advantages of economy and speedier justice with the more nebulous benefits of greater trust between prosecution and defence and an enhancement of the image of the criminal lawyer. However critics of the idea point to the ethical difficulties entailed in denying an accused person the right to choose his own legal representative and the problems

[1] See page 113 et seq.

inherent in adding yet another bureaucracy to the criminal justice process. The
Commission therefore recommended a compromise solution:

> there should be an experiment to assess whether or not a
> public defender system could with advantage be introduced
> into Scotland to run in parallel with the service provided by
> solicitors in private practice supported by legal aid. [RCLSS:
> 1980: 112]

The introduction of a public defender system to Scotland albeit somewhat
limited in scope would certainly have repercussions for the fiscal service.
Scottish prosecutors would be faced with defence agents who were Crown
servants like themselves and also had the resources of the state available to
them. It might therefore be more difficult for a fiscal to proceed with a case
where the evidence was weak or unsatisfactory since the public defender
would be in a position to detect any flaws at an early stage.

However the impact of such a scheme might not be as profound as might
be expected. If research in the United States can offer any useful parallels then
it is likely that the adversarial nature of the criminal justice process would
continue to diminish and that the number of trials would decrease under a
public defender system since the ingredients for successful plea negotiation
would more often be present. In effect the introduction of a public defender
system in Scotland would institutionalise and streamline existing practices rather
than presenting divergent strategies.

> The problem of the adversary system is maintaining the
> ethic of individuality and challenge in a system where the
> professionals will see greater advantage in co-operativeness
> than in conflict. Given the prevailing system of prosecutorial
> discretion the public defender operates on much the same
> principles as the private defense attorney. [Skolnick:
> 1967: 68]

CONCLUSION

This study set out to provide a description and analysis of the ways in
which Scottish prosecutors make initial decisions in relation to the prosecution
of criminal cases. In the rhetoric of Scottish criminal justice the fiscal apparently
exercises a wide and largely unfettered discretion in deciding which cases merit
prosecution and when he chooses to institute criminal proceedings in determining the nature of the charges and the appropriate forum for trial. Yet as our
research demonstrates parameters to decision-making are set by a wide variety
of constraints. Thus far from making extensive use of their discretion not to
proceed, we found that Scottish prosecutors *prosecute*; far from adopting an
active role in investigating crimes and offences, fiscals are largely dependent on
the quality and flow of information from the police; and far from making use
of their legal expertise in deciding whether or not to prosecute the majority of
cases are, in fiscals' eyes, routine. On the other hand, it is clear from our findings

that one area over which the Scottish prosecutor exercises considerable control is in relation to the negotiation of pleas. This important aspect of the fiscal's work is largely ignored in the accepted notion of what a fiscal does yet it has a profound impact on the way in which the Scottish criminal justice process operates.

However, as this final chapter has indicated, the fiscal service as well as the criminal justice system in Scotland has considerable potential for change at the present time. Different interpretations can certainly be made regarding the impact of future developments on the office of the fiscal. While the possibilities sketched in the preceding pages may appear to erode even further the Scottish prosecutor's autonomy and sphere of discretion, it can be argued that the placing of formal limitations on the scope of prosecutorial decision-making – by the extension of the fixed penalty system and other forms of diversion for example – may in fact paradoxically offer the fiscal a more active and independent part in the investigation and prosecution of crime.

APPENDIX

DECISION-MAKING BY FISCALS:
A CENSUS OF PROSECUTION
DECISIONS

INTRODUCTION TO THE CENSUS[1]

WITH THE CO-OPERATION of all fiscal offices in Scotland a census was held of reports received for the first time over a six day period in the autumn of 1977. Each report received for the first time which required the fiscal's decision whether to institute or drop proceedings against persons named therein was included in the census. However, to lessen the burden of extra work placed on both fiscals and office staff over the census period reports which dealt solely with speeding and parking offences were excluded and random samples of 1:3 were taken of all remaining reports in Glasgow and 1:2 in Edinburgh. Reports where all the accused were under sixteen or were subject to a Children's Panel Supervision Order were also left out since it was felt that they deserved separate scrutiny. Fiscals also completed a short questionnaire giving details of job experience and professional career. All fiscals except 33 members of the service whom it was known would not be marking cases during the census period were approached and 137 out of the 142 questionnaires sent out were completed and returned. This appendix summarises the results of the census exercise by considering the information provided by reporting agencies, decision-making by fiscals in relation to such reports and biographies of those fiscals who marked reports at the time of the census.

INFORMATION PROVIDED BY REPORTING AGENCIES

Since fiscals undertake all prosecutions in Scotland (with the exception of certain poaching offences and prosecutions under the Education Acts) reports naming a person or persons to be considered for prosecution are sent to fiscal offices by a variety of agencies. The police report the vast majority of cases; in the census 2,895 or 92 per cent[2] of all reports were submitted by them. The

---

[1] For a full description see *Decision-Making by Fiscals: A Census of Prosecution Decisions*, Susan Moody and Jacqueline Tombs, May 1978 available from the Social Research Branch, Scottish Home and Health Department.

[2] Percentages have been rounded up or down.

TV Licence Records Office report all cases under the Wireless Telegraphy Acts (98 cases or 3 per cent of the census) and the Traffic Commissioners have certain powers under the Road Traffic Acts to report certain minor road traffic offences as does the Motor Taxation Office with respect to vehicle excise cases (a cumulative total of 87 cases or 3 per cent of the census). Other reporting agencies include the Department of Health and Social Security (social security frauds amounted to 41 cases or 1 per cent of the census), British Transport Police, the Health and Safety at Work Executive, Customs and Excise, local Environmental Health Offices, other sections of local and regional government and the Fisheries Commission (a cumulative total of 1 per cent or 34 cases). Diagram I illustrates the contribution made by the different reporting agencies.

While there were 3,155 reports included in the census, the total number of charges was 4,929, of which 45 per cent appeared on reports involving one charge only and the remaining 55 per cent were distributed between multi-charge reports. It is important to emphasise the distinction between a report or case and a charge since in the discussion which follows the data is analysed using both of these measures and the results are different according to the measure adopted. For example, the contribution made by the police as a reporting agency may be analysed by case, so that 92 per cent of all *reports* are recorded as having been submitted by the police, or by charge, when the figure for the police is 94 per cent of all *charges*.

All charges were coded into thirteen different categories covering broadly similar types of offences. As Diagram II shows, the most frequent charge was

DIAGRAM I

REPORTING AGENCIES

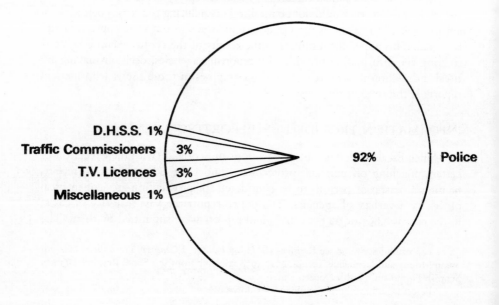

D.H.S.S. 1%
Traffic Commissioners 3%
T.V. Licences 3%
Miscellaneous 1%
92%   Police

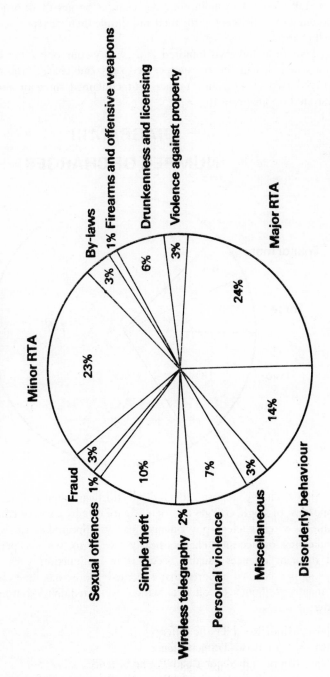

DIAGRAM II
TYPE OF CHARGES

Minor RTA 23%

Fraud 3%

Sexual offences 1%

Simple theft 10%

Wireless telegraphy 2%

Personal violence 7%

Miscellaneous 3%

Disorderly behaviour 14%

Major RTA 24%

Violence against property 3%

Drunkenness and licensing 6%

By-laws 3%

Firearms and offensive weapons 1%

L

for a major road traffic offence (1,202 or 24 per cent of all charges) with minor road traffic offences totalling 23 per cent.[1] Charges of disorderly behaviour amounted to 14 per cent of the total and simple theft was specified in 10 per cent of all charges.

Two thousand two hundred and twenty-four or 71 per cent of all the reports included in the census specified only one charge, 496 or 16 per cent involved two charges and 13 per cent contained three or more charges as illustrated by Diagram III.

DIAGRAM III

NUMBER OF CHARGES

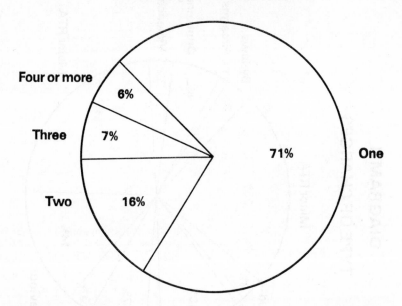

Single charge reports covered all thirteen offence categories but the proportion of single charges for each offence category varied considerably. For example, wireless telegraphy offences always appeared as the sole charge and drunkenness or licensing charges nearly always so, whereas personal violence and firearms offences usually occurred in conjunction with other charges. The 29 per cent of reports that specified more than one charge included six major groupings of offences which are listed in descending rank order below:

(a)   Minor Road Traffic Offences
(b)   Major Road Traffic Offences
(c)   Minor and Major Road Traffic Offences
(d)   Personal Violence and Disorderly Behaviour Offences

[1] This does *not* include speeding or parking.

(e)   Disorderly Behaviour Offences
(f)   Theft and Fraud Offences

Where there were two charges on a report (16 per cent of all cases) this order of frequency was particularly applicable but there was a tendency for the number of road traffic offences to increase with the number of charges on a report. For example, where there were four or more charges specified on a report, one at least of these charges was almost always for a road traffic offence.

When a report is submitted to the fiscal for a decision regarding prosecution the accused specified in the report will either be at liberty or in custody. In a substantial majority of census returns (2,463 or 78 per cent) the case was described as *cited* because the accused was at liberty and would, if prosecuted, normally be served with a citation to appear in court on a particular day. The remaining 22 per cent consisted of custody cases, where the accused had, generally, been arrested the day before and could then be held until *the next lawful day*.

Although custody reports specified charges drawn from all offence categories (except offences under the Wireless Telegraphy Acts), there was some considerable variation in the proportion of custody cases for different types of offence. For example, less than 6 per cent of all custody cases consisted of minor road traffic offences (although over 40 per cent of all reports contained one or more such charges) whereas 38 per cent of all custody cases consisted of drunkenness offences and 25 per cent of all custody cases involved an offence of personal violence (in spite of the relatively small number of such offences in the sample). It appeared, then, that offences involving violence against the person, cases of housebreaking or robbery and incidents of disorderly behaviour were more likely to appear on custody reports and that road traffic offences, fraud and byelaw contraventions were least likely to occur in custody cases as the following table shows.

The fact that in 14 per cent of cases involving females the accused were held in custody compared with 23 per cent of all cases involving males can usually be linked to the types of offences committed by women, a point which is discussed later. A greater number of charges also seemed to slightly increase the likelihood that an accused would be in custody, though only where the report specified an offence of personal violence or disorderly behaviour. For example, one third of all personal violence cases where there was only one charge involved a custody remand, whereas the figures for multi-charge personal violence cases was 47 per cent. There did not appear to be any correlation between the number of accused persons charged and the likelihood of the accused being held in custody. There was, however, some variation between different offices with larger urban offices having a higher proportion of custody reports. This is probably due to the distribution of particular kinds of charge between different fiscal offices. For example, urban offices receive a higher percentage of reports involving personal violence or disorderly behaviour than rural offices. In fact, in those offices which contributed more than 59 cases to the census 36 per cent of their reports consisted of disorderly behaviour or personal

TYPE OF CHARGE BY CITED/CUSTODY CASE

Offence Category	No of Custody Charges	% of Offence Category	No of Cited Charges	% of Offence Category
Violence against property	105	70%	44	30%
Sexual offences	16	50%	16	50%
Personal violence	170	47%	189	53%
Disorderly behaviour	307	44%	385	56%
Drunkenness	111	38%	180	62%
Simple theft	159	35%	299	65%
Firearms	22	34%	42	66%
Miscellaneous	33	27%	88	73%
Fraud	21	13%	134	87%
Byelaws	15	9%	144	91%
Major RTA	101	8%	1097	92%
Minor RTA	40	3%	1098	97%
Wireless telegraphy	–	–	98	100%
Total	682	22%	2462	78%

violence charges and 28 per cent of their reports were custody cases whereas in offices of caseloads with less than 50 the proportion of these reports was 28 per cent and the percentage of custody reports was 11 per cent.

In the great majority of reports (85 per cent) there was only one accused person, in 11 per cent of reports two persons were charged and in only 4 per cent of all reports were there three or more accused persons. Certain offence categories did tend to be associated with more than one accused, for example, disorderly behaviour, violence against property and personal violence, whereas incidents of fraud, drunkenness and sexual crimes tended to involve one person only. For certain offence categories the number of accused increased with the number of charges so that several charges of theft, road traffic offences or personal violence were more likely to involve several accused than a single charge report for the same offence categories.

Most of the reports (87 per cent) involved a male accused and only 11 per cent of reports related exclusively to females. The proportion of female accused did vary with different offence categories, so that 36 per cent of all wireless telegraphy offences were committed by women and 20 per cent of all thefts. Violence against property and firearms offences were almost exclusively committed by males. In just over 2 per cent of all cases both males and females were involved. There did not appear to be any association here with particular offence categories, though there was some correlation between multi-charge reports and a mixed group of accused persons so that where the accused persons specified on a report included males and females several charges were usually specified also.

DECISION-MAKING BY FISCALS

When a report is received for the first time by a fiscal there are a number of decisions which he is empowered to make by usage and Section 12 of the Sheriff Courts and Legal Officers (Scotland) Act 1927. Diagram IV shows how the 3,155 cases in the census were processed by the fiscal.

No Proceedings Cases

Two hundred and forty-nine or 8 per cent of all cases were marked *no proceedings* over the census period. All but 10 of the 56 offices contributed to this figure and it is noteworthy that the percentage of no proceedings cases was in inverse proportion to the total number of cases received, with the highest percentages being recorded in the smaller offices. This accords with analyses of no proceedings figures produced annually by fiscal offices for the seven years prior to the census. Only 3 per cent of no proceedings reports involved accused persons in custody although custody reports accounted for 22 per cent of the total sample. This is not surprising since almost 50 per cent of no proceedings cases entailed minor or major road traffic offences where the accused is generally not detained in custody. The most common offence was Section 3 of the Road Traffic Act 1972 (*careless driving*) often charged with the alternative of Section 2

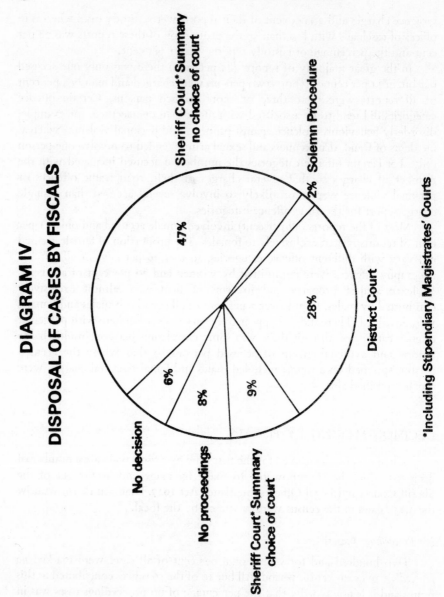

DIAGRAM IV

DISPOSAL OF CASES BY FISCALS

47%

Sheriff Court* Summary
no choice of court

2% Solemn Procedure

28%

District Court

9%

Sheriff Court* Summary
choice of court

8%

No proceedings

6%

No decision

*Including Stipendiary Magistrates' Courts

(*dangerous driving*)[1] which accounted for 20 per cent of all no proceedings cases. Minor road traffic offences comprised 15 per cent. The next largest group of no proceedings cases involved charges of theft (12 per cent) followed by disorderly behaviour (10 per cent) and personal violence (8 per cent). Eighty-seven per cent of no proceedings cases involved only one charge so that these reports were more likely to contain single charges than the total sample.

[1] Now *reckless driving* under Section 50 of the Criminal Law Act 1977, brought into effect on 1 December 1977.

The respondents were asked to specify up to three reasons from a list on the census form explaining why they did not institute proceedings. In over 50 per cent of no proceedings cases only one reason was given and this was usually *insufficient evidence* or the *trivial nature of the offence*. Where more than one reason was given it usually involved one of the two reasons already stated in association with *excusable conduct* or *sufficient but unsatisfactory evidence*. It is interesting that insufficient evidence did not always appear to the fiscals marking these cases to provide an adequate explanation on its own for dropping proceedings.

Different reasons did tend to be associated with different offence categories. For example, minor road traffic offences usually appear to have been dropped because of the trivial nature of the offence or because of this allied with the excusable nature of the conduct whereas theft was usually not proceeded with because of insufficient evidence. Disorderly behaviour was normally dropped because of the trivial nature of the offence while reports of personal violence involved several cases where the evidence was regarded as sufficient but un-satisfactory and the *complainer withdrew the complaint* or the *complainer was malicious*. In such cases although the fiscal had sufficient evidence in law the difficulty was that such evidence might prove unsatisfactory and unreliable when put to the test in court as, for instance, where the accused and the victim were closely related and the victim was the chief prosecution witness. Thus several of these cases involved wife assault charges. In 35 cases *office policy* was mentioned as a reason for not proceeding and this occurred in 21 offices and was particularly associated with careless driving cases and shoplifting reports. In 13 cases the decision not to proceed was taken because the problem was regarded as a social work or mental health matter and this occurred in a variety of offence categories from a sexual offence by a member of the National Health Service under Section 51 of the Criminal Law Act 1977 to a major road traffic offence.

Referrals to outside agencies, usually to social work departments, were made in almost all the cases specified as being social work matters but in only a very few others, several of which involved children. Cases were referred to the police for warning or the fiscal himself administered a warning in 11 per cent of no proceedings cases amounting to 1 per cent of all reports covered by the census. Only twelve offices used the warning and over half of these cases were concentrated in three offices. A wide range of offences was included in this group representing a good cross-section of the no proceedings cases. It would appear that no proceedings cases took longer to mark than reports where proceedings were instituted but this may be explained by the greater proportion of custody cases in the latter group that had to be marked on the day of receipt.

Choice of procedure

In only a small number of cases, 62 or 2 per cent of the total sample, did the fiscal decide to put an accused person on petition initially subject to verification by crown counsel. These cases were distributed among 25 offices, the majority of which were large ones, with Glasgow sheriff court office contributing the largest number. Just under half of these reports specified more than one charge and only one case involved a female accused. They thus differed significantly in these respects from the total sample. The most common charge was for personal violence or theft. Almost half of all the cases involved an offence of personal violence, either alone or in conjunction with an offence of disorderly behaviour, a firearms offence or a charge involving violence against property. A quarter of all these cases specified a charge of theft, either alone or in conjunction with a disorderly behaviour, firearms or road traffic offence. The remaining reports usually specified single charges of disorderly behaviour, violence against property, sexual offences and frauds. There were no crimes of murder or rape reported to fiscal offices over the census period. In almost half of these reports *gravity of the offence* was given as the main reason for deciding on solemn procedure and this was especially so in cases involving violence against the person. *The accused's previous record* was used in a quarter of all solemn proceedings cases and was usually associated with theft or fraud cases. *Sentencing powers* and the *accused's mental condition* were only mentioned in a handful of cases.

No Decision Cases

In 192 cases or 6 per cent of the census reports decisions concerning the institution or abandonment of proceedings were deferred by fiscals after an initial reading of the reports concerned. These reports involved 35 different offices and fiscals of various grades and diverse experience took the decision to defer exercising their discretion to prosecute. Only a few of these cases were custody reports, a quarter of them contained more than one charge and the largest group consisted of fraud charges usually involving violations of social security legislation. The majority of these cases were sent to the police for clarification or for further information where the police had not reported the case initially and a few were referred to a *foreign fiscal*, a fiscal in another office, where it seemed more appropriate that the report should be handled by that office. The next largest group comprised charges of personal violence, disorderly behaviour and firearms offences and these were generally returned to the police for full statements to be obtained from witnesses though several, probably difficult, cases where corroboration or identification might prove difficult were kept for re-reading. Minor and major road traffic offences accounted for almost a third and these were normally sent to the police for clarification. It appeared that more unusual cases, such as those involving breaches of Planning Acts, were kept for re-reading. Colleagues or a senior fiscal were apparently seldom consulted and referrals were made to crown counsel on two occasions only in those cases where decision-making was deferred.

Choice of Summary Court[1]

In 1,173 cases or 37 per cent of the census the fiscal had to make a decision as to the appropriate summary court in which the case should be heard, that is whether the accused should appear before the sheriff or the district court. This

---

[1] 31 cases were sent to the stipendiary magistrates' courts in Glasgow but the number was considered too small for separate analysis and in any case there are special arrangements in force for case distribution between the stipendiary and the other summary courts in Glasgow.

reinforces the impression gained from the foregoing analysis of charges that many reports are concerned with trivial offences. In 1,477 cases (47 per cent) the sheriff court had sole jurisdiction under Section 285 Criminal Procedure (Scotland) Act 1975.[1] Cases where there was a choice of summary court therefore excluded most road traffic offences, various other statutory offences such as prosecution under the Wireless Telegraphy Acts and some common law offences such as thefts over the value of £25. Certain other categories of offences are not referred to the district court by direction of the Lord Advocate, for example breaches of the peace at football matches.

Fiscals were asked which summary court they had chosen and why. Just under a quarter of all cases where such discretion could be exercised[2] went to the sheriff court and the remainder were channelled to the district court. This distribution of cases was similar for all fiscal offices except in Glasgow, Hamilton and Greenock where there are distinct sheriff and district court fiscal offices. Almost all cases sent to the district court involved only one charge (this amounted to 90 per cent of district court cases) whereas only 68 per cent of all sheriff court cases consisted of single charge reports. While the highest proportion of custody reports noted in the census came from four district court fiscal offices in the Strathclyde Region, for the rest of Scotland cases going to the sheriff court were twice as likely to be custody reports as those being sent to the district court. The following table shows those offence categories where the *choice of court* decision most frequently occurred and illustrates how the fiscal exercised this discretion.

An examination of the reasons for choosing the particular court points to *gravity of offence* as the main reason, followed by *lay court matter, office policy, the accused's record* and *court sentencing policy*. Other reasons given on the census form, *police recommendation, court caseload, legal complexity*, were hardly mentioned at all. Theoretically any of the 1,173 cases taken on summary procedure where there was a choice of court could have gone to the district court so it is worth looking in detail at the reasons why 22 per cent were sent to the sheriff court. Thirty-one per cent of them went to this court because of the gravity of the offence and 21 per cent because of the accused's record and in both these groups offences of personal violence and disorderly behaviour predominated. Office policy determined a further 22 per cent particularly for minor road traffic offences. It was interesting to note that court sentencing policy was the reason for the choice of district rather than sheriff court particularly for disorderly behaviour and drunkenness offences. Not surprisingly, where an offence was regarded as a lay court matter the district court was chosen and this was used particularly for drunkenness, disorderly behaviour and byelaw cases.

Amendment of charges

It is important that the complaint or petition should be clear and unambiguous so fiscals must carefully scrutinise the charge or charges libelled on

[1] See Chapter 5 p. 89 et seq. for the expansion of district court jurisdiction under the Criminal Justice (Scotland) Act 1980.
[2] A few areas of Scotland, such as Orkney, have no district court.

M

CHOICE OF SUMMARY COURT

Offence Category	Total no. of charges	Total no.of charges where choice of Summary Court	(2) as % of (1)	Total no. of charges sent to District court	(4) as % of (2)
Drunkenness & licensing	292	277	95%	260	94%
Disorderly Behaviour	692	581	84%	453	78%
Byelaw Offences	159	103	64%	95	92%
Personal violence	360	223	62%	120	54%
Simple theft	461	203	44%	175	86%
Minor road traffic	1141	377	33%	249	66%

reports submitted to them for their decisions regarding prosecution. In many statutory offences, there is a standard way of libelling specific charges, for example speeding, so that the fiscal need only draw the attention of his office staff to the existence of such a stylised format by writing *style* on the report. In other cases the fiscal may need to simplify some portion of the charge, for example superfluous details or outmoded language, or include relevant matters that the police have not specified such as the time and place that the particular offence or offences occurred and this is described as *redrafting for style*. Occasionally he may feel that a different offence is more appropriate than the one libelled and he may substitute another charge for that specified by the police, for example *careless* instead of *dangerous* driving. Forty-seven per cent of those charges proceeded with were redrafted for style, and a further 34 per cent consisting mainly of statutory offences, particularly offences under the Road Traffic Acts were marked *style*. In 88 per cent of all cases proceeded with in the census the same number and type of charges were specified before and after marking so only 12 per cent of cases involved substantial changes. The number of accused and the number of charges dropped slightly after marking in cases where proceedings were instituted (a drop of 3 per cent in the number of accused and 1 per cent in the number of charges).

Time

Sixty-three per cent of all census cases were marked on the day they were received and only 5 per cent took longer than eight working days (excluding those where no decision was taken at initial reading). Offices varied considerably, so that in one office 58 per cent took longer than three working days whereas in another all cases were marked on the day of receipt.

Decisions made in collaboration with others

One interesting aspect of decision-making is the extent to which decisions are made in collaboration with others. In the census fiscals were asked whether their decisions not to prosecute, their choice of procedure and their choice of summary court had been decided with help from colleagues or a senior person in the fiscal office. Information was also collected on instances when one fiscal referred a case to another. Where it was decided not to proceed fiscals were asked if this decision had been made with the assistance of the reporting agency or other bodies outwith the fiscal office. Question 7 on the census form was devoted entirely to contacts with agencies outside the fiscal service either instituted by the fiscal or by the agency. Possible contacts were the reporting agency, a social worker, a general practitioner, a psychiatrist, the complainer or prison authorities. In the overwhelming majority of cases (96 per cent) decisions appear to have been made by one fiscal only. The remaining 4 per cent where consultation took place did not appear to be significantly different from the total sample in terms of offence category or decision-making. The most common instance of such contact was, surprisingly, not with other fiscals, but with the reporting agency, usually the police (3 per cent of all cases).

BIOGRAPHIES OF MARKING FISCALS

It was originally hoped that it would be possible to link information collected from the fiscal questionnaires to the cases marked by each fiscal to see if there was any association between such biographical material and decisions made by fiscals in the census. After collation of the data from both sources, however, it was decided that the validity of any such correlation would be dubious, because of the small number of *unusual* decisions, their fairly even distribution among offices and between fiscals, the large number of single fiscal offices (in 29 offices only one fiscal marked all the cases received over the census period) and the problem of drawing inferences about complex associations between behaviour and background from the census material. In the following discussion, therefore, no attempt is made to link data though it is, of course, possible to speculate on the relevance to marking of variations in such factors as age and experience.

Sixty-five per cent of those who completed the questionnaire had been recruited into the fiscal service within the seven years prior to the census (from November 1970 to November 1977) as a consequence of the general rise in the level of reported crime and the absorption by the fiscal service of district court and other formerly independent prosecution responsibilities (such as prosecutions under the Factories Acts and British Rail Statutes). In conjunction with such developments, the number of part-time fiscals has decreased (there was only one in 1977 compared with four in 1970) and many offices have expanded their staff considerably. The position of regional procurator fiscal has been created and these senior members of the service each administer one of six regions into which Scotland has been divided. Fiscals completing the questionnaire who had joined the service since 1970 can be described in four different profiles. The remaining 35 per cent who had been in the fiscal service for more than 7 years will be looked at separately.

Recent recruits to the fiscal service

(1) *No previous job experience* (28 cases) – This group (20 per cent of the total sample) had no previous experience as professional lawyers or in other permanent employment and joined the fiscal service immediately upon qualifying as solicitors, generally within the three years preceding the census. Most of the group were under twenty-six and their main reason for joining the fiscal service was a desire to gain experience of courtwork and criminal law, for example several fiscals commented that the fiscal service provides an ideal opportunity to develop skills in the criminal field. A few also mentioned the starting salary, describing it as good for someone only recently qualified. The great majority of these entrants had held no permanent postings in any fiscal office other than their present one and one third had joined the service within the previous six months.

Obviously these young inexperienced deputes would require time and help from more experienced colleagues initially in tackling the whole range of a fiscal's responsibilities, including marking. It is interesting to note that virtually all of these deputes marked some cases over the census period, whatever their length of service, and between them they were responsible for marking 23 per cent of all cases. From the census information it did not appear that they were more likely than those with previous experience to consult their seniors or colleagues about cases or actually refer cases to more experienced fiscals, though it is possible that very new recruits had their marked reports scrutinised by a senior.[1] It may also be that cases were allocated among fiscals on the basis of experience after scrutiny and selection by a senior.

(2) *Some previous legal experience* (27 cases) – These fiscals (20 per cent of the total sample) usually in their late twenties or early thirties had spent a few years as professional lawyers in private practice or local government. A small number of them also had job experience in other fields and two had experience of legal work in England and Wales. Their main reason for joining the service was an interest in criminal work and a consequent dissatisfaction with the opportunities for this in private practice or local government. A third of this group had worked in at least one other fiscal office and had been in the service for over three years. Two of this group had achieved the status of senior legal assistant and one was a procurator fiscal. Between them, they marked 18 per cent of all cases and it is to be noted that their experience of other legal jobs, while useful, would not necessarily have given them any special expertise in the skills of prosecution.

(3) *Considerable legal experience* (16 cases) – This group (12 per cent of the total) comprised those fiscals with considerable experience in private practice and/or local government or occasionally as a Reporter to the Children's Panels or as a district prosecutor before 1975. A third of them had experience abroad as magistrates in British colonies or with courts martial. Their primary motivation for joining the fiscal service seems to have been loss of job satisfaction in private practice combined with their experience in criminal work, which made them particularly well equipped to act as prosecutors. An additional factor was the chance to be recruited as senior legal assistant, the status of most of this group, four of whom were procurators fiscal in small fiscal offices. The group marked 13 per cent of all cases and obviously their experience, particularly in criminal work, would be a most valuable asset.

(4) *Law as a second career* (22 cases) – These fiscals (16 per cent of the total sample) usually in their thirties had qualified as solicitors after pursuing a different career for a number of years. The majority had held administrative jobs in government or industry, a few had been teachers and a fairly high percentage (31 per cent) had been policemen either in Scotland or in a British colony. Not surprisingly, this group had the most varied non-legal job experience of any of the profiles discussed. Interest in criminal law was the main incentive for joining the service though job satisfaction and work in the public service were also mentioned. Ex-policemen saw the job as an appropriate one providing the best opportunity for the utilisation of their considerable

[1] See Chapter 3 p. 38 et seq.

experience in the investigating and prosecution of crime. Most of these recruits had less than two years service, were legal assistants and had worked in other fiscal offices. While this group had no previous legal experience, their maturity and previous careers might be an advantage in those aspects of the fiscal's work, like marking, that may involve more than strictly legal decisions. This group marked 17 per cent of all cases.

Fiscals with 7 years service or more

(5) *Seven to 15 years service* (20 cases) – This group (15 per cent of the total sample) usually in their forties had been in the service for more than 7 but less than 15 years. Before 1970 there was an age-bar on entry to the fiscal service (the aspiring recruit had to be 26) so that all of this group had experience as qualified lawyers, usually in private practice and sometimes in the Colonial legal service. A few of the group also had non-legal job experience usually as National Service conscripts or as clerks. Three-quarters of these fiscals held the rank of procurator fiscal, usually in a small fiscal office. For them also a desire to specialise in criminal law was the main reason for joining the service, the fiscal service seemed the *obvious* choice and good prospects were also mentioned. Naturally, all of this group had worked in other fiscal offices apart from their present one though, perhaps surprisingly, almost 50 per cent had spent time in one other office only. The great majority had been in their present office for two years or more. These fiscals marked 14 per cent of all cases.

(6) *Over 15 years service* (25 cases) – These fiscals (17 per cent of the total sample) were members of the service with over 15 years experience, usually in their fifties. The majority had been qualified for over 25 years and had joined the service within a few years of qualifying, generally after a number of years in private practice. Most of this group had served in the Second World War and almost a quarter had been involved in military law. Their reasons for joining the fiscal service were similar to the other groups and a few also mentioned a desire to serve the public interest. Virtually all this group were procurators fiscal in large offices and most had been in their present offices for over two years with over a third staying in the same office for more than 10 years. This group obviously represented the top echelons of the service and included all the regional procurators fiscal. They marked 15 per cent of all cases though a third did not mark any cases. It may, in fact, be considered surprising that procurators fiscal in large offices with such a wide range of responsibilities should contribute to marking at all.

Diagram V illustrates the percentage of fiscals in each of the six categories described above and also shows the distribution of the different fiscal grades within each category as of November 1977.

CONCLUSIONS

Information obtained from the census, then, made it possible to advance several broad generalizations about the fiscal's task of marking. Firstly, it appeared that the vast majority of reports received by fiscal offices concerned

DIAGRAM V

PROFILES OF FISCALS

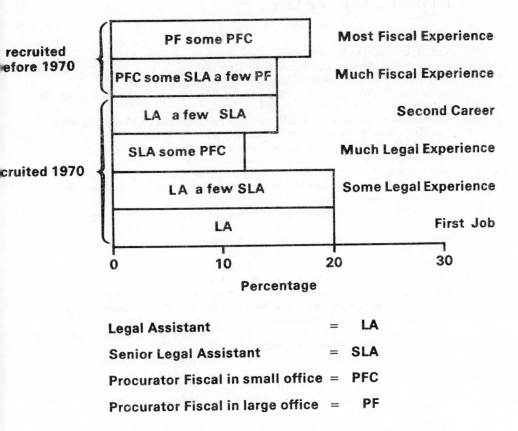

minor offences only, offences involving serious violence against the person or damage to property being rarely mentioned. Secondly, it seemed that a substantial proportion of all cases referred to the fiscal were processed by him in a routine straightforward way and this trend was reflected across the country. The large number of cases marked by fiscals, the use of *styles* in the production of a complaint and the rarity of unusual decisions (to drop proceedings, to put a case on petition or to defer taking any action) all supported this view. Thirdly, the census findings suggested that marking was very much a solitary task with fiscals making decisions alone without involving colleagues or other agencies outside the fiscal service. The overall impression of marking, then, was of an unproblematic process which did not often entail conscious deliberation over the choices available to the fiscal in each case.

BIBLIOGRAPHY

ABEL, R. L. 1979, 'The Rise of Professionalism', *British Journal of Law and Society*, 6(1):82–98.
——1981, 'Conservative Conflict and the Reproduction of Capitalism: The Role of Informal Justice', *International Journal of the Sociology of Law*, 9:245–67.
ALSCHULER, A. W. 1979, 'Plea Bargaining and Its History', *Columbia Law Review*, 79(1):1–43.
AMERICAN BAR ASSOCIATION, 1958, 'Report of Joint Committee on Professional Responsibility', *American Bar Association Journal*, 44:1159.
BAKER, N. F. 1933, 'The Prosecutor – Initiation of Prosecution', *Journal of Criminal Law, Criminology and Police Science*, 23(5):770–96.
BALDWIN, J. & McCONVILLE, M. 1977, *Negotiated Justice*. London, Martin Robertson.
——1978, 'Preserving the Good Face of Justice: Some Recent Plea Bargain Cases', *New Law Journal*, September, 7:2–4.
——1978, 'Sentencing Problems Raised by Guilty Pleas: An Analysis of Negotiated Pleas in the Birmingham Crown Court', *Modern Law Review*, 41:544–88.
BANKOWSKI, Z. & McMANUS, J. 1980, 'Lay Justice: Some Preliminary Observations', *Scottish Legal Action Group Bulletin*, 45:80–2.
BARCLAY, W. 1853, *Digest of the Law of Scotland*. Edinburgh.
BLUMBERG, A. S. 1967, *Criminal Justice*. Chicago, Quadrangle Books.
BOTTOMLEY, A. K. 1973, *Decisions in the Penal Process*. London, Martin Robertson.
BLOOR, M. 1978, 'On the Routinized Nature of Work in People Processing Agencies'. In Davis (ed.), *Relationships Between Doctors and Patients*. Aldershot, Saxon House.
CAMPBELL, C. M. 1976, 'Lawyers and Their Public'. In D. N. McCormick (ed.), *Lawyers in their Social Setting*. Edinburgh, Greens.
CAMPBELL, C. M. & WILSON, R. J. 1972, *Public Attitudes to the Legal Profession: Report to the Law Society of Scotland*. Edinburgh, Greens.
CAPPELLETTI, M. 1978–9, *Access to Justice*. Netherlands, Sijthoff and Noordhoff.
CASPER, J. D. 1979, 'Reformers v. Abolitionists: Some Notes for Further Research on Plea Bargaining', *Law and Society Review*, 13:567–72.
CHALMERS, W. G. 1978, 'The Role of the Crown Office in the Scottish System of Criminal Procedure', paper given at the *Council of Europe Study Visit* to Edinburgh.
CHINKIN, C. M. & GRIFFITHS, R. C. 1980, 'Resolving Conflict by Mediation', *New Law Journal*, January, 3:6–8.
CHISWICK, D., McCLINTOCK, F. H. & McISAAC, M. 1982, *Discretion in Arrest and Prosecution: The Problem of the Mentally Abnormal Offender*. Aberdeen, Aberdeen University Press.
CHRISTIE, N. 1978, 'Conflicts as Property'. In C. Reasons & R. Rich (eds.), *The Sociology of Law: A Conflict Perspective*. London, Butterworths.
CHURCH, T. N. 1979, 'In Defence of "Bargain Justice" ', *Law and Society Review*, 13:509–25.
CURRAN, J. & CHAMBERS, G. 1982, *Social Enquiry Reports in Scotland*. Edinburgh, HMSO.
DOBASH, R. E. & DOBASH, R. 1979, *Violence Against Wives*. New York, Free Press.
DUNPARK COMMITTEE, 1977, 'Reparation by the Offender to the Victim in Scotland', *Cmnd. 6802*. Edinburgh, HMSO.
EGGLESTON, W. 1978, *Evidence, Proof and Probability*. London.
ERIKSON, K. T. 1964, 'Notes on a Sociology of Deviance'. In H. S. Becker (ed.), *The Other Side*. New York, Free Press.
FELKENES, G. T. 1976, 'Plea Bargaining: Its Pervasiveness on the Judicial System', *Journal of Criminal Justice*, 4:133–45.
FRANK, J. R. 1949, *Courts on Trial*. Princeton, Princeton University Press.

FREIDSON, E. 1973, 'The Production of Deviant Populations'. In E. Rubington & M. S. Weinberg (eds.), *Deviance: The Interactionist Perspective*. New York, Macmillan.

GANE, C. H. W. & STODDART, C. N. 1980, '*A Casebook on Scottish Criminal Law*'. Edinburgh, Greens.

GOLDSTEIN, A. S. & MARCUS, M. 1977, 'The Myth of Judicial Supervision in Three "Inquisitorial" Systems: France, Italy and Germany', *Yale Law Journal*, 87:240–83.

GORDON, G. H. 1978, *The Criminal Law of Scotland*. Edinburgh, Greens.

——1981, *The Criminal Justice (Scotland) Act 1980* [Annotated]. Edinburgh, Greens.

GROSMAN, B. A. 1969, *The Prosecutor: An Inquiry into the Exercise of Discretion*. Toronto, University of Toronto Press.

——1970, 'The Role of the Prosecutor in Canada', *American Journal of Comparative Law*, 18:498–507.

HARVARD LAW REVIEW, 1970, 'Notes: Plea Bargaining and the Transformation of the Criminal Process', 90:564–95.

HERMANN, J. 1974, 'The Role of Compulsory Prosecution and the Scope of Prosecutorial Discretion in Germany', *University of Chicago Law Review*, 49(3):468–505.

HETHERINGTON, T. 1980, 'Speech as Director of Public Prosecutions to the Media Society', *Guardian Newspaper*, May 22.

HUME, D. 1797, *Commentaries on the Law of Scotland Respecting Crimes*. Edinburgh.

HUNTER, LORD. 1978, 'Historical Development of Criminal Law in Scotland', paper given at the *Council of Europe Study Visit* to Edinburgh.

IRVINE SMITH, J. 1936, 'Criminal Procedure.' In Stair Society, *Introduction to Scottish Legal History*. Edinburgh.

JOHNSON, T. J. 1972, *Professions and Power*. London, Macmillan.

JOURNAL OF JURISPRUDENCE, 1877–8, 'A Procurator Fiscal – What He Was, What He Is, and What He Will Be', 21:25 et seq.

JUSTICE, 1970, 'The Prosecution Process in England and Wales', *Criminal Law Review*, 668–83.

——1978, 'Notes on English Criminal Prosecution and Trial', paper presented at a *Meeting Between The Royal Commission on Criminal Procedure in England and Wales and Justice* in London.

——1980, *Breaking The Rules*. London, Justice.

JUSTICES' CLERKS' SOCIETY, 1981, 'Decriminalisation – An Argument For Reform', *New Law Journal*, July 23:766.

KING, M. 1981, *The Framework of Criminal Justice*. London, Croom Helm.

KRESS, J. M. 1976, 'Progress and Prosecution', *Annals of the American Academy for Political and Social Sciences*, 423:99–116.

LANGBEIN, J. H. 1974, 'Controlling Prosecutorial Discretion in Germany', *University of Chicago Law Review*, 41(3):439–67.

LARSON, M. S. 1977, *The Rise of Professionalism: A Sociological Analysis*. Berkeley, University of California Press.

LAW REFORM COMMISSION OF CANADA, 1975, *Studies On Diversion: East York Community Law Reform Project*. Ottawa, Information Canada.

LEIGH, L. H. & HALL WILLIAMS, J. E. 1981, *The Management of the Prosecution Process in Denmark, Sweden and the Netherlands*. London, James Hall.

McCLUSKEY, LORD. 1977, 'Public Prosecutors and Public Defenders: The Scottish Experience', paper given at the *Commonwealth Law Conference* in Edinburgh.

——1980, 'The Prosecutor's Discretion', *International Journal of Medical Law*, 1(1):5–9.

McDONALD, W. F. (ed.) 1980, *The Prosecutor*. London, Sage Publications.

McPHAIL, I. D. 1979, *Research Paper on the Law of Evidence in Scotland*. Edinburgh, Scottish Law Commission.

MARKHAM, G. R. 1980, 'The Elderly Offender and the Police', *Justice Of The Peace*, 144(7):97–8.

MARKS, F. R. 1972, *The Lawyer, the Public and Professional Responsibility*. Chicago, American Bar Foundation.

MILLER, F. W. 1969, *Prosecution: The Decision to Charge a Suspect with a Crime*. Boston, Little, Brown & Co.

MOLEY, R. 1929, *Politics and Criminal Prosecution*. Chicago, Minton Balch & Co.

NAGEL, S. S. & NEEF, M. 1976, 'The Impact of Plea Bargaining on the Judicial Process', *American Bar Association Journal*, 62:1020–2.

NARDULLI, P. F. 1978, 'Plea Bargaining: An Organisational Perspective', *Journal of Criminal Justice*, 6:217–31.

NACRO, 1975, *Diversion From Criminal Justice in an English Context: Report of a NACRO Working Party under the Chairmanship of Michael Zander*. London, Barry Rose.

NATIONAL COMMISSION ON CRIMINAL JUSTICE STANDARDS AND GOALS, 1973, *Report of Corrections Task Force*. Washington, US Department of Justice.

NATIONAL CRIMINAL JUSTICE REFERENCE SERVICE, 1975, *Prosecutorial Discretion: The Decision to Charge: An Annotated Bibliography*. Washington, National Institute of Law Enforcement and Criminal Justice.

NATIONAL INSTITUTE OF LAW ENFORCEMENT AND CRIMINAL JUSTICE, 1975, *Exemplary Projects*. Washington, US Department of Justice.

——1975, *The Dilemma of Diversion: Resource Materials on Adult Pre-Trial Intervention Programmes*. Washington, US Department of Justice.

NEWMAN, D. J. 1966, *Conviction: The Determination of Guilt or Innocence Without Trial*. Boston, Little, Brown & Co.

NORMAND, W. G. 1938, 'The Public Prosecutor in Scotland', *Law Quarterly Review*, 54:345–57.

PACKER, H. L. 1969, *The Limits of the Criminal Sanction*. Stanford.

PARK, W. n.d., *The Truth About Oscar Slater*. London, Psychic Press.

PODMORE, D. 1980, 'Bucher and Strauss Revisited – The Case of the Solicitors' Profession', *British Journal of Law and Society*, 7(2):1–21.

PRESIDENT'S COMMISSION ON LAW ENFORCEMENT AND ADMINISTRATION OF JUSTICE, 1967, *Reports*. Washington, US Department of Justice.

REID, W. n.d., 'The Origins of the Office of Procurator Fiscal in Scotland', unknown journal, 154–160.

RENTON, R. W. & BROWN, H. H. 1972, *Criminal Procedure According to the Law of Scotland*. 4th Edition, G. H. Gordon. Edinburgh, Greens.

RITCHIE, W. 1824, 'Office of Lord Advocate in Scotland', *The Edinburgh Review*, 39:363 et seq.

ROYAL COMMISSION ON CRIMINAL PROCEDURE IN ENGLAND AND WALES, 1981, 'Final Report', *Cmnd. 8092*. London, HMSO.

ROYAL COMMISSION ON LEGAL SERVICES IN SCOTLAND, 1980, 'Final Report', *Cmnd. 7846*. Edinburgh, HMSO.

RUESCHEMEYER, D. 1969, 'Doctors and Lawyers: A Comment on the Theory of the Professions'. In V. Aubert (ed.), *Sociology of Law*. London, Penguin.

SCOTTISH HOME AND HEALTH DEPARTMENT, 1972, *Working Party on the Lay Summary Courts*. Edinburgh.

——1979, 'Criminal Statistics Scotland 1978', *Cmnd. 7676*. Edinburgh, HMSO.

——1981, 'Criminal Statistics Scotland 1979', *Cmnd. 8215*. Edinburgh, HMSO.

SCOTTISH INFORMATION OFFICE, n.d., *Children's Hearings*. Edinburgh, HMSO.

SCOTTISH OFFICE, 1978, *Handbook for Newly Appointed Justices of the Peace in Scotland*. Edinburgh.

SESSAR, K. 1980, 'Prosecutorial Discretion in Germany'. In W. F. McDonald (ed.), *The Prosecutor*. London, Sage Publications.

SHEEHAN, A. V. 1975, *Criminal Procedure in Scotland and France*. Edinburgh, HMSO.

SKOLNICK, J. H. 1967, 'Social Control in the Adversary System', *Journal of Conflict Resolution*, XI(1):52–70.

SOUTHERN CALIFORNIA LAW REVIEW, 1969, 'Prosecutorial Discretion and the Initiation of Criminal Complaints', 42:137–49.

STEWART COMMITTEE, 1980, 'The Motorist and Fixed Penalties', *Cmnd. 8027*. Edinburgh, HMSO.

STODDART, C. N. 1979, *The Law and Practice of Legal Aid in Scotland*. Edinburgh, Greens.

THOMAS, D. A. 1978, 'Plea Bargaining in England', *Journal of Criminal Law and Criminology*, 69:170–8.

THOMAS, P. 1969, 'An Exploration of Plea Bargaining', *Criminal Law Review*, 69–79.

THOMSON COMMITTEE, 1975, 'Criminal Procedure in Scotland' (Second Report), *Cmnd. 6218*. Edinburgh, HMSO.

TOMASIC, R. & BULLARD, C. 1979, 'Lawyers and Legal Culture in Australia', *International Journal of the Sociology of Law*, 7:417–32.

WALKER, A. G. & WALKER, N. M. L. 1964, *The Law of Evidence in Scotland*. Edinburgh.

WEBER, M. 1954, *Economy and Society*. M. Rheinstein (ed.). Harvard.

WILCOX, A. M. 1972, *The Decision to Prosecute*. London, Butterworths.

WILLIAMS, G. 1979, 'The Mathematics of Proof', *Criminal Law Review*, 297–308.

INDEX

advocates depute *see* crown counsel

alternatives
  to prosecution, 70-4, 133-6
    see also decriminalization; detoxifica-
    tion centres; diversion; fixed penalties;
    warnings
  to traditional adjudication, 136-8

Book of Regulations, 20, 24, 50
burgh courts *see* district courts

caseload, 48, 49
  impact on fiscals' work, 63-4, 87-8, 134
  individual offices in, 35, 36, 38, 40, 42, 43
charges
  bargaining over *see* plea negotiation
  drafting of, 43-4, 46-7, 51-2, 53, 54,
    106-8
compensation, 123 n.1, 132
complaint *see* procedure, summary
court
  choice of, 89-99
courts Scotland *see* district courts; high
  court; procedure; sheriff courts
criminal cases
  cited, 9, 32, 45, 114, 115
  custody, 9, 32, 35, 46, 113-14, 115
  statistics on, 22, 23
criminal justice systems
  adversarial, 11, 29, 100, 102, 119, 136-7,
    140
  inquisitorial, 11, 103
Crown Agent, 8 n.1, 20, 21, 105 n.1
crown counsel
  historical development of, 19
  recommendations to, 84-5, 105 n.1
  role of, 26, 28, 87
Crown Office
  circulars, 19-20, 28, 75 n.1, 105, 113, 114
  historical development of, 19-20
  role of, 8, 24, 28, 37-8, 50-1

decriminalization, 133-4, 135
defence agents
  relations with fiscals, 116, 117-19
  role in plea negotiation, 29-30, 104,
    106-9, 110, 111-14, 139-40
deterrence, 59, 71, 89
detoxification centres, 74

Director of Public Prosecutions, 13-14
district courts, 27, 64, 80-2, 89-99
  clerks to, 92, 94, 95
  see also lay justices
diversion, 70-4, 76, 134-6
domestic violence, 52, 67-9, 75, 95
Dunpark Committee, 132
duty solicitors, 93, 113, 139

Faculty of Advocates, 19, 20
fiscals
  accountability of, 8, 28, 50-1, 60
  as administrators, 37, 40-1
    bureaucrats, 7-8, 48, 50
    investigators, 26-7, 48, 130, 134
    lawyers, 4-5, 43-4, 51-2
    professionals, 5-7, 53, 79, 118
  biographical details of, 156-8, 159
  educational background of, 5, 22, 34,
    54-5
  future directions for, 132-3, 134, 135-6,
    138, 140, 141
  impartiality of, 8, 28-9, 37, 120
  training of, 34-5, 38, 39-40, 41, 42-3, 54
fiscal service
  historical development of, 18-22
  structure of, 22-30
fixed penalties, 27 n.1, 73, 134-6

high court, 26, 28, 80, 81, 84

indictment *see* procedure, solemn

judicial examination, 81, 82, 131, 136
juries, 80, 81, 82, 88, 121

lay justices
  fiscals' assessment of, 93-9
  selection of, 91, 92, 96-7
  sentencing policies of, 97-9
  training of, 95
legal aid, 61, 93, 113-14, 120, 139-40
Lord Advocate, 8, 19-22, 24-6, 28, 29, 50,
  57, 84, 91, 112, 139

marking
  definition of, 1, 31-2
  legal requirements in, 43-4, 51-2, 110-11